跟安迪学英语系列2
ENGLISH WITH ANDY 2

SELECTED EXTRACTS FROM ENGLISH LITERATURE
英国文学选读

Andrew Harrison / 安德鲁·哈里森　著/插图

石百楠　译

西北工业大学出版社
西安

【内容简介】《英国文学选读》提供了众多作家的文学选集,不失为大学和高中的优秀教育资源,每个节选后的任务不仅有助于增加学生的阅读技巧和提高学生对文章的理解力,而且有助于学生提高运用语法的能力和增加词汇量。每个单元的导言都有一个中文译本,确保读者能够正确地学习每个单元的主题。

图书在版编目(CIP)数据

英国文学选读 /(英)安德鲁·哈里森(Andrew Harrison)著. —西安:西北工业大学出版社,2020.9
(跟安迪学英语系列)
ISBN 978-7-5612-7225-1

Ⅰ. ①英… Ⅱ. ①安… Ⅲ. ①英语-阅读教学-高等学校-教材 ②英国文学-文学欣赏 Ⅳ. ①H319.37

中国版本图书馆CIP数据核字(2020)第185025号

YINGGUO WENXUE XUANDU
英 国 文 学 选 读

责任编辑:朱辰浩	策划编辑:黄 佩
责任校对:李 欣	装帧设计:李 飞

出版发行:西北工业大学出版社
通信地址:西安市友谊西路127号   邮编:710072
电   话:(029)88491757,88493844
网   址:www.nwpup.com
印 刷 者:陕西向阳印务有限公司
开   本:720 mm×1 020 mm   1/16
印   张:28.375
字   数:421千字
版   次:2020年9月第1版   2020年9月第1次印刷
定   价:92.00元

如有印装问题请与出版社联系调换

Preface

I have written this book for students of English, especially those who are studying English Literature. It is the second book in the *English with Andy* series, and aimed at undergraduate English majors, although it is also a vital resource for all university and middle school students and teachers.

Selected Extracts from English Literature provides a wide selection of samples of original, fluent standard English from a variety of original, literary sources from the British Isles. These literary sources are also respected worldwide, and are therefore representative of sound International English.

Additional notes and exercises are situated throughout the book to enable the reader to understand the extracts better, and glossaries at the end of each unit (listing the meanings of the underlined words in each unit) support a clear understanding of the contexts in which the extracts were originally written. These study aids will also help the reader to improve in areas of vocabulary and grammar. Older samples of English Literature also have a modern version alongside them, and additional glossaries are provided where necessary, to ensure all the extracts are understood in today's English.

After using this book faithfully, the reader will have a sound overview of English Literature and its background from the time of the origins of the English language to today.

I hope you will enjoy this book as much as I have enjoyed writing it.

Andrew Harrison

June 2020

前　言

我为英语专业学生，特别是那些学习英国文学的学生写了这本书。它是《跟安迪学英语》系列中的第二本书，面向英语专业的本科生，同时它对所有大学、中学的学生和教师而言也是重要的资源。

《英国文学选读》提供了从不列颠群岛各种原始的文学资源中所选择的大量原始、流利的标准英语样本。这些文学资源在世界范围内也受到推崇，因此具有良好的国际英语代表性。

在整本书中都有附加的注释和练习，以便读者更好地理解节选内容，而每一单元末尾的词汇表（表中列出了每一单元带下画线的单词及其含义）为读者能够清晰理解节选原文的语境提供了支持。这些学习辅助也将帮助读者增加词汇和语法方面的知识。在古时的英国文学样本旁边也有一个现代版本，并在必要时提供额外的词汇表，以确保所有的摘录都能用现代英语理解。

在充分地使用这本书之后，读者将对从英语起源到如今的英国文学及其背景有一个较为全面的了解。

我希望你们享受阅读这本书，就像我享受写它一样。

安德鲁·哈里森
2020年6月

Introduction

English language began in England one thousand five hundred years ago, and it spread throughout the British Isles from England long before it became an international language. Various dialects of English were present in England before the language began to become more standardised under, among others, the influence of two Williams—William Caxton and his printing press in the fifteenth century, and William Shakespeare in the sixteenth century.

It was not until these influences had been deeply embedded that English became an international language. It was from the British Isles that English spread, first to the Americas, and then to every populated continent on Earth. By the early twentieth century, the British Empire had covered almost a quarter of the Earth's population and land area, and as a consequence, the English language has remained vital for international communication and business. Although the British Empire no longer exists in the same form, there remains the British Commonwealth (the Commonwealth of Nations), which is an intergovernmental organisation of over 50 member states that were mostly territories of the British Empire in the past. It goes without saying that English remains extremely important in these countries. About a third of the population of the world now belongs to the Commonwealth of Nations.

Another consequence of this spread of the English language has been the recognition and appreciation of English Literature, the term originally referring to literature written in the English language in the British Isles. Now, it also refers to exceptional literature written in English elsewhere in the world.

In *Selected Extracts from English Literature*, I will focus on British English Literature, which actually began well over a thousand years ago. Every extract chosen will be explored to ensure it is understood in today's English, with a bias towards the standard English of England, as every international variety was founded upon it, and its influence remains just as strong today.

简 介

英语起源于1 500年前的英格兰，在它成为国际语言很久之前，它就从英格兰传遍了不列颠群岛。英语的各种方言在英语开始变得更加标准化之前就存在于英格兰，而后的两位威廉——15世纪的威廉·卡克斯顿和他的印刷机，以及16世纪的威廉·莎士比亚对英语的标准化产生了重要影响。

直到这些影响根深蒂固，英语才成为一种国际语言。英语的传播从不列颠群岛开始，首先到美洲，然后到地球上每个有人口居住的大陆。到20世纪初，大英帝国已经覆盖了地球上近1/4的人口和土地面积，因此，英语对于国际交流和商业至关重要。尽管大英帝国不再以之前的形式存在，但仍存在英联邦（英联邦国家），它是一个由50多个成员国组成的政府间组织，这些成员国在过去大多属于大英帝国的领土。毫无疑问，英语在这些国家仍然极为重要。全世界约1/3的人口都属于英联邦国家。

英语传播的另一个结果是对英国文学的承认和欣赏，英国文学这个词最初指的是在不列颠群岛用英文书写的文学。如今，它也指世界其他地方用英文书写的杰出文学作品。

在《英国文学选读》中，我将重点介绍英国文学，它实际上在1 000多年前就存在了。本书将以标准英式英语为导向，探索每一个节选的内容，以确保它能用现代英语来理解，因为国际上不同国家的英语都是建立在英式英语基础之上的，英式英语如今的影响力依然强大。

Extract List
节选书目

Throughout this book we have 116 extracts of literature by authors from the British Isles during the period from approximately 500 AD to 2020 AD. There are also numerous quotations from other works of literature in the text. Here is a list of the 116 extracts.

In most cases, I have listed the author, the work, then the date.

1   The Franks Casket, Early 8th Century AD
2   *The Dream of the Rood*, Early 8th Century AD
3   Bede, *Ecclesiastical History*, 9th Century AD
4   Bede, *Ecclesiastical History*, 9th Century AD
5   Bede, *Ecclesiastical History*, 9th Century AD
6   *Beowulf*, 1000 AD
7   Seamus Heaney, *Beowulf*, 1999
8   Pearl Poet, *Sir Gawain and the Green Knight*, Late 14th Century
9   Pearl Poet, *Sir Gawain and the Green Knight*, Late 14th Century
10 Pearl Poet, *Sir Gawain and the Green Knight*, Late 14th Century
11 Geoffrey Chaucer, *The Canterbury Tales*, 1387-1400
12 Geoffrey Chaucer, *The Canterbury Tales*, 1387-1400
13 Geoffrey Chaucer, *The Canterbury Tales*, 1387-1400
14 Geoffrey Chaucer, *The Canterbury Tales*, 1387-1400
15 William Caxton, *Prologue to Eneydos*, 1490

16 *The Geneva Bible*, 1560

17 *Shakespearean Sayings*, 1590-1612

18 *Shakespearean Insults*, 1590-1612

19 William Shakespeare, *Hamlet*, 1599-1602

20 William Shakespeare, *Hamlet*, 1599-1602

21 William Shakespeare, *King Lear*, 1608

22 William Shakespeare, *Sonnet I and Sonnet II*, 1598-1609

23 *The King James Version (KJV) of the Bible*, 1611

24 *The King James Version (KJV) of the Bible*, 1611

25 John Milton, *Paradise Lost*, 1667

26 John Bunyan, *The Pilgrim's Progress*, 1678

27 John Bunyan, *The Pilgrim's Progress*, 1678

28 John Bunyan, *The Pilgrim's Progress*, 1678

29 Daniel Defoe, *Robinson Crusoe*, 1719

30 Daniel Defoe, *Robinson Crusoe*, 1719

31 Jonathan Swift, *Gulliver's Travels*, 1726 and 1735

32 Robert Burns, *Auld Lang Syne*, 1788

33 Robert Burns, *My Heart is in the Highlands*, 1789

34 William Blake, *The Tyger*, 1794

35 William Blake, *Jerusalem*, 1804

36 Jane Austen, *Pride and Prejudice*, 1813

37 Jane Austen, *Pride and Prejudice*, 1813

38 Jane Austen, *Emma*, 1815

39 Jane Austen, *Emma*, 1815

40 Mary Shelley, *Frankenstein*, 1818

41 Mary Shelley, *Frankenstein*, 1818

42 Jane Taylor, *The Star*, 1806

43 William Wordsworth, *I Wandered Lonely as a Cloud*, 1807

44 Percy Shelley, *To a Sky-Lark*, 1820

45 John Keats, *Ode to a Nightingale*, 1819

46　Robert Southey, *The Story of the Three Bears*, 1837

47　Charles Dickens, *Oliver*, 1838

48　Charles Dickens, *A Christmas Carol*, 1842

49　Charlotte Bronte, *Jane Eyre*, 1847

50　Emily Bronte, *Wuthering Heights*, 1847

51　Emily Bronte, *Wuthering Heights*, 1847

52　Alfred Tennyson, *Ulysses*, 1842

53　Alfred Tennyson, *In Memoriam A.H.H.*, 1850

54　Robert Browning, *The Laboratory*, 1845

55　William Thackery, *Vanity Fair*, 1848

56　Thomas Hughes, *Tom Brown's Schooldays*, 1857

57　Charles Kingsley, *The Water Babies*, 1863

58　Lewis Carroll, *Alice's Adventures in Wonderland*, 1865

59　Lewis Carroll, *Through the Looking Glass*, 1871

60　Edward Lear, *The Owl and the Pussycat*, 1871

61　Robert Louis Stevenson, *Treasure Island*, 1883

62　Robert Louis Stevenson, *Strange Case of Dr. Jekyll*, 1886

63　Robert Louis Stevenson, *Strange Case of Dr. Jekyll*, 1886

64　Robert Louis Stevenson, *Strange Case of Dr. Jekyll*, 1886

65　Thomas Hardy, *Far from the Madding Crowd*, 1874

66　Thomas Hardy, *Tess of the D'Urbervilles*, 1891

67　Arthur Conan Doyle, *The Speckled Band*, 1892

68　Arthur Conan Doyle, *The Speckled Band*, 1892

69　Rudyard Kipling, *The Jungle Book*, 1894

70　Oscar Wilde, *The Picture of Dorian Gray*, 1890

71　Oscar Wilde, *The Picture of Dorian Gray*, 1890

72　H.G. Wells, *The Time Machine*, 1895

73　H.G. Wells, *The Invisible Man*, 1897

74　Bram Stoker, *Dracula*, 1897

75　Bram Stoker, *Dracula*, 1897

76 Bram Stoker, *Dracula*, 1897

77 E.M. Forster, *Howards End*, 1910

78 J.M. Barrie, *Peter and Wendy*, 1911

79 D.H. Lawrence, *Sons and Lovers*, 1913

80 Virginia Woolf, *To the Lighthouse*, 1927

81 A.A. Milne, *Winnie-the-Pooh*, 1926

82 A.A. Milne, *The House at Pooh Corner*, 1928

83 Agatha Christie, *Hercule Poirot Quotations*, 1920–1974

84 Agatha Christie, *Murder on the Orient Express*, 1933

85 Agatha Christie, *By the Pricking of My Thumbs*, 1968

86 J.B. Priestly, *An Inspector Calls*, 1945

87 Daphne Du Maurier, *Rebecca*, 1938

88 Enid Blyton, *Five on a Treasure Island*, 1942

89 Enid Blyton, *The Naughtiest Girl is a Monitor*, 1945

90 J.R.R. Tolkien, *The Hobbit*, 1937

91 J.R.R. Tolkien, *The Fellowship of the Ring*, 1954

92 J.R.R. Tolkien, *The Two Towers,* 1954

93 J.R.R. Tolkien, *The Return of the King*, 1955

94 C.S. Lewis, *The Screwtape Letters*, 1942

95 C.S. Lewis, *The Magician's Nephew*, 1955

96 C.S. Lewis, *The Lion, the Witch and the Wardrobe*, 1950

97 C.S. Lewis, *The Silver Chair*, 1953

98 C.S. Lewis, *The Last Battle*, 1956

99 John Wyndham, *The Day of the Triffids*, 1951

100 Ian Fleming, *Casino Royale*, 1953

101 Philippa Pearce, *Tom's Midnight Garden*, 1958

102 Roald Dahl, *Charlie and the Chocolate Factory*, 1964

103 Roald Dahl, *Matilda*, 1988

104 Richard Adams, *Watership Down*, 1972

105 Douglas Adams, *The Hitchhiker's Guide to the Galaxy*, 1979

106 Colin Dexter, *The Daughters of Cain*, 1994

107 David West, *The Aeneid*, 1990

108 E.V. Rieu and D.C.H. Rieu, *Homer: the Odyssey*, 1991

109 E.V. Rieu and D.C.H. Rieu, *Homer: the Odyssey*, 1991

110 J.K. Rowling, *Chamber of Secrets*, 1998

111 J.K. Rowling, *Order of the Phoenix*, 2003

112 J.K. Rowling, *Deathly Hallows*, 2007

113 J.K. Rowling, *Deathly Hallows*, 2007

114 Ruth Rendell, *Tigerlily's Orchids*, 2010

115 Andrew Harrison, *As Time Approaches*, 2015

116 Andrew Harrison, *Death and Hades*, 2018

I would like to formally express gratitude to all the authors referred to in this book, posthumously in most cases, who have contributed so much to the development of English over the last 1,500 years and made the language what it is today, creating what we call International English, enabling the world to communicate effectively in every aspect of life.

Almost every book that has been used for the above extracts has been adapted for film or television.

Many of these writers were educated at Cambridge University, England, or Oxford University, England. According to the telegraph in September 2019, Oxford University is still ranked as the best performing university in the world, for the fourth year running. This is according to the Times Higher Education (THE), which ranks the universities of the world on five areas: teaching, research, citations, industry income, and international outlook.

目录
CONTENTS

Unit 1 Old English Texts 古英语文本

Chapter 1　Early Old English Texts　第1章　早期古英语文本 003
Chapter 2　Later Old English Texts　第2章　晚期古英语文本 009
Additional Notes for Unit 1　第1单元附加注释 018

Unit 2 Chaucer and Middle English 乔叟与中世纪英语

Chapter 3　A Major Change　第3章　重大变化 023
Chapter 4　Chaucer's *Canterbury Tales*
　　　　　　第4章　乔叟的《坎特伯雷故事集》 034
Additional Notes for Unit 2　第2单元附加注释 042

Unit 3 Shakespeare and Standardisation 莎士比亚与标准化

Chapter 5　The Rise of Early Modern English
　　　　　　第5章　早期现代英语的出现 047
Chapter 6　The Beginning of International English
　　　　　　第6章　国际英语的开端 057
Additional Notes for Unit 3　第3单元附加注释 068

Unit 4 17th to 18th Century Literature   17—18世纪文学

Chapter 7   More Features of Early Modern English
　　　　　第7章　早期现代英语的其他特点 075
Chapter 8   Daniel Defoe and Jonathan Swift
　　　　　第8章　丹尼尔·笛福和乔纳森·斯威夫特 096
Additional Notes for Unit 4   第4单元附加注释 107

Unit 5 Literature from the Romantic Period   浪漫主义时期文学

Chapter 9   The Modern English Period   第9章　现代英语时期 117
Chapter 10   Romantic Novelists   第10章　浪漫主义小说家 128
Chapter 11   Romance Poets   第11章　浪漫主义诗人 140
Additional Notes for Unit 5   第5单元附加注释 155

Unit 6 Literature from the Victorian Period   维多利亚时期文学

Chapter 12   Charles Dickens and the Bronte Sisters
　　　　　 第12章　查尔斯·狄更斯与勃朗特姐妹 161
Chapter 13   Poetry from the 1840s   第13章　19世纪40年代的诗歌 180
Chapter 14   More Novels from the 1840s to the 1860s
　　　　　 第14章　19世纪40—60年代的小说 187
Chapter 15   Nonsense Writing   第15章　荒诞文学 194
Chapter 16   The 1870s and 1880s   第16章　19世纪70与80年代 204
Chapter 17   The 1890s   第17章　19世纪90年代 224
Additional Notes for Unit 6   第6单元附加注释 238

Unit 7　Literature from the First Half of the 20th Century
20世纪上半叶文学

Chapter 18　The Second and Third Decade of the 20th Century
　　　　　　第18章　20世纪20与30年代 243
Chapter 19　Mysteries and Whodunnits　第19章　推理和侦探小说 258
Chapter 20　The 1930s and 1940s　第20章　20世纪30与40年代 267
Chapter 21　Tolkien and Lewis　第21章　托尔金与刘易斯 279
Additional Notes for Unit 7　第7单元附加注释 296

Unit 8　Literature from Late 20th to Early 21st Century
20世纪下半叶到21世纪初的文学

Chapter 22　The 1950s　第22章　20世纪50年代 301
Chapter 23　The 1960s to 1990s　第23章　20世纪60—90年代 309
Chapter 24　Translations and a Resurgence of Murder Mysteries
　　　　　　第24章　谋杀推理小说的翻译与复兴 317
Chapter 25　The 21st Century　第25章　21世纪 330
Additional Notes for Unit 8　第8单元附加注释 349

Appendices　附录

Timeline　时间线 367
Task Answers　问题答案 372
Sample Essay　范文 430
Acknowledgements　致谢 433

Unit 1

Old English Texts 古英语文本

Chapter 1   Early Old English Texts
第1章   早期古英语文本

Chapter 2   Later Old English Texts
第2章   晚期古英语文本

Additional Notes for Unit 1
第1单元附加注释

Chapter 1　Early Old English Texts

第1章　早期古英语文本

Before the English language existed, that is, prior to 450 AD, the local languages in the British Isles were Celtic, called Brythonic or common Brittonic. However, many communities were bilingual, speaking Celtic and Latin, as Latin became the language of government after the Roman invasion of Britain in 55 BC. But a great change began to take place after the Romans decided to leave the British Isles. This change came by way of the Anglo-Saxon invasion of 449 AD. However, Latin remained, and is even still noticeable in the names of the Romans' major settlements from that time, for example in the names of English towns ending in '-chester'. In contrast, Celtic languages had very little influence on the development of English, adding only a few words such as 'crag' 'cross' and 'tor', for example.

In the fifth century, the Anglo-Saxons came mainly from what is now northern Germany, bringing with them a variety of Germanic dialects. These dialects formed the basis of English. So this foundation language base is referred to as 'Anglo-Saxon' or 'Old English', representing a period of development from 450–850 AD. During the first 300 years of this Anglo-Saxon settlement in England, the Celtic Britons moved to the west and north of the British Isles, to places such as Scotland, Wales and Cornwall.

The Anglo-Saxons named their new country 'Engla Land' (England) and their language 'Englisc' (English). And so, English language has its roots in England.

在英语出现之前，即公元450年之前，不列颠群岛的当地语言是凯尔特语，被称为布立吞语或普通布立吞语。然而，拉丁语在公元前55年罗马人入侵不列颠后成为官方语言，因此许多社区讲双语——凯尔特语和拉丁语。但在罗马人决定离开不列颠群岛后，发生了巨大的变化。这个变化是由公元449年盎格鲁-撒克逊人入侵造成的。然而，拉丁语仍然存在，而且从罗马人定居时起，它在罗马人主要定居点的名字中显而易见，例如以"切斯特"结尾的英格兰城镇名字。相反，凯尔特语对英语的发展影响很小，例如只增加了"crag""cross"和"tor"等几个词。

在5世纪，盎格鲁-撒克逊人主要从现在的德国北部来到英格兰，带来了各种日耳曼方言。这些方言构成了英语的基础。因此，这个基础语言的基础被称为"盎格鲁-撒克逊"或"古英语"，代表了公元450—850年的发展时期。在盎格鲁-撒克逊人定居英格兰刚开始的300年中，凯尔特人搬到了不列颠群岛的西面和北面，如苏格兰、威尔士和康沃尔。

盎格鲁-撒克逊人把他们的新国家命名为"Engla Land"，后来改为现在的"England"（英格兰），把他们的语言命名为"Englisc"，也就是现在的"English"（英语）。因此，英语在英格兰开始生根发芽。

Writing

The first inscriptions we have in Old English date from the sixth century. These are written in the runic alphabet, which the Anglo-Saxons brought with them. The runic alphabet that was used is called 'futhorc'. It looks like this, with the equivalent Roman letters written beneath:

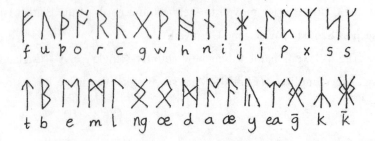

The 'futhorc' runic alphabet

You can see from the shapes how easy it would be to carve these letters (runes) with a blade. The English word 'write' actually comes from the Old English verb 'writan' which means 'to scratch runes into bark'.

The Franks Casket

A well-known example of Old English in <u>runic script</u> is the Franks Casket, now in the British Museum. You can see a picture of a panel from the casket below:

A panel of the Franks Casket in the British Museum

It is a carving into whalebone, and was produced in Northumbria, England, in the early eighth century. Around the perimeter can be seen the runic text referring to <u>Romulus and Remus</u>, the legendary founders of Rome.

The first part of the <u>inscription</u> in Old English is written as follows:

Extract 1

ᚱᚠᛗᛈᚠᛚᛞᛋᛖᚼᚱᛗᛚᚪᛈᚠᛚᛋᛏᛈᛟᛉᛉᛖᛏ

A sample of the Old English inscription on the Franks Casket

Interestingly, there are no spacings between words. The system of word endings in Latin made this less important, but in Old English, the endings of words were less predictable, so it soon became the norm after this to use spacing.

Task 1

Using the futhorc alphabet illustrated above as a key, transliterate this first part of the inscription into Roman letters.

The full inscription on the panel reads as follows in modern English:
Romulus and Remus, two brothers, a she-wolf nourished them in Rome, far from their native land.

The Ruthwell Cross

The Ruthwell Cross, now displayed in Ruthwell Village near Dumfries, Scotland

Due to the importance of Latin in England at the time, runic inscriptions in Old English often appeared alongside Latin inscriptions, and the Franks Casket is an example of this; another example is the Ruthwell Cross. In both examples, the Latin text is inscribed in the Roman script, the origin of the English alphabet today and the Old English is inscribed in runes.

The Ruthwell Cross is an eighteen foot high Anglo-Saxon cross dating from the early eighth century. Ruthwell was part of the Anglo-Saxon Kingdom of Northumbria at the time, but now it is part of Scotland. A section of the Old English poem, *The Dream of the Rood* is carved into the cross. This carving is the oldest surviving example of Old English poetry. 'Rood' comes from the Old English word 'rod', meaning 'pole' or 'crucifix'.

In the poem, the narrator has a vision of the cross of Jesus Christ. Here is a part of the inscription, with the Old English <u>transliteration</u> underneath the runes using the <u>Roman letters</u> to help you:

Extract 2

This part of the poem describes the cross itself speaking about its experience of being formed from a tree into a cross, and then bearing the powerful King and Lord of Heaven. Men did not only hammer nails into the Saviour's hands, but also into the cross, which became drenched in blood when Jesus was pierced by the spear. The cross felt mocked too when men mocked the King that it bore.

Here are the modern English translations of the words above, written in the same format and order as the original:

lifted up I a great king

heaven's lord

bend I not did dare

mocked us two men

both together I was with

blood drenched

ahof ic riicnae kyninge

heafunaes hlafard

haelda ic ni dorstae

bismaeraedu ungket men

ba aetgadrae ic waes miþ

blodae bistemid

A part of *The Dream of the Rood* on the Ruthwell Cross

We can see that the word order is different to modern English; indeed, Old English was fairly free in its word order due to it having been an <u>inflectional language</u>. Today, the meaning of a sentence in English is strongly connected with word order, making modern English difficult to learn in a non-native English language environment.

Task 2

Now write this extract of poetry in modern English, thinking carefully how to change the word order. After doing this exercise, check your version with the one at the end of the book.

The production of Latin literature in England abounded after the arrival of Roman missionaries under the direction of Augustine at the end of the sixth century. Many Latin manuscripts were written, especially the Bible and other religious texts, and Old English glossaries were added to Latin texts around 700 AD.

Anglo-Saxon scholars were first introduced to the Roman (Latin) alphabet in Lindisfarne (Holy Island) just off the coast of Northumbria in England. By the eighth century, the Church basically controlled the skill of writing, so it is no surprise that Old English started to use the Roman alphabet with the addition of some extra letters which were taken from the futhorc runic alphabet when Latin letters could not represent certain sounds in English.

As more and more people became Christians in the British Isles, the demand grew for the Bible to be written in English. Bede (672/673–735 AD), the most respected of the Northumbrian monks, produced one of the first <u>Gospels</u> in Old English. It was through translations like this that Latin words were taken into English, because during translation, where English did not have a word to replace a Latin one, the Latin word was used. These words were mostly connected with the Church, such as 'disciple' 'hymn' 'monk' 'noon' 'temple' 'nun' 'offer' 'priest' 'psalm' and 'rule' . But there were also everyday words such as 'cap' 'sock' 'mat' 'pear' 'cook' 'plant' 'school' and 'verse' .

This trend of adding Latin words continued up until the eighteenth century through not only the Church, but also from Legal Institutions, Education and Science (Incidentally, the words 'educate' and 'education' entered English from Latin as late as the fifteenth century).

Chapter 2　Later Old English Texts

第2章　晚期古英语文本

Later Old English is classified by the period 850–1100 AD. The language became influenced by Scandinavian languages in the north of England due to the Viking (Norse) invaders from the eighth to the eleventh century. It is believed that as a consequence, the inflections typical of Old English began to disappear. Many manuscripts were inevitably burned by the invaders in the eight century, but we have surviving manuscripts dating after the reign of King Alfred (849–899) who had many Latin works translated into Old English, including Bede's *Ecclesiastical History*. The basic alphabet used for these was the Roman alphabet rather than runes.

Bede's *Ecclesiastical History*

Below is a short extract from Bede's *Ecclesiastical History of the English People* in Old English translation. It was one of the original Latin texts that King Alfred had translated into Old English. This section concerns the Anglo-Saxon story about a poet called Caedmon. Above each line of the Old English text is a word for word translation to help you.

Extract 3

```
      When he  that  on a certain  occasion  did,    that  he  left    the house of the
  1   þa  he  þæt  þa sumre     tide    dyde, þæt he forlet þæt hus  þæs

      feast            and out was    going      to of cattle the shed  whose
  2   gebeorscipes ond ut wæs gongende to neata  scipene,  þara

      care to him was  that    night   entrusted   when he     there at
  3   heord him wæs þære neahte beboden,    þa he ða þær in

      the appointed tide his   limbs   in rest laid down   and fell asleep
  4   gelimplice  tide his leomu on reste gesette   ond onslepte

      then  stood him  a certain man  below in (a)  dream  and  him   hailed   and
  5   þa  stod him   sum  mon  æt  þurh swefn ond hine halette ond

      greeted and  him  by  his   name   called:    'Caedmon sing me
  6   grette ond hine be his noman nemnde: 'Cedmon sing me

      something'.   Then   answered    he and   said:    'Not know I not (how)
  7   hwæþwugu'. þa ondswarede he ond cwæð : 'Ne con ic noht
```

Taken from *English: History, Diversity and Change* by David Graddol, Dick Leith and Joan Swann (1996), Routledge and the Open University

Task 3a

Now rewrite this extract in today's modern English, using the given translations for each Old English word to help you.

Task 3b

Carefully compare the word order of your translation with that of the original language, looking particularly at the position of the verbs. You can use my translation at the back of the book for Task 3 to help you.

The sequence of the words is often different to modern English, due to Old English being an inflectional language. Today's English is an SVO (Subject then Verb then Object) language, so we usually put the Verb immediately after the

Subject and before the Direct Object. In the following example from line 6 of the extract 3, we have the pattern SOV (Subject then Object then Verb):

ond   hine   be   his   noman   nemde
and   him   by   his   name   called

The word order needs to be changed to get the following correct translation in Modern English: 'and called him by his name'.

However, sometimes the word order is the same, such as in the phrase 'Caedmon sing me something' (from the last two lines of the extract 3).

In the following extract of the poem, line 20 and 21, we can see evidence of <u>alliteration</u>:

Extract 4

He first   made   on earth   for men
He ærest sceop   *   eorðan bearnum

heaven   as a roof   the holy   Creator
heofon to hrofe,   *   halig Scyppend

Taken from *English: History, Diversity and Change* by David Graddol, Dick Leith and Joan Swann (1996), Routledge and the Open University

Task 4a

Find the line containing alliteration. Which Old English words display this poetic device? Does the same effect occur in the modern English equivalent of this line?

Task 4b

Write out the translated four half-lines together in order as a sentence, and consider the word order to see in what way it differs from modern English. Then write it in modern English by rearranging the words.

The next extract from Bede's *Ecclesiastical History* is taken from the same poem, but it is already translated into prose in today's modern English. Read and study the extract carefully before doing the following task.

Extract 5

On a certain occasion, he left the house of the feast and went out to the cattle shed, whose care was entrusted to him that night, and there, at the appointed time, he laid down his limbs in rest and fell asleep. Then a certain man stood before him in a dream and hailed and greeted him, and called him by his name, "Caedmon, sing me something!" Then he answered and said, "I don't know how to sing, and it was for this very reason that I left the feast, and came here, because I don't know how to sing anything." Again, he who was speaking with him said, "However, can't you sing for me?" Then he said, "What shall I sing?" He said, "Sing to me about the creation." Then, having received this answer, he immediately began to sing these lines and words which he had never heard before, in praise of God the Creator, in this form:

'Now we must praise the Guardian of Heaven's Kingdom, the Creator's power and his existence, and the work of the Father of Glory, as he, the Eternal Lord, established the beginning of every wonder. He, the Holy Creator, first made Heaven as a roof for the people on Earth. Then the Guardian of humankind, the Everlasting Lord, afterwards adorned the Earth for the people.'

Then he woke up from that sleep and all that he had sung while sleeping was firmly implanted in his memory, and he was immediately able to add to those words many more lyrics worthy of God in the same metre.

Task 5

Answer the following comprehension questions:
a List all the different names for God.

b What are we told the Creator did first?

c What did the Creator do after this?

d What does 'adorned' mean in the given context?

e What did God want Caedmon to do and why?

f What was the consequence of having this dream?

Beowulf

The most well-known work in Old English is the epic poem (heroic poem) *Beowulf*. We only have one old copy which was written in England around 1000 AD (250 years after it was originally composed). It is now in the British Library. Beowulf was a Scandinavian, and the events of the story took place in Scandinavia, where he fought a man-eating monster called Grendel and its mother. As victor, he ruled as king for fifty years until faced with a dragon, which he killed while losing his own life.

The following is an extract from *Beowulf* when the Danes are describing their warrior kings, the

A page of *Beowulf* in the British Library

most famous one being Shield Sheafson. It represents tenth century Old English. Try to read it yourself before you look at the translation below it.

Extract 6a

Oft Scyld Scēfing   sceaþena þrēatum,
monegum mǣgþum   meodosetla oftēah,
egsode eorl[as],   syððan ǣrest wearð
fēasceaft funden;   hē þæs frōfre gebād,
wēox under wolcnum,   weorðmyndum þāh,
oðþæt him ǣghwylc þ[ǣr]   ymbsittendra
ofer hronrāde   hȳran scolde,
gomban gyldan.   Þæt wæs gōd cyning!

Taken from Seamus Heaney's *Beowulf* published
by Faber and Faber in 1999

Seamus Heaney (1939-2013) was an Irish poet who received the 'Nobel Prize in Literature' in 1995. He wrote his own excellent translation of *Beowulf* into modern English in 1999. Here is his modern English translation of this Old English passage:

Extract 6b

There was Shield Sheafson, scourge of many tribes,
a wrecker of mead-benches, rampaging among foes.
This terror of the hall-troops had come far.
A foundling to start with, he would flourish later on
as his powers waxed and his worth was proved.
In the end each clan on the outlying coasts
beyond the whale-road had to yield to him
and begin to pay tribute. That was one good king.

Glossary

scourge   a cause of misery or death
wrecker   destroyer

mead-benches	Mead is an alcoholic drink made by fermenting honey.
terror	This warrior king caused people to feel terrified.
hall-troops	soldiers who live in and around the hall of a kingly building
foundling	orphan
flourish	grow strong
waxed	increased
worth	value
whale-road	sea

Here, Seamus Heaney has stayed faithful to *Beowulf* as a poem by translating it as a poem. He has also retained the cultural aspects of the society in which Beowulf existed by using terms such as 'mead-benches' and 'hall-troops'. And to help the reader to keep in mind the longevity of the story, he has used words that may be considered 'old-fashioned', although they are still found in modern English, in such words as: 'scourge' 'foundling' and 'waxed'.

Task 6

Using your understanding of the words and phrases from the given glossary, rewrite the above extract of poetry, at the same time changing it from poetry into modern English prose.

The following selection of extracts from the same translation describe the occasion when the fierce dragon was woken up from its sleep, and Beowulf took up the challenge of fighting it. The extracts are in chronological order, missing out parts of the narrative for the sake of creating the following exercise.

Extract 7

[The dragon] guarded a hoard; there was a hidden passage,

unknown to men, but someone managed
to enter by it and interfere
with the heathen trove. He had handled and removed
a gem-studded goblet ...
When the dragon awoke, trouble flared again.
He rippled down the rock, writhing with anger
when he saw the footprints of the prowler who had stolen
too close to his dreaming head.
The dragon began to belch out flames
and burn bright homesteads ...
Then Beowulf was given bad news,
a hard truth: his own home,
the best of buildings, had been burnt to a cinder,
the throne-room of the Geats.
... the fire-dragon
had rased the coastal region and reduced
forts and earthworks to dust and ashes,
so the war-king planned and plotted his revenge.

Glossary

hoard	a hidden collection of items
heathen trove	A trove is hidden treasure. In this case, it is heathen in the sense that it is connected in some way with uncivilised behavior. These treasures, guarded by the dragon, may include items of gold, such as goblets, plates and rings.
gem-studded goblet	A goblet is an ornate cup, sometimes used in ceremonies. This one is studded with precious stones and jewels.
prowler	A prowler is someone who sneaks about with bad

	intentions.
stolen too close	came too close
dreaming head	This refers to the head of the sleeping dragon.
homesteads	homes and the land around them owned by families
hard truth	fact difficult to bear
burnt to a cinder	destroyed by fire
throne-room	This is the main hall of the king's residence.
Geats	This is the name of a Scandinavian tribe in the days of Beowulf.
fire-dragon	dragon that breathes out fire
rased	This means to tear down flat.
forts	A fort was a building used by soldiers to defend a place.
earthworks	This was a wide pile of earth to help protect a castle or city.
war-king	This refers to a king who is familiar with and good at fighting in battle.

Task 7

Study the five extracts above until they are fully understood, using the given glossary. Then, changing them from poetry into continuous prose, in today's English, use your own language to rewrite and then retell this part of the story. Be flexible with your language to fully express everything implied in the poetic phrases. As long as you do not contradict the given content, allow your imagination to take over.

Additional Notes for Unit 1
第1单元附加注释

The Days of the Week

From our analysis of the Ruthwell Cross extract, we can see how vocabulary and pronunciation has changed. Take the following as examples:

ahof	lifted up
ic	I
hlafard	lord
ni	not
ba	both

However, some Old English words remain similar, such as:

freo	free
freond	friend, lover
freondleas	friendless
freondlice	in a friendly manner (friend-like)

The Anglo-Saxons named the days of the week after the pagan gods and planets they worshipped before they were converted to Christianity. Compare the Old English with the modern English below and see how the pronunciation has changed due to the original significance of these words becoming unimportant, allowing for slurred speech and changes in spelling conventions to take over:

Monandaeg (Monday)   the day of the Moon

Tiwesdaeg (Tuesday)	the day of Tiw, the god of the sky and war
Wodnesdaeg (Wednesday)	the day of Woden, the god of war, wisdom and poetry
Thunresdaeg (Thursday)	the day of Thunor, the god of thunder, weather and sky
Frigesdaeg (Friday)	the day of Frig, the goddess of love and fertility
Saeternesdaeg (Saturday)	the day of Planet Saturn
Sunnandaeg (Sunday)	the day of the Sun

Now, the days of the week are just names, and their original meanings are not commonly known.

The word 'holiday' has also lost its original meaning. It comes from the Old English 'haligdaeg' meaning 'a holy day'.

Inflections

Modern English adds inflections to verbs, but there are only two forms in verbs like 'to sing' in the present tense (i.e. sing, sings), whereas Old English had four (i.e. singe, singest, singeth, singath) as follows:

	Singular		Plural	
First Person:	I sing	ic singe	we sing	we singath
Second Person:	you sing	thu singest	you sing	ge singath
Third Person:	he sings	he singeth	they sing	hie singath
	she sings	heo singeth		
	it sings	hit singeth		

Modern English does not distinguish the singular and plural of 'you', but Old English did. The singular of 'you' was 'thu' and the plural of 'you' was 'ge'. This distinction continued into Early Modern English as we shall see later, by which time the forms had changed to 'thou' and 'ye' respectively.

Glossary for Unit 1

runic script 如尼文

This was the writing system used by the Anglo-Saxons when they invaded England. The individual carved letters are called runes. The particular runic script used for Old English was the 'futhorc' alphabet.

Romulus and Remus 罗慕路斯与雷穆斯

These were twin brothers who were abandoned by their parents and suckled by a wolf. Romulus was the founder of the city of Rome, which was named after him.

inscription 铭文

This is a text which is engraved or carved onto something. In this case, the letters were inscribed onto bone.

eighteen foot high 18英尺高

This is approximately five and a half metres.

transliteration 转写

This is copying text into the letters of an alternative alphabetic system.

Roman letters 罗马字母

This is the alphabet used for English today. It was originally used for Latin, the language of the Roman Empire.

inflectional language 屈折语

Inflection is the alteration of words for grammatical reasons, for example, signifying different tenses (past, present and future), number (singular, plural or dual) and gender (male, female or neuter). Inflectional languages are those that use a lot of inflections, such as Greek, French and German.

Gospels 福音

There are four Gospels in the New Testament section of the Bible, and they are called Matthew, Mark, Luke and John.

alliteration 头韵

Alliteration is a poetic effect in which the initial consonants of words are repeated, for example: The slithery, slimy snake slipped into my slipper. Here the 's' is repeated to emphasise the presence and actions of a snake.

Unit 2

Chaucer and Middle English
乔叟与中世纪英语

Chapter 3   A Major Change
第3章   重大变化

Chapter 4   Chaucer's *Canterbury Tales*
第4章   乔叟的《坎特伯雷故事集》

Additional Notes for Unit 2
第2单元附加注释

Chapter 3　A Major Change
第3章　重大变化

It was in 1066 AD, at the Battle of Hastings, that William, Duke of Normandy (William the Conqueror) defeated King Harold of England (King Harold Ⅱ), and as a result the French invaded and ruled England for 200 years. During this time and after, English vocabulary and spelling became very strongly influenced by the French language. One example of a change in spelling that took place due to French scribes was the letters 'qu' at the beginning of words. For example, the Old English words 'cwic' and 'cwen' became 'quick' and 'queen'.

After the defeat of King Harold Ⅱ, French became the official language of England. The upper classes and church leaders of England were replaced by French people and the educated English people became trilingual, speaking French, English and Latin.

So the eleventh century marked a transition from Old English to what we call Middle English (Middle English covers the period from 1100-1450). In the twelfth century, English language began to spread from England to the whole of the British Isles.

It was not until the fourteenth century that English became the most important language again in England, and education was taught in English instead of French, although Latin remained an important part of the curriculum.

Middle English is understandable to modern readers, but not easily, and this can be illustrated by a study of the following extracts.

公元1066年，在黑斯廷斯战役中，诺曼底公爵威廉（征服者威廉）打败了英格兰国王哈罗德（哈罗德二世），致使法国入侵并统治了英格兰200

年。在这段时间及之后，英语词汇和拼写受到法语的巨大影响。由于法文书吏的缘故，拼写发生变化的一个例子是单词开头的字母"qu"。例如，古英语单词"cwic"和"cwen"变成了"quick"和"queen"。

在国王哈罗德二世战败后，法语成为英格兰的官方语言。英格兰的上层阶级和教会领袖被法国人取代，受过教育的英格兰人成为三语习得者，他们讲法语、英语和拉丁语。

因此，11世纪标志着一个从古英语向我们所说的中世纪（中古）英语的过渡（中世纪英语在1100—1450年被广泛应用）。12世纪时，英语开始从英格兰传播到整个不列颠群岛。

直到14世纪，英语才再次成为英格兰最重要的语言，教育的开展改用了英语而非法语，但拉丁语仍然是课程的重要组成部分。

中世纪英语对现代读者来说是可以理解的，但并不容易，这可以通过对以下内容的研究来说明。

Piers Plowman and *Sir Gawain and the Green Knight*

One of the greatest works of English Literature from the Middle Ages, and one that influenced Chaucer's *Canterbury Tales*, is *The Vision of Piers Plowman* by William Langland (1330–1400). It is believed to have been written between 1370 and 1390. This work contains the first mention of Robin Hood, who is elsewhere recorded to have been born in South Yorkshire, in England. He was an outlaw who lived with his Merry Men in Sherwood Forest, in Nottingham, England. This literary reference in *Piers Plowman* dates to 1377. Middle English ballads about Robin Hood were very popular in the second half of the fourteenth century.

An equally important work of English Literature written in the late fourteenth century is *Sir Gawain and the Green Knight*, a story from English folklore about chivalry and romance. We call the writer the 'Gawain Poet' or the 'Pearl Poet', who wrote the book in stanzas of alliterative verse. It is an Arthurian story, that is, one of the many stories about King Arthur, who is believed to have been the King of the Britons in the sixth century. According to *The History of the Britons*,

Arthur was a war lord, a Christian soldier associated with miracles. *The History of the Kings of Britain*, written by Geoffrey of Monmouth in the first half of the twelfth century includes Celtic legends about King Arthur. This Latin work also contains the earliest known version of the story of King Lear and his three daughters.

Many stories have arisen in memory of King Arthur, including characters such as Merlin the Magician, the Lady of the Lake, Queen Guinevere, and the Knights of the Round Table, the most famous knight being Sir Lancelot who had a love affair with the king's Queen Guinevere. Among the well-known stories is the one when Arthur pulls a sword from a stone, signifying he was the true King. Many stories have also been written in relation to the sword <u>Excalibur</u>, Merlin's magic, and other events such as the Quest for the <u>Holy Grail</u>.

Sir Gawain and the Green Knight

Sir Gawain was King Arthur's nephew, and one of his Knights of the Round Table. The Round Table was believed to have been made by wise Merlin; the fact that it was round encouraged respect and equality among the 100 knights. The capital of Arthur's kingdom was Camelot.

The following extract, taken from near the beginning of the story of *Sir Gawain and the Green Knight*, sets the scene just before the Green Knight arrives. You can see how this example of Middle English is easier to understand than Old English.

Extract 8

This kyng lay at Camylot vpon Krystmasse
With mony luflych lorde, ledez of the best,
Rekenly of the Rounde Table alle tho rich brether,
With rych reuel orygt and rechles merthes.
Ther tournayed tulkes by tymez ful mony,

Justed ful jolile thise gentyle knigtes,
Sythen kayred to the court caroles to make.
For ther the fest watz ilyche ful fiften dayes,
With alle the mete and the mirthe that men couthe avyse;
Such glaum ande gle glorious to here,
Dere dyn vpon day, daunsyng on nygtes,
Al watz hap vpon hege in hallez and chambrez
With lordez and ladies, as leuest him thogt.

Glossary

kyng	king
Camylot	Camelot, the capital of King Arthur's kingdom
Krystmasse	Christmastime
mony luflych lorde	many lovely lords/many noble lords
Rounde Table	This was a table made by Merlin the Magician to bring a sense of equality between the knights.
rich brether	rich brotherhood
merthes	mirth/happy mood
tournayed	This refers to the jousting tournaments that knights took part in, involving two knights on horseback riding quickly towards one another holding a blunted lance each.
gentyle knigtes	gentle knights
caroles	Carols/Christmas songs
fest	feast
mete	meat
gle	glee
daunsyng on nigtes	dancing by night
hallez and chambrez	halls and chambers

Task 8

Using the glossary above, study the extract and see how much you can understand. Then check the modern English version at the back of the book.

Also present at the feast with King Arthur and the knights was his beautiful Queen Guinevere who sat beside Sir Gawain. It was New Year's Eve, and Arthur refused to begin eating until he had heard an amazing story, a tale of bravery, or until he had witnessed a challenge from one knight to another for a jousting competition. Nobody rose to this demand until a terrifying knight burst into the banquet hall on his horse and challenged the bravest person there to a contest.

The next extract from *Sir Gawain and the Green Knight* has been adapted from Middle English poetry into modern English prose. It is the lengthy description of the Green Knight who has entered the hall. Two small sections describing the Green Knight's horse have been omitted.

Extract 9

A mysterious rider burst in through the hall door, a being bigger and stronger than any other person there. His neck, waist and thighs were thick, and his muscular legs were long. He was half the size of a giant, but still taller than any human. However, he looked handsome and well-proportioned on his horse in spite of his bulk; his waist and stomach were in good trim although the sense of his presence was grim. All around him was an air of dread, causing everyone in the hall to be in awe at the strange sight of him, especially as he was green everywhere — his face, hands, clothes and gear were all green!

The visitor wore a close fitting coat adorned by an attractive cloak, well-designed with a costly fur lining. His hood was slung down from his head and laid on his shoulders. The tight hose on his legs was green too, but golden spurs were fastened to his heels beside his attractive riding shoes. The studs on his belt and the precious jewels in his noble clothing were also green ...

The Green Knight

The hair on his head was like the tresses of his horse, flowing over and covering his shoulders. His beard was as big as a bush, hanging over his chest along with his thick hair, reaching to just above his elbows so that the tops of his arms were completely covered, like a cape covering his neck ...

The stranger's glances were like flashes of lightning so the guests were afraid to look at him.

Task 9

Read and study this extract and then, in your own words, describe the Green Knight to a partner.

The next extract from *Sir Gawain and the Green Knight* continues the story.

Having hurtled through the hall door, the Green Knight on horseback addresses his audience and issues a challenge. It is written in prose narrative, <u>paraphrased</u> from the original.

Extract 10

'Where is the captain of this crowd?' asked the strange Green Knight, glaring around threateningly, but nobody made a sound as they all awaited King Arthur's response.

King Arthur finally spoke fearlessly, 'Welcome to you! I am the head of this hall. My name is Arthur. Get off your horse and tell us your tale!'

'I will not stay, even though your people are considered to be the best throughout the World, your every knight bearing weaponry of steel on the backs of steeds,' responded the green visitor.

The Knights of Camelot held still even though their noble pride was rising up within them.

The visitor continued, 'I come in peace and would part as friends. I am not here to fight as I left my weapons at home, and I only brought my axe so that I could take part in a simple game.'

King Arthur responded by saying, 'Sir, you are very courteous in your words, but if it is a fight you are truly looking for, then we are more than willing even without weapons'.

'No. Fighting is far from my mind; I only want to play a little Christmas game.'

'What is this game?' asked the king.

'If there is anyone among your young blood here who is brave enough, let him be willing to come here and exchange blows from my axe.'

There was silence in the hall, so the Green Knight continued, 'Your man can strike my neck first, and if he is successful, he can keep my axe. But after I have received his strike, he must yield his neck to me and allow my turn.'

The Green Knight stirred in the saddle of his steed, while his red flashing eyes looked around at his audience. Laughing, he said, 'What! Isn't this the house of famous King Arthur, renowned for valour and many victories? Is every courageous Knight of the Round Table afraid of the words of one man?'

King Arthur's sense of embarrassment flushed his face red with rage, so he stepped towards the Green Knight and said, 'You are mistaken! Nobody here is afraid of you. We are just surprised at your foolish words. Give me your axe and I will do as you ask in God's name.' Arthur took the axe from the Green Knight who descended from his horse. As everyone looked on, Arthur swung the axe around his head to get a feel for it, while the visitor just stood there stroking his thick beard, totally relaxed.

Suddenly, Gawain the knight called out to the king, 'Before everyone here, I entreat you my king to allow me to take up this challenge. And if Queen Guinevere does not object, I will leave my seat and come and stand beside you now. It isn't fitting for a king to respond to the foolish words of this stranger, but as for me, I am the feeblest of all the knights, and the loss of my life would be of least significance. The only value I have is the honour of being the king's nephew.'

Everyone in the hall agreed to give Sir Gawain the challenge and release the king. 'Come to my side!' shouted King Arthur to Gawain, who responded without hesitation, rushing to the king's side. Bowing before the king, Gawain took the axe from him. Raising a hand in the air, the king blessed Gawain: 'May God keep your hand and heart strong!'

Approaching the Green Knight, Sir Gawain prepared to strike the visitor's neck with the axe.

'What's your name?' asked the Green Knight.

'I am Gawain.'

'Sir Gawain, before we begin, promise me now that after you strike my neck, you will come and find me at my home to allow me my turn to finish the game.'

'Where do you live?' asked Gawain, 'And what's your name? If you tell me these things, I will do as you promise.'

The Green Knight replied, 'Strike me first, then I will tell you my name and where I live; and if I don't, then you are released from your promise. Now, hold the axe steady and chop with all your strength.'

'Gladly sir, I will.'

The Green Knight bowed his head, baring the flesh from under his hair, clearly displaying the nape of his neck. Gawain gripped tightly onto the axe and lifted it high into the air, positioning his left foot forward to keep a steady pose. Gawain brought the axe down quickly onto the Green Knight, slicing straight through and hitting the ground, completely severing the Green Knight's head from his neck. The huge head fell to the ground and rolled around as blood gushed from the decapitated body. But the Green Knight's body did not fall. Instead, it reached out to grab its own head by the hair. The body then straightened up, lifting the head high in the air, and then it climbed onto the horse, putting its feet into the stirrups. The decapitated Green Knight sat there on his horse as though nothing had happened, and King Arthur's people quaked in fear.

Holding his head high in the air by its hair, the Green Knight faced the head towards King Arthur, Queen Guinevere and Sir Gawain. Then the grotesque lips of the head spoke: 'Sir Gawain, do not forget what we agreed. Look for me until you find me, just like you promised before these proud knights, otherwise you will be remembered by all as a coward. You can find me at the Green Chapel where you will receive a strike on your neck from me on New Year's morning, one year and a day from now. I am called the Knight of the Green Chapel and am known by many, so you cannot fail to find me.'

After speaking these words, the Green Knight pulled the reins of his steed and hurtled out of the hall door with his head in his hand.

King Arthur's heart was greatly disturbed by these events, but he hid it well and said aloud to Queen Guinevere, 'Do not be dismayed, these strange things are normal at Christmastime, and we can now enjoy our feast, because I have without a doubt witnessed a marvellous challenge.'

To Gawain, King Arthur said, 'Now Sir Gawain, hang up that axe, it has done enough chopping for now; it is time to eat. Just remember to fulfil your vow with courage when the time draws near.' So King Arthur, Sir Gawain and all the people feasted together.

Glossary

tale	short story
young blood	young men in their prime/strong young men
steed	war horse
valour	courage, bravery
get a feel for it	become acquainted with it so he could use it skilfully
nape	The nape is the bottom part of the back of the neck.
severing	detaching
stirrups	These are metal hoops into which the feet of a horse rider are placed.
grotesque	revolting, ugly
Chapel	A chapel is a small church.

Task 10

Answer the following comprehension questions:

a In your own words, explain why the Green Knight came to King Arthur's hall.

b Describe in what ways the Green Knight insults his audience.

c Describe in what ways the Green Knight compliments his audience.

The story continues with Sir Gawain setting off on the long journey to find the Green Chapel, until on Christmas Eve, he entered a castle and was entertained by an old hero called Sir Bertilak and his wife who was the most beautiful woman Gawain had ever seen. There he heard he was very close to the Green Chapel. Whenever the old hero was out hunting, Gawain faithfully refused the beautiful woman's advances.

On New Years' Day, he visited the Green Chapel where the Green Knight was sharpening an axe. The Green Knight's strikes failed to chop off Gawain's head due to Gawain's faithfulness to his promises, although his neck was gashed due to not being totally honest. The Green Knight reveals himself to be Sir Bertilak himself, the lord of the castle. The game had been organised by Morgan le Fay (a wicked enchantress who was the half-sister of King Arthur) who wanted to discredit Arthur and his knights. Gawain returned to Camelot to tell the tale, carrying with him his prize of a green belt.

Thereafter, all the Knights of the Round Table would wear a similar green belt in honour of Sir Gawain and his faithfulness to his promises.

Chapter 4 Chaucer's *Canterbury Tales*

第4章 乔叟的《坎特伯雷故事集》

By the fourteenth century, English was established as the most important language in England again, and it had already spread throughout the British Isles. The 14th century also produced *The New Testament* in English, translated by John Wycliffe in the 1380s. This helped in the process of establishing English as a literary language. However, the writer considered to be the father of English Literature is Geoffrey Chaucer, who was probably born in 1343 and died in 1400. He was later buried in Poet's Corner in Westminster Abbey in 1556, the first poet to have this honour. Chaucer wrote *Parlement of Foules* in 1382, which is the first recorded evidence of Valentine's Day being associated with romantic love. But the work he is most famous for is *The Canterbury Tales* which he wrote from 1387 to 1400.

In Chaucer's *Canterbury Tales*, there is a gathering of pilgrims in an inn in London. The host at the inn offers to judge the tales that the pilgrims tell on the way to Canterbury, and to judge the winner. Canterbury, which is also in England, in the County of Kent, southeast of London, is where Saint Thomas Becket was martyred in 1170.

The General Prologue

The first part of *The Canterbury Tales* is called the General Prologue. It was written in Middle English, and the following extract is taken from the first section of the prologue in its original form:

Extract 11

Whan that Aprill, with his shoures soote
The droghte of March hath perced to the roote
And bathed every veyne in swich licour,
Of which vertu engendred is the flour;
Whan Zephirus eek with his sweete breeth
Inspired hath in every holt and heeth
The tendre croppes, and the yonge sonne
Hath in the Ram his halfe cours yronne,
And smale foweles maken melodye,
That slepen al the nyght with open eye
(So priketh hem Nature in hir corages);
Thanne longen folk to goon on pilgrimages
And palmers for to seken straunge strondes
To ferne halwes, kowthe in sondry londes;
And specially from every shires ende
Of Engelond, to Caunterbury they wende,
The hooly blisful martir for to seke
That hem hath holpen, whan that they were seeke.

Glossary

Zephirus This is Zephyr, meaning a soft, gentle wind.
the Ram This is a constellation of stars, here indicating a position of the sun viewed from the Earth.

Task 11a

Underline or write down in a list every word in the extract that is exactly the same as a modern English word.

Task 11b

Underline or write down in a list every word in the extract that looks almost the same as a modern English word and therefore can be easily understood.

Task 11c

Underline or write down in a list every word in the extract that looks different to a modern English word, and you therefore cannot understand it.

The following extract is the same passage from the prologue converted from Middle English into modern English. Read it carefully and compare it with the original Middle English version above.

Extract 12

> When April with his sweet showers
> Has pierced the drought of March to its roots
> And bathed every vein with such liquor,
> Whose virtues give the flowers birth;
> When the gentle breeze with his sweet breath
> Has inspired life to each forest and field
> To each tender branch, and the young sun
> Has run to the Ram on half its course,
> And small birds have begun to make melody,
> And sleep through the whole night with open eye
> (This is the way Nature stirs their hearts);
> Then folk long to go on pilgrimages

And pilgrims yearn to seek out strange places,
Foreign shrines renowned in sundry lands;
And from every County's end
It is to the Canterbury of England they go,
To seek the holy blessed martyr there
Who had helped them when they were sick.

Task 12a

Now you have spent time analysing the two extracts, two versions of the same passage, look back at the words you underlined or listed for Task 11b, and check the meanings of the words that look almost the same as modern English words and see if you understood them correctly now.

Task 12b

Now look back at the words you underlined or listed for Task 11c, and see if you can identify the meanings of the words that looked different to modern English words.

The next extract taken from the General Prologue of *The Canterbury Tales* concerns a worthy knight just back from war. This version has been adapted from Middle English poetry into modern English prose. A section mentioning various place names has been removed in my version for ease of reading.

Extract 13

A knight was there, and what a gentleman worthy of recognition!

From the first moment he began to ride his horse throughout the World, he loved chivalry, truth, honour, freedom and courtesy. He was highly valued on his King's campaigns, and for noble causes he rode through Christendom and heathen lands, greeted with honour everywhere for his conduct, ranking above all knights internationally on his quests ... fighting in fifteen deadly battles for our Faith!

The knight also fought three duels, defeating his opponent each time, winning widespread fame by his strength, skill and bravery.

In addition to these things, he was also very wise and gentle, as meek as a young lady. He never spoke any unkind or vile word to any person; he was a truly perfect, noble knight.

However, although his horse was good, he himself looked plain, wearing simple clothes that were stained with rust from his coat of chain mail, but this was only because he had just returned to England from his most recent expedition.

He was determined to go on this pilgrimage.

Glossary

Christendom — This was everywhere where Christianity was adhered to.

heathen lands — These were lands (countries and regions) where Christianity was not adhered to.

Faith — This was his belief in God as he was a Christian.

coat of chain mail — This is the sleeveless coat made out of metal to protect a knight's torso.

Task 13a

List all the qualities (descriptive words) that are attributed to the knight.

Task 13b

Some of these descriptive qualities seem almost contradictory. Using the descriptive words in your list for Task 13a, devise two contrasting lists of qualities that the knight has according to the extract.

Task 13c

Discuss how these two different aspects of the knight's character can be united in the same person.

Task 13d

For how long has the knight been such a good person?

Task 13e

Why did the knight look so plain?

The Miller's Tale

The Miller's Tale, in *The Canterbury Tales*, concerns an old rich Oxford carpenter called John and his beautiful young wife Alison. There are two competing lovers, Nicholas the poor student lodger and Absolon the parish clerk and local barber. The story is a 'fabliau', a style of writing popular in France in the thirteenth century among aristocrats, written to poke fun at the rising middle classes. It is typically obscene in its content and is intended to make the readers and listeners laugh.

The extract below, taken from *The Miller's Tale*, describes Alison the heroine. It begins by saying she is beautiful, but then likens her body to that of a weasel, which is not very flattering as weasels are considered to be aggressive little animals. We are then told in great detail what she is wearing.

Extract 14

Fair was this yonge wyf, and therwithal
As any wezele hir body gent and smal.
A ceint she werede, barred al of silk,
A barmclooth eek as whit as morne milk
Upon hir lendes, ful of many a goore.
Whit was hir smok, and broiden al bifoore
And eek bihinde, on hir coler aboute,
Of col-blak silk, withinne and eek without.
The tapes of hir white voluper
Were of the same suite of hir coler;
Hir filet brood of silk, and set ful hye.

Glossary

wezele	weasel
ceint	girdle
barred al of silk	made of silk and striped
barmclooth	apron or overskirt
whit as morne milk	white as morning milk
lendes	the skirt around her hips
many a goore	lots of gores or pieces of material
smok	smock
broiden al bifoore and eek bihinde	embroidered front and back
on hir coler aboute	the same applies to her collar (embroidered inside and outside)
col-blak silk	coal-black silk
withinne and eek without	inside and outside/on both sides
tapes	These are the tapes that held her cap in place.
voluper	cap

same suite of hir coler	matched her collar
filet	headband
brood	broad
set ful hye	high off her brow

Task 14

Using the extensive glossary, rewrite this extract in modern English. Then compare it with the example at the end of the book.

Additional Notes for Unit 2
第2单元附加注释

French Words that came into English

As England was ruled by the French at the beginning of the development of Middle English, it is not surprising that French words concerning Government, Law, the Church and the Arts found their way into the English language. Here are a few examples:

mayor, parliament, army, battle, captain, navy, peace, soldier, city, tax, constable, crime, jury, justice, prison, baptise, bible, saint, sermon, vicar, comedy, fashion, luxury, poetry, satin

Because of the influence of other languages, including French, the English language has multitudes of synonyms. Below, I have paired up some English words with an accompanying synonym that originated from the French language:

English	English Synonym (originating from French)
ask	question
book	volume
smell	scent
sorrow	grief

French Cuisine

French words concerning food, cooking and eating, have become an essential part of English vocabulary. Here are some examples:

café, restaurant, menu, dessert, dinner, dine, picnic, sauce, pie, tart, gateau, sausage, beef, pork, mutton

French was, and still is, an inflectional language, including the classification of words into male and female. Even though French had a huge influence on the development of English, especially in the area of vocabulary, English moved away from being an inflectional language such that, by the time Middle English Period had ended, most gender classifications were gone.

Glossary for Unit 2

Battle of Hastings 黑斯廷斯战役

This battle took place in England and was between the French, led by William the Conqueror, and the Anglo-Saxons of England under King Harold Ⅱ. Hastings is in the county of Sussex in the south of England. England's defeat allowed France to invade the country.

Normandy 诺曼底

This is a region in the north of France.

the French 法国人

French people

scribes 书吏、抄写员

Scribes used to make written copies of official documents.

Robin Hood 罗宾汉

Robin Hood was famous for stealing from the rich to give to the poor. He is believed to have existed in the twelfth century during the reign of King Richard the Lionheart.

Britons 布立吞人

This word is used to refer to the Celtic peoples who inhabited the British Isles prior to the Anglo-Saxon invasions. Nowadays it can also be used in a general way to refer to the native inhabitants of Great Britain.

Excalibur 圣剑、断钢剑

This is the legendary sword of King Arthur associated with magic power.

Holy Grail 圣杯

This is the cup or chalice that was used by Jesus Christ at the Last Supper 2,000 years ago.

paraphrased 释义

To paraphrase is to express the meaning of a text in a different way to make the original meaning clear to a specific reader.

pilgrims 朝圣者

Pilgrims are people who go on a journey to a holy place.

martyred 殉道

A martyr is someone who dies for their religious beliefs and is admired by people because of this.

Unit 3

Shakespeare and Standardisation
莎士比亚与标准化

Chapter 5　The Rise of Early Modern English
　　　　　　第5章　早期现代英语的出现

Chapter 6　The Beginning of International English
　　　　　　第6章　国际英语的开端

Additional Notes for Unit 3
　　　　　　第3单元附加注释

Chapter 5 The Rise of Early Modern English

第5章 早期现代英语的出现

The Early Modern English period covers 1450 to 1750 and includes the Renaissance Period, the Elizabethan Era and what is referred to as the Age of Shakespeare.

At the beginning of this period, Latin and French declined further and English became the language of government and science. Eventually, English became thoroughly established as a national language, and became more standardised. This was helped along very significantly by the use of the printing press because William Caxton, the first man to start a business using the printing machine, required consistency of language for his printing work to be efficient. This in turn enabled the development of officially recognised dictionaries and grammars (books about correct grammar), and the ensuing reliance on such books standardised English language further.

现代英语早期指1450—1750年，包括文艺复兴时期、伊丽莎白时代和莎士比亚时代。

从这一时期开始，拉丁语和法语进一步衰落，英语成为政府和科学的语言。最终，英语被完全确立为国家语言，并变得更加标准化。这得益于印刷机的使用。因为第一个使用印刷机创业的人——威廉·卡克斯顿，为了使他的印刷工作高效率地完成，提出了语言一致性的要求。这反过来又促进了官方认可的词典和语法（关于正确语法的书）的发展，随后对这些书的依赖进一步推动了英语标准化。

Caxton's Printing Press

William Caxton (1422–1491) trained as a printer in Holland and set up his printing press in England. When using the printing press for English works, there was a sea of English dialects in the country to choose from; he chose the dialect of London and the south east of England.

The first book ever to have been printed in English was *The History of Troy*. It was a translation from French, the English translation being printed by Caxton in 1473. Here is a page from the book:

A page from *The History of Troy* (1473)
from John Rylands University Library in Manchester

The following extract is taken from William Caxton's prologue to his English translation *Eneydos* (*The Aeneid*), written in Early Modern English prose in 1490. This prologue confirms the fact that Caxton had to deal with the many problems associated with a diverse variety of English dialects.

In the prologue, Caxton tells a story about some merchants from the north of England who were trying to buy eggs from a woman in the south of England. The northerner used the Old Norse (Viking) word 'egges' while the southern woman used the word 'eyren' from Old English. Modern English of course eventually chose the word 'egges' which is now spelt 'eggs'.

Extract 15

And certaynly our language now vsed varyeth ferre from that whiche was vsed and spoken whan I was borne. For we Englysshe men ben borne vnder the somynacyon of the mone, whiche is neuer stedfaste but euer wauerynge, wexynge one season, and waneth and dyscreaseth another season. And that comyn Englysshe that is spoken in one shyre varyeth from a nother. In so moche that in my dayes happened that certayn marchauntes were in a shippe in Tamyse for to haue sayled ouer the see into Zelande, and for lacke of wynde thei taryed atte Forlond, and wente to lande for to refreshe them; And one of theym named Sheffelde, a mercer, cam in-to an hows and axed for mete; and specyally he axyd after eggys: And the goode wyf answerde, that she coude not speke no Frenshe. And the marchaunt was angry, for he also coude speke no Frenshe, but wolde haue hadde egges, and she vnderstode hym not. And thenne at laste a nother sayd that he wolde haue eyren: then the good wyf sayd that she vnderstod hym wel. Loo, what sholde a man in thyse dayes now wryte, egges or eyren. Certaynly it is harde to playse eueryman by cause of dyuersite and chaunge of langage.

Glossary

certaynly	certainly
vsed	used
ferre	fairly

whiche	which
whan	when
borne	born
Englysshe	English
ben	been
vnder	under
somynacyon	dominion
mone	moon
neuer	never
stedfaste	steadfast
euer	ever
wauerynge	wavering
wexynge	waxing
waneth	wanes
dyscreaseth	decreases
comyn	common
shyre	shire, county
a nother	another
moche	much
dayes	days
marchauntes	merchants
shippe	ship
Tamyse	Thames (River Thames in London)
haue	have
sayled	sailed
ouer	over
see	sea
Zelande	Zeeland (a province in the Netherlands on mainland Europe)
wynde	wind
taryed atte Forlond	tarried at the foreland (the verb 'to tarry' means 'to wait')

wente	went
refreshe them	refresh themselves
mercer	A mercer is a dealer in textiles (fabrics).
axed	asked
mete	meat
egges	This term for 'eggs' comes from the language of Scandinavia.
eyren	This term for 'eggs' comes from Anglo-Saxon (Old English).
by cause	because
dyuersite	diversity

Task 15

Using the extensive glossary, rewrite this extract in today's modern English, and after you have written your own version, compare your version with the one at the back of the book.

You may have found the above task difficult as the grammar and usage of Early Modern English was still quite different. After carefully comparing your version of the extract with mine at the back of the book, you will be in a position to understand the notes below, where I explain the reasons behind some of the significant changes. Studying these notes will also help you to grasp some important aspects of English grammar today.

it is certainly true that (certaynly)

The word 'certainly' is not used on its own like this today. My version is typical of today's English even though it is much longer.

has a usage varying to some extent (vsed varyeth ferre)

The three original words used together, even when changed into their word-for-word equivalents, make no sense, so we need more words to express the same meaning as the original.

have been born (ben borne)

We need the auxiliary verb 'have' here as today's grammar uses more complex structures to make meanings more precise.

still (stedfaste)

'Steadfast' is not an appropriate word here although the meaning is completely understandable to a modern reader. The reason why we need to change 'steadfast' to another word such as 'still', is because 'steadfast' these days is primarily used when speaking of a person's virtues, and not when describing an object.

it happened that (happened that)

Omitting the pronoun in this phrase does not follow today's conventions.

some merchants (certayn marchauntes)

The use of the word 'certain' in 'certain merchants' is acceptable, but not conventional today, as we would usually use the word 'some'.

on the Thames (in Tamyse)

Using the preposition 'in' today implies that the ship was under water.

with the intention of sailing (for to naue sayled)

'for to have' is considered to be old-fashioned English and will only be heard when watching a film based on a period several hundred years ago. Today we would say something like 'with the intention of'.

went inland (wente to lande)

Now, 'to land' means to come from the sky onto the earth as though they were in an aeroplane. Caxton's meaning is 'to go inland'.

to refresh themselves (for to refreshe them)

The addition of 'for' in the original (making 'for to') created the meaning 'for the purpose of ...' which would today require the phrase to be adapted to 'for the purpose of refreshing themselves'. But for a simple statement as this today, the meaning is completely expressed in the simple word 'to' as long as we change 'them' to 'themselves'.

called Sheffield (named Sheffelde)

'named' is used correctly here, but it is more common these days to use the word 'called' in this context.

went into a house (cam in-to an hows)

Using the word 'came' suggests that Caxton was in the house himself, which is too subjective (although it is possible he was there). But the story is being recounted objectively, so 'went' is more appropriate.

Using the indefinite article 'an' before words beginning with a vowel is normal practice today, but in the past, it was also used before words beginning with 'h'. Now, the indefinite article 'a' is used before words beginning with 'h'.

he especially (specyally he)

Using 'specially' is not correct in today's English. It seems strange perhaps because the word 'special' is used when referring to very important people or objects, and not used this way when describing actions. 'Especially' is better here. Correct grammar today would also require the adverb and the pronoun to be inverted. However, if the same word order was desired, then 'specially' could become 'most importantly' creating 'most importantly he'.

asked for eggs (axyd after eggys)

The phrase 'asked after' in the context of wanting to obtain an object is not correct today.

answered by saying that she (answerde, that she)

The original is acceptable but it is common today to be more precise. The word 'that' has less significance now [see the example of '*it happened that (happened that)*' above].

could not speak any French (she coude not speke no Frenshe)

In the original we have a double negative, which conveys the opposite meaning. But if we change the second negative 'no' into 'any', then the meaning is clear in today's English.

because he could not speak French either (for he also coude speke no Frenshe)

Here there is only one negative, so the meaning is very clear. In Early Modern English the word 'for' was often used when we require 'because' in

English today. In regard to changing 'also' in the middle of the clause to 'either' at the end of the clause, this is really due to my personal preference, but it is just as likely to find 'because he also could not speak French'. In both cases, to be correct in today's English, the word order of the original 'speak no French' must change, and as a consequence, 'no' must change to 'not', making 'not speak French'.

he wanted eggs (wolde haue hadde egges)

The original form is not correct in today's English. However, in a different context, the phrase 'would have had eggs' is correct, for example in the sentence, 'If he had bought some hens, he would have had eggs for breakfast'. But the intended meaning in Caxton's prologue means 'he wanted eggs'. I have also added the pronoun 'he' to make the meaning clear.

write these days (in thyse dayes now wryte)

Today's English does not require the word 'now' to be added here, and the word 'in' is also not required for such a common phrase as 'these days'.

Indeed (Certaynly)

'Certainly' is not used like this in today's English, so I have replaced it with a word that is more acceptable.

everyone (eueryman)

'Everyman' is not used with this meaning these days and Caxton is probably not only referring to men. 'Everyone' is more inclusive.

the diversity (dyuersite)

Here I have added the definite article 'the' because today we would be very specific in our language. Caxton is presumably not referring to 'diversity' as a phenomenon or a concept, but rather the diversity between languages in particular. To make this specificity understood, it is better to add 'the' in today's English. This requirement is partly due to the popularity of the word 'diversity' in reference to diversity in the qualities and attributes among people and different cultures nowadays, so a lack of the definite article may distract the reader from the context of the passage.

changes in language (chaunge of langage)

A 'change of language' implies a change from the language of one country to the language of another country. But here Caxton is referring to different dialects within one language, so 'of' must be replaced by 'in'.

The Geneva Bible

By the sixteenth century, English writers had great pride in their language. The Reformation (1517-1648) was responsible for this to a large extent, including King Henry Ⅷ's new status as the head of the English Church.

The translation of *The Holy Bible* into English, and then its dissemination in print, also helped to focus the English language. *The Geneva Bible* was printed in England in 1560, preceding the world-renowned King James Version of *The Bible* by 51 years.

The Geneva Bible was the primary Bible of sixteenth century Protestantism, and was used by William Shakespeare, Oliver Cromwell, John Bunyan and John Milton. It was the first Bible to divide scriptures into numbered verses, at the advice of John Calvin. It was even taken on board the Mayflower, the ship in which the Pilgrim Fathers from England sailed to North America in 1620.

Below is a photograph of the beginning of the book of Genesis in *The Geneva Bible*, and the extract below it is Genesis chapter 1, verses 1-6, taken from the photograph.

The beginning of *The Geneva Bible*, printed in 1560

Extract 16

In the beginning God created the heauen and the earth. And the earth was without forme and uoyde, and darknesse was upon the deepe, and the Spirit of God mooued upon the waters. Then God saide, Let there be light: and there was light. And God sawe the light that it was good, and God separated the light from the darkenesse. And God called the light, Day, and the darkenesse, hee called Night. So the Euening and the Morning were the first day. Againe God saide, Let there bee a firmament in the middes of the waters: and let it separate the waters from the waters.

Glossary

without forme and uoyde	without form and void
firmament in the middes	dome in the middle/dome in the midst

It is interesting to see that there is little or no need to include a glossary for this passage as the language is so close to today's modern English.

Task 16a

Underline or make a list of all the spellings that are different to English today.

Task 16b

Study the spellings of the words in your list and find the two most common spelling differences.

Chapter 6 The Beginning of International English

第6章 国际英语的开端

Through trade and exploration, Britain began to acquire colonies abroad, and as a consequence, the English language was taken to the Americas, Australia and Asia. In addition to this, the dreadful slave trade removed Africans and relocated them to North America and the Caribbean, combining English with native African languages, eventually giving rise to English Creoles. So every populated continent on earth was exposed to the English language, the language of England.

However, due to exposure to local languages within the various continents, the English language began to develop some new characteristics and new vocabulary. As a result, linguists can today identify different varieties of Standard English throughout the world, such as Standard English English (i.e. Standard English in England), Standard American English, Standard Australian English and Standard Indian English. But the differences between these standard varieties are not significant enough to hinder communication between the continents. This phenomenon is called International English.

William Shakespeare

William Shakespeare (1564–1616) was born in Stratford-upon-Avon in England, and even during his days, English was in a state of transition. For example, word endings that gave fluidity in the order of words in a sentence were being abandoned, but the strict word order of today's English had not yet been fully established. This makes it difficult for us to fully understand Shakespeare's original meaning at times, hence the need for all fans of Shakespeare to study the work of specialists who have researched Shakespeare in depth.

Shakespeare had access to a huge stock of vocabulary, but he also invented words that we still use today, such *as accommodation, apostrophe, assassination, dislocate, obscene, reliance, and submerged.*

Shakespeare used typical sixteenth century verbal phrases, as use of the auxiliary verb 'do' was not common yet and neither were progressive verb forms. For example, he would write 'What do you read, my Lord?' instead of 'What are you reading, my Lord?' . The latter progressive structure, with which we are very familiar today, was a later development. Another example of a change in verbal phrase is Shakespeare's 'Arthur, who they say is killed tonight,' where today we would have 'Arthur, who they say has been killed tonight,' making clear the fact that it has already taken place, but very recently.

During the medieval period, there were no theatres, as plays were performed outside or on carts at Christian festivals, and plays were usually religious. So, when the theatre that Shakespeare used was built, this situation began to change.

Shakespeare wrote nearly 40 plays, including Histories, Comedies and Tragedies, written between 1590 and 1612. Here are a handful in chronological order:

King Henry VI, The Comedy of Errors, The Taming of the Shrew, Romeo and Juliet, A Midsummer Night's Dream, The Merchant of Venice, King Henry IV, Much Ado About Nothing, The Life and Death of Julius Caesar, Twelfth Night, The Tragedy of Hamlet Prince of Denmark, Troilus and Cressida, All's Well That Ends Well, Othello the Moore of Venice, King Lear, The Tragedy of Macbeth, Antony and Cleopatra, Timon of Athens, The Tempest, The Life of Henry VIII.

As well as his histories, tragedies and comedies, Shakespeare wrote poems and sonnets.

Many of today's expressions and idioms are based on Shakespeare, such as:
It's all Greek to me
It vanished into thin air
To refuse to budge an inch
To be tongue-tied

To be in a pickle
To not sleep a wink

Task 17a

Study the idioms above with a partner and try to work out what they mean.

We also have to thank Shakespeare for many famous sayings, some of which are listed below.

Extract 17

The lady doth protest too much.
All the world's a stage, and all the men and women merely players.
To be, or not to be, that is the question.
O Romeo, Romeo, wherefore art thou Romeo?
All that glisters is not gold.
The course of true love never did run smooth.
Friends, Romans, countrymen, lend me your ears.

Task 17b

With a partner, try to identify the meanings of the above sayings before rewriting them in today's English.

On a more humorous note, Shakespeare has produced a great number of insults in his plays. Have a look at the following list.

Extract 18

Thy words are blunt and so art thou (Henry VI)

Base dunghill villain (Henry VI)

There's no more faith in thee than in a stewed prune (Henry IV)

A goodly apple rotten at the heart (The Merchant of Venice)

Not worth a gooseberry (Henry IV)

You are not worth the dust which the rude wind blows in your face (King Lear)

No more brain than a stone (Twelfth Night)

Thou hast in thy skull no more brain than I have in mine elbows (Troilus and Cressida)

Thy lips rot off! (Timon of Athens)

Would thou wert clean enough to spit upon (Timon of Athens)

Were I like thee, I'd throw away myself (Timon of Athens)

Task 18

Change the above insults into today's English.

Dramatic Irony and Monologues

Dramatic Irony is a major feature in Shakespeare's plays. For example, characters may speak of things to come in the plot of the story in an ironic way, because they are not aware of the significance of their words in regard to events that are going to occur afterwards. This helps the audience to possess information that the characters do not have.

Another dramatic technique is the soliloquy. The word 'soliloquy' comes from the Latin, which means 'to speak alone'. A soliloquy is often called a monologue. It is an opportunity for the audience to know the inner thoughts, feelings and decisions of a character in a play as the speaker speaks out loud to himself in front of the audience.

These are just two examples of how Elizabethan plays acknowledge the presence of the audience, which is also achieved through the use of prologues, epilogues and choruses.

The Shakespearean saying 'To be, or not to be', comes from Hamlet's Soliloquy in *The Tragedy of Hamlet, Prince of Denmark* (written somewhere between 1599 and 1602), Act 3, Scene 1. During this monologue Hamlet contemplates death and suicide because of the pain of life. The following extract is taken from this soliloquy.

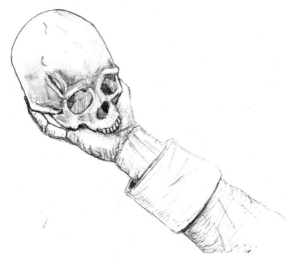

Alas, poor Yorick!

Extract 19

To be, or not to be: that is the question:
Whether 'tis nobler in the mind to suffer
The slings and arrows of outrageous fortune,
Or to take arms against a sea of troubles,
And by opposing end them? To die: to sleep;

No more; and by a sleep to say we end
The heart-ache and the thousand natural shocks
That flesh is heir to, 'tis a consummation
Devoutly to be wish' d.

Task 19

Read this extract from Hamlet's Soliloquy several times until you gain a general understanding of its meaning. Then in your own words, rewrite it in prose in today's English remaining as closely as possible to the original.

The following extract is an example of how the extract above could be converted into today's English.

Extract 20

To be, or not to be, that is the question:
Whether it is considered more noble to suffer the slings and arrows of outrageous fortune, or to take up arms against a sea of troubles; and by opposing them, put them to an end?
Or to enter the sleep of death—no more—and by this sleep we could end the heartache and the thousand disasters that people naturally inherit. That is a consummation to be greatly desired.

Glossary

slings and arrows	These are missiles from weapons of Hamlet's time. They are used here to symbolise the afflictions received by bad or unlucky circumstances.
take up arms	get ready to fight
sea of troubles	Here, 'sea' expresses a huge quantity of problems.

consummation　　　result, final outcome

Task 20

Here are the first few lines of the two versions. The first one is the original, and the second one is my version in prose in today's English. Practice reading the two versions out loud and choose one to memorise. Then recite it to your partner from memory.

Original

To be, or not to be: that is the question:
Whether 'tis nobler in the mind to suffer
The slings and arrows of outrageous fortune,
Or to take arms against a sea of troubles,
And by opposing end them?

Modernised Version

To be, or not to be, that is the question:

Whether it is considered more noble to suffer the slings and arrows of outrageous fortune, or to take up arms against a sea of troubles; and by opposing them, put an end to them?

King Lear

Shakespeare's *King Lear* was first published in 1608. It is written in blank verse, in which there are five stressed syllables and five unstressed syllables in each line. However, Shakespeare breaks the rules when he uses shorter lines for emphasis.

Characters of low status usually speak in prose in Elizabethan drama, and scenes of madness use prose too. When King Lear goes mad, Shakespeare shifts from prose to verse to prose to symbolise the confusion in his mind. Lear also uses the third person pronoun in the form of the royal 'we' at the beginning of the play, which is an expression of his high position and influence, however, later on, when he becomes powerless, he uses the more humble first person pronoun 'I' and the expression 'methinks' (meaning 'I think'). This shows the King's change from being a powerful king to a 'foolish old man'.

The plot of *King Lear* is as follows:

King Lear is getting old and wants a life without too many responsibilities, so he decides to divide his kingdom between his three daughters: Gonerill, who turns out to have a lust for power, Regan and Cordelia. The king wants to test the extent of their love for him, hoping his favourite, his youngest daughter Cordelia, will win, so he can give her the largest part of the kingdom. But Cordelia refuses to take part in such a test. This makes Lear angry, and as a result he divides his kingdom between his other two daughters, who eventually throw Lear out.

King Lear himself is the protagonist who goes mad because of his serious mistake, and the story traces his tragic downfall. The play is therefore called a tragedy. Shakespeare's tragedies typically concentrate on the downfall of powerful men who are not necessarily good. In Lear's case, whether or not he deserves his downfall is unclear.

The play also explores the struggle between good and evil, and the issue of justice.

The next extract is taken from the beginning of *King Lear*'s Act III, Scene 2. In this scene, Lear is in a violent and confused state of mind. He seeks revenge even though he recognises that he has made mistakes himself. Lear is the storm described in the passage; his actions have caused chaos and this state of affairs is reflected in nature. He has caused others to suffer, and he feels he should suffer too.

Extract 21

> **Lear:** *Blow, winds, and crack your cheeks! Rage! Blow!*
> *You cataracts and hurricanoes, spout*
> *Till you have drenched our steeples, drowned the cocks!*
> *You sulphurous and thought-executing fires,*

Vaunt-curriers of oak-cleaving thunderbolts,
Singe my white head! And thou all-shaking thunder,
Strike flat the thick rotundity o' the world,
Crack Nature's moulds, all germens spill at once
That makes ingrateful man!

Fool: O, nuncle, court holy-water in a dry house is better than this rain-water out o' door. Good nuncle, in; ask thy daughters' blessing. Here's a night pities neither wise men nor fools.

Lear: Rumble thy bellyful! Spit, fire! Spout, rain!
Nor rain, wind, thunder, fire are my daughters.
I tax not you, you elements, with unkindness;
I never gave you kingdom, called you children.
You owe me no subscription; then let fall
Your horrible pleasure. Here I stand, your slave,
A poor, infirm, weak and despised old man.
But yet I call you servile ministers,
That will with two pernicious daughters join
Your high-engendered battles' gainst a head
So old and white as this. O, ho! 'Tis foul!

Task 21a

Consider the following statements by 'Lear' taken from the extract above, and for each one, describe what is being conveyed:

Blow, winds, and crack your cheeks! Rage! Blow!

... oak-cleaving thunderbolts,
Singe my white head! And thou all-shaking thunder,
Strike flat the thick rotundity o' the world ...

Rumble thy bellyful! Spit, fire! Spout, rain!

Nor rain, wind, thunder, fire are my daughters.
I tax not you, you elements, with unkindness ...

Task 21b

Consider the following sentence by 'Fool' taken from the extract above and describe what is being conveyed:

Here's a night pities neither wise men nor fools.

The Sonnets

Shakespeare wrote many sonnets. They were written somewhere between 1598 and 1609. A sonnet is a poetic verse consisting of 14 lines with a fixed rhyming pattern. Shakespeare's sonnets had the following rhyme pattern. His sonnets I and II are written below.

Extract 22

<u>Sonnet I</u>
From fairest creatures we desire increase,
That thereby beauty's rose might never die,
But as the riper should by time decease,
His tender heir might bear his memory:
But thou contracted to thine own bright eyes,
Feed'st thy light's flame with self-substantial fuel,
Making a famine where abundance lies,
Thy self thy foe, to thy sweet self too cruel:

Thou that art now the world's fresh ornament,
And only herald to the gaudy spring,
Within thine own bud buriest thy content,
And, tender churl, mak'st waste in niggarding:
Pity the world, or else this glutton be,
To eat the world's due, by the grave and thee.

<u>Sonnet II</u>
When forty winters shall besiege thy brow,
And dig deep trenches in thy beauty's field,
Thy youth's proud livery so gazed on now,
Will be a totter'd weed of small worth held:
Then being asked, where all thy beauty lies,
Where all the treasure of thy lusty days;
To say, within thine own deep sunken eyes,
Were an all-eating shame, and thriftless praise.
How much more praise deserv'd thy beauty's use,
If thou couldst answer 'This fair child of mine
Shall sum my count, and make my old excuse,'
Proving his beauty by succession thine!
This were to be new made when thou art old,
And see thy blood warm when thou feel'st it cold.

Task 22

Read and enjoy sonnets I and II. Note down which lines rhyme amongst the 14 lines of sonnet I, and then do the same with sonnet II. For example, you can start the analysis of sonnet I as follows:

Sonnet I :
Lines 1 and 3, lines 2 and 4 …

Additional Notes for Unit 3
第3单元附加注释

Silent Letters

There are 26 letters in the English alphabet, but only five of them are never silent. They are f,j,q,v and x. I will give some examples of silent letters below:

The 'k' in the letter combination 'kn' at the beginning of a word used to be pronounced, but now it is silent. Consider the following: **knee, knife, knit, knock, knot** and **know**.

The 'w' in the letter combination 'wr' at the beginning of a word used to be pronounced, but in the following examples it is silent: **wrestle, wrinkle, write** and **wrong**. But many people still pronounce not only the letter 'w' in words such as **where** and **what**, but also the 'h.' Listen out for this.

The fact that the silent letters have not disappeared from spelling can cause frustration, but there are advantages for writing. For example, if you were to speak the phrase '**write** and **wrong**' from the previous paragraph, it would give the impression of 'right and wrong,' a very common phrase in English, but when read there is absolutely no confusion, as the difference in spelling makes it clear. The pronunciation of the word 'write' could also be misunderstood as a third word with exactly the same pronunciation, that is, 'rite'. The meanings of the three words **write**, **right** and **rite** are completely different.

Since the sixteenth century onwards, words have come into English from Greek and Latin by scientists and scholars, but the sound of the first letter of some words was soon dropped due to the sounds being difficult for a native English speaker. Two examples from Greek are the 'p' in 'pn' or 'ps,' and the 'm' in the combination 'mn.' Consider the following: **pneumonia**, **psychology** and **mnemonic**. Now try to say the words pronouncing the first and second letters of each word. This will help you to see the reasons why English speakers soon made the first 'p' and 'm' silent.

In your answers to Task 16, you can see many examples of an additional 'e' at the end of words, when we would not have the 'e' in today's English; this extra 'e' seemed to be added freely by the printer. Extract 16 has the following examples: **forme, uoyde, darknesse, deepe, saide, sawe, hee, againe** and **bee**. In every case, the final 'e' has been dropped today. But a special type of 'final e' that we have not discarded, was introduced in the sixteenth century by Richard Mulcaster who wrote a book on spelling. He suggested that a letter 'e' should be added to words of one syllable that have only one vowel in the middle. This 'e' would indicate that the vowel sound in the middle would be a long one. This suggestion was adopted and is still present today. Consider the inner vowel sounds of the following examples: **hat** and **hate, bit** and **bite, con** and **cone**. The first word from each pair has a short vowel sound, whereas the second word in each pair has a long vowel sound.

However, printers took advantage of this trend and the result was that the letter 'e' was used at the end of words even where the rule did not apply. Consider the following: **come, done, give, gone, have, love** and **some**.

Further Notes on Extract 17

O Romeo, Romeo, wherefore art thou Romeo?

After looking at my answers at the back of the book, you may be surprised to see the interpretation, *'Oh Romeo, Romeo, why are you like this Romeo?'*

'Wherefore' does not mean 'where', but rather 'why'. In the play, there was a feud between Juliet's Capulet family and Romeo's Montague clan. Romeo and Juliet were from different sides. So Juliet is asking, 'Why are you a Montague, Romeo!' She suggests that if he will not change his allegiance, then she will change hers:

O Romeo, Romeo! Wherefore art thou Romeo?
Deny thy father and refuse thy name;

The story of Shakespeare's *Romeo and Juliet* goes as follows:

The play begins with a fight between Montague and Capulet servants in Verona, Italy, setting the scene of rivalry between the masters of each.

Later, Count Paris approaches Capulet about his wish to marry his daughter Juliet, and she is put under pressure to do so. Romeo (a Montague) attends Capulet's ball where Paris and Juliet are, and Romeo falls in love with Juliet. Juliet's cousin Tybalt wants to kill Romeo but Juliet's father does not want blood spilt in his house, so he stops him.

After the ball, Romeo sneaks into the Capulet orchard and overhears Juliet at her window talking of her love for him. During the balcony scene, they agree to marry, which they do secretly the next day. Then in a feud, Romeo ends up killing Juliet's cousin Tybalt which results in Romeo being thrown out of Verona under threat of death if he returns. In spite of this, Romeo secretly spends the night in his wife Juliet's bedroom.

Meanwhile, unaware of her marriage to Romeo, Juliet's family pressures her to marry Paris and the wedding day is set. In an attempt to help, Friar Laurence gives Juliet a potion that will put her into a deathlike coma for forty-two hours. She takes it the night before the wedding. The plan is for her to be happily reunited with Romeo when she wakes up, but the plan fails. After taking the potion, Juliet's family thinks she is dead and Romeo hears that news before he hears that it is all part of a plan to help them to be reunited. Romeo visits Juliet's crypt and, believing her to be dead, drinks poison in his grief. Juliet then wakes up, and seeing Romeo is dead, she stabs herself with his dagger to join him.

All that glisters is not gold

The saying '*All that glitters is not gold*' comes from *The Merchant of Venice* (1596). The original word that Shakespeare used for 'glitters' was 'glisters,' but in spite of this, whenever the original is quoted, it is changed to 'glitters', making 'All that glitters is not gold', as the word 'glisters' is unfamiliar. The saying is set in the context of Hell and Death, and close to the words '*Gilded tombs do worms enfold*', so the meaning is clear. Wealth does not guarantee happiness or long lasting power, and you cannot take your riches with you when you die.

Glossary for Unit 3

The Aeneid 《埃涅阿斯纪》

The Aeneid was originally written in Latin by the poet Virgil over 2,000 years ago. It is an epic poem about the Trojan Aeneas who, after the defeat of Troy, fled from the great city carrying his father Anchises on his shoulders. Aeneas' descendants founded the city of Rome in Italy.

inclusive 范围广泛的

One of the primary reasons for the use of inclusive language is to ensure men and women are considered equal. Another example would be the word 'mankind' which actually includes men and women in its meaning; however, using the word 'humankind' would be considered more appropriate.

Protestantism 新教

This refers to the separation of the Church from Roman Catholicism during the Reformation.

Pilgrim Fathers (英国1620年前到达北美洲的)清教徒前辈移民

These were the English people that travelled by ship in 1620 to settle in North America, hoping for an earthly paradise without the dominance of selfishness and sin.

blank verse 无韵诗、素体诗

Blank verse is poetry written in regular metrical but unrhymed lines, usually iambic pentameters. Blank Verse has been the most commonly used poetic form for English language since the sixteenth century.

stressed syllables 重读音节

Every word has a number of syllables or individual sounds; for example, 'attitude' has 3 syllables, and the first syllable is stressed or emphasised, making the initial 'a' the loudest part of the word.

royal 'we' 英国皇室的自称（类似中国皇帝自称"朕"或"寡人"，译者注）

The plural pronoun could be used by a person such as a monarch, to express his/her high position. Queen Victoria of England (1819–1901) has often been quoted as saying, 'We are not amused!'

protagonist 主人公、主角

The word 'protagonist' comes from the ancient Greek meaning 'player of the first part'. So the word is used to identify the 'main character/actor' in a play.

tragedy 悲剧

A tragedy follows the downfall of an individual. In tragedies, there is often a connection between the protagonist's downfall and their preceding behaviour, and the story will highlight moments when the protagonist learns the truth of their situation.

Unit 4

17th to 18th Century Literature
17—18世纪文学

Chapter 7 More Features of Early Modern English
  第7章 早期现代英语的其他特点

Chapter 8 Daniel Defoe and Jonathan Swift
  第8章 丹尼尔·笛福和乔纳森·斯威夫特

Additional Notes for Unit 4
  第4单元附加注释

Chapter 7   More Features of Early Modern English

第7章　早期现代英语的其他特点

The Early Modern English Period lasted for three-hundred years, ending in about 1750. Here we will look at English Literature from the latter half of the period.

The language of England was beginning to spread throughout the world and even until today the English language has not fragmented into mutually unintelligible languages, unlike Latin which developed into languages such as French, Spanish and Romanian. The establishment of English-speaking colonies in North America was the first real step in making English an international language. But before this, mainland Europeans, such as the Portuguese and Spanish, had already settled in South America, so these languages also influenced the development of English in the Americas. Within twenty years of the most successful settlement in North America by the Pilgrim Fathers (in 1620), 25,000 more Europeans had migrated to North America.

The English language that was implanted in North America was of course that of England during the Early Modern English Period.

Today, American English has acquired approximately 300 <u>Native American loanwords</u>. Half of these entered English in the seventeenth century. Here are a few of those early loanwords: *caribou, moccasin, moose, possum, persimmon, powwow, skunk, squash, terrapin* and *wigwam*.

早期现代英语持续了300年，大约在1750年结束。在这一单元，我们将研究后半期的英国文学。

英格兰的语言开始在全世界传播。不像拉丁语发展成法语、西班牙语和罗马尼亚语,直到今天,英语尚未分裂成互不可知的语言。在北美建立讲英语的殖民地是英语成为国际语言的第一步。但在此之前,本土欧洲人如葡萄牙人和西班牙人已经在南美殖民定居,因此他们的语言也影响了美洲英语的发展。在清教徒祖先在北美顺利定居的20年内(1620年),又有25 000名欧洲人移居北美。

  当然,在北美植根的英语是早期现代英语的英格兰语言。

  如今,美式英语有大约300个美国本土的借词。其中一半是在17世纪介入了英语语言的发展。以下是一些早期的借词:驯鹿、鹿皮鞋、驼鹿、负鼠、柿子、讨论会(帕瓦仪式)、臭鼬、西葫芦、水龟和棚屋。

The King James Version (KJV)

  Of course, English continued to develop in England itself, its place of origin. A book in English that was to have a huge influence on the stability of English language was the King James Version of the Bible, the Bible translation of The Church of England. It was published in 1611, at a time when *The Geneva Bible* was still popular, but *The Geneva Bible* was displaced after a several decades. The Bible translators of the KJV said, 'God's sacred Word... is that inestimable treasure that excelleth all the riches of the earth.' It is named 'The noblest monument of English prose.' It was the only authorized Bible for the English-speaking world for 250 years.

  The following extract is taken from the original KJV of 1611. It is the text of Genesis chapter 1, verses 1-6.

Extract 23

  In the beginning God created the Heauen, and the Earth. And the earth was without forme, and voyd; and darkenesse was upon the face of the deepe: and the Spirit of God mooued upon the face of the waters. And God said, Let there be light: and there was light. And God saw the light, that it was good: and

God diuided the light from the darkenesse. And God called the light, Day, and the darkenesse he called Night: and the euening and the morning were the first day. And God said, Let there be a firmament in the midst of the waters: and let it diuide the waters from the waters.

Task 23a

List or underline all the words that have an 'e' at the end when it is not needed in today's English. Then compare these with the examples you found in the equivalent extract (Extract 16) from *The Geneva Bible*, which is 51 years older. What do you find?

Task 23b

Carefully examine the two versions of the text from the Book of Genesis (Extracts 16 and 23) and list all the differences in the use of vocabulary and phrases. Why do you think these differences exist?

Task 23c

Look at the punctuation in Extract 23. Which punctuation symbols are missing? Why is this?

Here is another extract from the KJV in its original form. This is the most well-known Psalm in *the Bible*. It was written by David who was the most famous of all the kings of Israel. He was also the ancestor of Jesus Christ.

Extract 24

Psalm 23

The LORD is my shepheard, I shall not want.
He maketh me to lie downe in greene pastures:
he leadeth mee beside the still waters.
He restoreth my soule:
he leadeth me in the pathes of righteousnes, for his names sake.
Yea though I walke through the ualley of the shadowe of death, I will feare no euill:
for thou art with me, thy rod and thy staffe, they comfort me.
Thou preparest a table before me, in the presence of mine enemies:
thou anointest my head with oyle, my cuppe runneth ouer.
Surely goodnes and mercie shall followe me all the daies of my life:
and I will dwell in the house of the LORD for euer.

Glossary

I shall not want	I shall lack nothing
… me to lie downe	... me lie down
Yea though	Even though
dwell	live

It is worth noting from this extract that another important feature of today's punctuation is missing. In the phrase, 'for his names sake,' there should be an apostrophe before the final 's' in 'names', giving, 'for his name's sake'.

There are also a lot of spelling differences, such as:

shepheard (shepherd), downe (down), greene (green), mee (me), soule (soul), pathes (paths), walke (walk), shadowe (shadow), feare (fear), euill (evil), staffe (staff), cuppe (cup), followe (follow).

Task 24a

Scan through the extract and find 2 words that have a suffix spelt differently to today's English.

Task 24b

Scan through the extract and find 3 words that have their 'i' or 'y' confused by today's expectations.

Task 24c

In the psalm, there are many examples of a pronoun with an accompanying verb, and some possessive pronouns. Underline them or write them in a list like this:

He maketh ...
He leadeth ...

Task 24d

Study the examples of pronouns with their accompanying verbs, and the examples of possessive pronouns. What patterns can you see? Discuss this with your partner and note down your descriptions before checking my notes at the back of the book.

Task 24e

Now you have analysed Psalm 23 in depth, you are in a position to change it into today's modern English. Keep the poetic pattern of the lines as you do so, and keep your version as accurate as possible to the original KJV.

You will have noticed that the Second Person Singular Pronoun in the extract is 'Thou' and the Second Person Singular Possessive Pronoun is 'Thy'. In today's English, these are 'You' and 'Your' respectively, and 'You' and 'Your' are used for the Singular and the Plural today. In the past, the old 'Thou' and 'Thy' could only be used for the Singular, and the Second Person Plurals were 'Ye' and 'Your' respectively.

John Milton's *Paradise Lost*

A famous poet from England at this time was John Milton (1608–1674), the last major poet of the Renaissance period. He is well-known for his work *Paradise Lost* which was published in 1667. *Paradise Lost* is an epic poem in blank verse. It concerns Adam and Eve, the first man and woman of God's creation. It also concerns Satan (Lucifer) who with his wicked angels was defeated by God and banished to Hell (Tartarus). However, Satan decides to corrupt the newly created Earth and its people. He finds his way to the Garden of Eden, where Adam and Eve are living a blissful existence. Adam and Eve have been told by God, their Creator, that they can eat the fruit of any tree in the garden except for the Tree of the Knowledge of Good and Evil. But Satan, disguised as a serpent, tempts Eve to eat from the forbidden tree, and Adam follows suit; they feel guilt and shame for the first time. God punishes Satan and his evil angels who turn into snakes, unable to walk and talk.

God's Angel Michael tells Adam that one day, the Messiah (the Christ),

Jesus Christ, will provide a way of forgiveness for humankind, but for now Adam and Eve are thrown out of the Garden of Eden.

The extract below is taken from the beginning of the first book of *Paradise Lost*. A couple of short sections of the poem have been removed for ease of reading.

Extract 25

Of man's first disobedience, and the fruit
Of that forbidden tree, whose mortal taste
Brought death into the world, and all our woe,
With loss of Eden, till one greater man
Restore us ......
Say first, for Heaven hides nothing from thy view
Nor the deep tract of Hell, say first what cause
Moved our grand parents in that happy state,
Favoured of Heaven so highly, to fall off
From their Creator, and transgress his will
For one restraint, lords of the world besides.
Who first seduced them to that foul revolt?
Th' infernal serpent; he it was, whose guile
Stirred up with envy and revenge, deceived
The mother of mankind, what time his pride
Had cast him out from Heaven, with all his host
Of rebel angels, by whose aid aspiring
To set himself in glory above his peers,
He trusted to have equalled the most high,
If he opposed; and with ambitious aim
Against the throne and monarchy of God
Raised impious war in Heaven and battle proud
With vain attempt. Him the Almighty Power

Hurled headlong flaming from th' ethereal sky
With hideous ruin and combustion down
To bottomless perdition, there to dwell
In adamantine chains and penal fire,
Who durst defy th' Omnipotent to arms.
Nine times the space that measures day and night
To mortal men, he with his horrid crew
Lay vanquished, rolling in the fiery gulf
Confounded though immortal: But his doom
Reserved him to more wrath; for now the thought
Both of lost happiness and lasting pain
Torments him; round he throws his baleful eyes
That witnessed huge affliction and dismay
Mixed with obdurate pride and steadfast hate:
At once as far as angels ken he views
The dismal situation waste and wild,
A dungeon horrible, on all sides round
As one great furnace flamed, yet from those flames
No light, but rather darkness visible
Served only to discover sights of woe,
Regions of sorrow, doleful shades, where peace
And rest can never dwell, hope never comes
That comes to all; but torture without end
Still urges, and a fiery Deluge, fed
With ever-burning sulphur unconsumed:
Such place eternal justice had prepared
For those rebellious, here their prison ordained
In utter darkness, and their portion set
As far removed from God and light of Heaven
As from the centre thrice to th' utmost pole.

Oh how unlike the place from whence they fell!
There the companions of his fall, o'erwhelmed
With floods and whirlwinds of tempestuous fire,
He soon discerns, and weltering by his side
One next himself in power, and next in crime,
Long after known in Palestine, and named
Beelzebub. To whom th' arch-enemy,
And thence in Heaven called Satan, with bold words
Breaking the horrid silence thus began.

If thou beest he; But O how fallen! how changed
From him, who in the happy realms of light
Clothed with transcendent brightness didst outshine
Myriads though bright: if he whom mutual league,
United thoughts and counsels, equal hope
And hazard in the glorious enterprise,
Joined with me once, now misery hath joined
In equal ruin: into what pit thou seest
From what height fallen, so much the stronger proved
He with his thunder: and till then who knew
The force of those dire arms? yet not for those,
Nor what the Potent Victor in his rage
Can else inflict, do I repent or change,
Though changed in outward luster; that fixed mind
And high disdain, from sense of injured merit,
That with the mightiest raised me to contend,
And to the fierce contention brought along
Innumerable force of spirits armed
That durst dislike his reign, and me preferring,
His utmost power with adverse power opposed
In dubious battle on the plains of Heaven,

And shook his throne. What though the field be lost?
All is not lost; the unconquerable will,
And study of revenge, immortal hate,
And courage never to submit or yield:
And what is else not to be overcome?
That glory never shall his wrath or might
Extort from me. To bow and sue for grace
With suppliant knee, and deify his power,
Who from the terror of this arm so late
Doubted his empire, that were low indeed,
That were an ignominy and shame beneath
This downfall; since by fate the strength of gods
And this empyreal substance cannot fail
……
    Fallen Cherub, to be weak is miserable
Doing or suffering: but of this be sure,
To do aught good never will be our task,
But ever to do ill our sole delight,
As being the contrary to his high will
Whom we resist. If then his providence
Out of our evil seek to bring forth good,
Our labour must be to pervert that end,
And out of good still to find means of evil;
Which oft times may succeed, so as perhaps
Shall grieve him, if I fail not, and disturb
His inmost counsels from their destined aim.
But see the angry Victor hath recalled
His ministers of vengeance and pursuit
Back to the gates of Heaven: The sulphurous hail
Shot after us in storm, o'erblown hath laid

The fiery Surge, that from the precipice
Of Heaven received us falling, and the thunder,
Winged with red lightning and impetuous rage,
Perhaps hath spent his shafts, and ceases now
To bellow through the vast and boundless deep.
Let us not slip th' occasion, whether scorn,
Or satiate fury yield it from our foe.
Seest thou yon dreary plain, forlorn and wild,
The seat of desolation, void of light,
Save what the glimmering of these livid flames
Casts pale and dreadful? Thither let us tend
From off the tossing of these fiery waves,
There rest, if any rest can harbour there,
And reassembling our afflicted powers,
Consult how we may henceforth most offend
Our enemy, our own loss how repair,
How overcome this dire calamity,
What reinforcement we may gain from hope,
If not what resolution from despair.

Glossary

forbidden tree	The forbidden tree is called The Tree of the Knowledge of Good and Evil. Adam and Eve were told by God, their Creator, that they could eat the fruit of any tree, except for this one.
Eden	This is the Garden of Eden, a beautiful garden like an earthly Heaven (an earthly Paradise); this is where Adam and Eve lived happily.
greater man	This is Jesus Christ, the Messiah.
Heaven	The perfect place where God lives and where his

	followers will eventually live in bliss forever.
fall off	fall from
Th'infernal serpent	The Infernal Serpent/The Serpent from Hell, is Satan, the most powerful evil angel that was originally created by God.
Almighty Power	God is the Almighty Power because he possesses almighty power.
th'ethereal sky	This is the upper atmosphere.
adamantine	unbreakable
as far as angels ken	as far as angels can see
urges	afflicts
utter	complete
Beelzebub	This is the name of a god worshipped among the Philistines of past history. The literal meaning of the name is 'The Lord of Flies'. Here it is used as an alternative name for Satan.
Satan	adversary
study	pursuit
fail	cease to exist
Fallen Cherub	Satan (Lucifer) is also referred to as the Chief Cherub, 'cherub' being another name for an angel. Satan is described as 'fallen' because he has fallen away from God as a result of his sinful rebellion.
To do aught good	To do anything good
to do ill	'To do ill' means to do bad or evil things.
yon dreary plain	'Yon' is an old fashioned word meaning 'distant'.
livid flames	glowing flames of death

Task 25

Read the above extract several times, using the glossary and checking any other words you do not know in a dictionary. Then convert the following section of the extract into today's English prose, staying as close to the original as possible:

Of man's first disobedience, and the fruit
Of that forbidden tree, whose mortal taste
Brought death into the world, and all our woe,
With loss of Eden, till one greater man
Restore us ……
  Say first, for Heaven hides nothing from thy view
Nor the deep tract of Hell, say first what cause
Moved our grand parents in that happy state,
Favoured of Heaven so highly, to fall off
From their Creator, and transgress his will
For one restraint, lords of the world besides.
Who first seduced them to that foul revolt?
Th' infernal serpent; he it was, whose guile
Stirred up with envy and revenge, deceived
The mother of mankind, what time his pride
Had cast him out from Heaven, with all his host
Of rebel angels, by whose aid aspiring
To set himself in glory above his peers,
He trusted to have equalled the most high,
If he opposed; and with ambitious aim
Against the throne and monarchy of God
Raised impious war in Heaven and battle proud

With vain attempt. Him the Almighty Power
Hurled headlong flaming from th' ethereal sky
With hideous ruin and combustion down
To bottomless perdition, there to dwell
In adamantine chains and penal fire,
Who durst defy th' Omnipotent to arms.

The Pilgrim's Progress by John Bunyan

One of John Milton's contemporaries was John Bunyan (1628-1688), who was from a poor background. He suffered many hardships during this extremely difficult period in the history of England. Amongst the many events, we had 'The English Civil Wars' which took place from 1642-1651, involving England, Scotland and Ireland. The Civil Wars came to an end by the hand of Oliver Cromwell in 1651. 'The Great Plague' also struck and lasted from 1665-1666, and 'The Great Fire of London' took place in 1666 which many believe to have eradicated The Great Plague.

Bunyan had a traumatic life. He was a Christian preacher, for which he was imprisoned from 1661-1666. After this, he was imprisoned again for another six years. However, he had the freedom to write books in prison. His first book was an autobiography called *Grace Abounding*, published in London in 1666. In 1675 he was arrested for preaching again and jailed for 6 months in Bedford, England. It was during this prison term that he began the book he is most famous for. It is called *The Pilgrim's Progress*, which was published in 1678. Since then the book has been translated into over 200 languages. It is considered to be the first novel in English. It was also unique in that the novel was written as an <u>allegory</u> from beginning to end.

George Bernard Shaw (1856-1950), the Irish playwright, wrote:

'All that you miss in Shakespeare you find in Bunyan ... The world to him [Bunyan] was a more terrible place than it was to Shakespeare; but he saw through it

a path at the end of which a man might look ... forward to the Celestial City.'

John Bunyan <u>coined the phrase</u> 'Vanity Fair' (amongst many others) in his work *The Pilgrim's Progress*, a phrase that has been used many times over the centuries. For example, the nineteenth century novelist William Makepeace Thackery is most famous for his <u>satirical novel</u> called *Vanity Fair*.

In *The Pilgrim's Progress*, Vanity Fair refers to an allegorical place called Vanity, in which there is a Fair that continues perpetually. It symbolises idle pleasures and the vain arrogance of human beings.

Below is an extract from *The Pilgrim's Progress*. The pilgrim called Christian is in the Valley of Humiliation where he meets a monster called Apollyon.

Extract 26

But now, in this Valley of Humiliation, poor Christian was hard put to it; for he had gone but a little way before he espied a foul fiend coming over the field to meet him: his name is Apollyon. Then did Christian begin to be afraid, and to cast in his mind whether to go back or to stand his ground. But he considered again that he had no armour for his back, and therefore thought, that to turn the back to him might give him greater advantage with ease to pierce him with his darts. Therefore he resolved to venture, and stand his ground; for, thought he, had I no more in my eye than the saving of my life, it would be the best way to stand.

So he went on, and Apollyon met him. Now the monster was hideous to behold; he was clothed with scales like a fish, and they are his pride; he had wings like a dragon, feet like a bear, and out of his belly came fire and smoke; and his mouth was as the mouth of a lion. When he was come up to Christian, he beheld him with a disdainful countenance, and thus began to question with him.

APOLLYON: Whence came you; and whither are you bound?

CHRISTIAN: I am come from the City of Destruction, which is the place of all evil, and am going to the City of Zion.

APOLLYON: By this I perceive that thou art one of my subjects; for all that country is mine, and I am the prince and god of it. How is it, then, that thou hast run away from thy king? Were it not that I hope that thou mayest do me more service, I would strike thee now, at one blow, to the ground.

CHRISTIAN: I was indeed born in your dominions, but your service was hard, and your wages such as a man could not live on; for the wages of sin is death; therefore, when I was come to years, I did, as other considerate persons do, look out, if perhaps I might mend myself.

APOLLYON: There is no prince that will thus lightly lose his subjects, neither will I as yet lose thee; but since thou complainest of thy service and wages, be content to go back, and what our country will afford, I do here promise to give thee.

CHRISTIAN: But I have let myself to another, even to the King of princes; and how can I with fairness go back with thee?

APOLLYON: Thou hast done in this according to the proverb, 'Changed a bad for a worse:' but it is ordinary for those that have professed themselves his servants, after a while to give him the slip and return again unto me. Do thou so too, and all shall be well.

CHRISTIAN: I have given him my faith, and sworn my allegiance to him; how then, can I go back from this, and not be hanged as a traitor?

APOLLYON: Thou didst the same to me, and yet I am willing to pass by all if now thou wilt yet turn and go back.

CHRISTIAN: What I promised thee was in my nonage; and, besides, I count that the Prince under whose banner I now stand is able to absolve me; yea, and to pardon also what I did as to my compliance with thee. And besides, O thou destroying Apollyon! to speak truth, I like his service, his wages, his servants, his government, his company and country better than thine; therefore leave off to persuade me further: I am his servant, and I will follow him.

Glossary

Valley of Humiliation   As an allegory, the story has locations that symbolise aspects of a person's life. It is in the Valley of Humiliation that Christian fights with the monster, because the monster tries to humiliate him.

was hard put to it	facing great difficulties
foul fiend	offensive and evil monster
venture	take a risk
hideous to behold	extremely ugly to look at
When he was come up to	When he had come up to
disdainful countenance	contemptuous (facial) expression
to question with him	to question him
Whence came you; and whither are you bound?	Where did you come from; and where are you going?
I am come from the City of Destruction	I have come from the City of Destruction.
one of my subjects	one of the people under my authority
born in your dominions	born in the place that is under your authority
nonage	This means the time before he was legally responsible for his decisions.

Task 26

You will see from the extract and the glossary, that the text has many old fashioned words and phrases. Underline them or write them down in a list. Then study them and try to describe their meanings to a partner. Then write down alternative phrases in today's English for each example.

The glossary has already given some examples to start you off.

Now we continue the story in the following extract which brings Christian and the monster Apollyon to the beginning of their fight.

Extract 27

APOLLYON: Thou hast already been unfaithful in thy service to him; and how dost thou think to receive wages of him?

CHRISTIAN: Wherein, O Apollyon, have I been unfaithful to him?

APOLLYON: Thou didst faint at first setting out, when thou wast almost choked in the gulf of Despond. Thou didst attempt wrong ways to be rid of thy burden, whereas thou shouldest have stayed till thy Prince had taken it off. Thou didst sinfully sleep, and lose thy choice things. Thou wast, also, almost persuaded to go back at the sight of the lions. And when thou talkest of thy journey, and of what thou hast seen and heard, thou art inwardly desirous of vainglory in all that thou sayest or doest.

CHRISTIAN: All this is true, and much more which thou hast left out; but the Prince whom I serve and honour is merciful, and ready to forgive. But, besides, these infirmities possessed me in thy country; for there I sucked them in, and I have groaned under them, being sorry for them, and have obtained pardon of my Prince.

APOLLYON: Then Apollyon broke out into a grievous rage, saying, I am an enemy to this Prince; I hate his person, laws, and people: I am come out on purpose to withstand thee.

CHRISTIAN: Apollyon, beware what you do, for I am in the King's highway, the way of holiness; therefore take heed to yourself.

APOLLYON: Then Apollyon straddled quite over the whole breadth of the way, and said, I am void of fear in this matter. Prepare thyself to die; for I swear by my infernal den that thou shalt go no farther; here will I spill thy soul.

The battle between the two opponents raged for over half a day. At one point, Christian's sword flew out of his hand, but he managed to retrieve it and thrust it into the dragon-like monster, which then flew away defeated; Christian never saw Apollyon again.

Task 27

Extract 27 has many examples of Early Modern English personal pronouns and verbs that are not used today. List them and write their equivalents in today's modern English.

The next extract is an updated version of Extract 26 and 27. Read it carefully and then answer the comprehension questions beneath it.

Extract 28

But now, in this Valley of Humiliation, poor Christian was in for trouble again, because he had only gone a little distance before he could see an evil looking creature coming over the field to meet him; his name is Apollyon. Then Christian began to be afraid, and considered in his mind whether to go back or to stand his ground. But he considered again how he had no armour for his back, and therefore thought that turning his back to him might give the monster a greater advantage because he could easily pierce him with his arrows. Therefore he resolved to take a risk, and stand his ground, because he thought, 'If I had nothing more in mind than to save my life, this would be the best way to succeed'.

So he continued, and Apollyon met him. Now the monster was hideous to look at; he was clothed with scales like a fish, and they are his pride; he had wings like a dragon, feet like a bear, and out of his belly came fire and smoke; and his mouth was like the mouth of a lion. When he was close to Christian, he looked down upon him with disdain, and began to question him like this:

APOLLYON: Where have you come from, and where are you going?

CHRISTIAN: I have come from the City of Destruction, which is the place of all evil, and am going to the City of Zion.

APOLLYON: By this I perceive that you are one of my subjects, because all of that country is mine, and I am the prince and god of it. How is it, then, that you have run away from your king? If it wasn't for the fact that I am hoping you may offer me some service, I would strike you to the ground now, with one blow.

CHRISTIAN: I was indeed born in one of the areas that you control, but serving you was hard, and your wages were not suitable for a man to live on, because the wages of sin is death; so, when I was old enough, I looked beyond, just like other sensible people do, with the intention of mending my ways.

APOLLYON: There is no prince that will so lightly let his subjects go, and neither will I; but since you have complained about your duties and wages, be content to go back, and whatever our country can afford, I promise to give you.

CHRISTIAN: But I have given myself to another, to the King of princes; so how can I with fairness go back with you?

APOLLYON: You have done what the proverb says; you have 'Changed a bad situation for a worse one.' But it is quite normal for those that have professed themselves to be his servants, after a while to give him the slip and return to me. Do the same, and all will be well.

CHRISTIAN: I have given him my faith, and sworn my allegiance to him; how then, can I go back from this, and not be hanged as a traitor?

APOLLYON: You did the same to me, and yet I am willing to forget it all as long as you turn round and go back.

CHRISTIAN: What I promised you was in my young ignorance; and, anyway, I believe that the Prince under whose banner I now stand is able to absolve me, and also pardon me for what I did in accordance with your expectations. And besides, you destroying Apollyon! to be honest, I like serving him; I like his wages, his servants, his governance, his company and country better than yours. So, stop trying to persuade me anymore; I am his servant, and I will follow him. ...

APOLLYON: You have already been unfaithful in your service for him, so how do you think you are going to get any wages from him?

CHRISTIAN: How, Apollyon, have I been unfaithful to him?

APOLLYON: You fainted when you first set out, when you were almost choked in the gulf of Despond. You attempted to use wrong ways to get rid of your burden, instead of staying until the Prince took it off. You sinfully slept and lost your special possessions. You were also almost persuaded to go back at the sight of the lions. And when you talk about your journey, and about the things you have seen and heard, you are always longing for 'vainglory' in all that you say and do.

CHRISTIAN: All this is true, and there's much more that you've left out, but the Prince whom I serve and honour is merciful, and ready to forgive. Anyway, I had those infirmities in your country, and it was there that they took hold of me, and I groaned under the weight of them, being sorry for them, and I have obtained a pardon from my Prince.

APOLLYON: (Breaking into an extreme rage) I am an enemy of this Prince; I hate him, his laws and his people; I have come out on purpose to stop you.

CHRISTIAN: Watch out, Apollyon, because I am on the King's highway, the way of holiness; so be careful what you do.

APOLLYON: (Straddling across the whole breadth of the highway) I have no fear over this. Prepare to die, because I swear by my infernal den that you shall go no farther; I will spill your soul right here.

Glossary

vainglory   This is excessive pride in yourself, boasting about your achievements.

Task 28

Answer the following comprehension questions on the extract above.

a Why did Christian decide not to turn back when he saw Apollyon in the distance?

b In your own words, describe to your partner what Apollyon looks like.

c Give 5 reasons why Christian left the City of Destruction.

d What 5 things does Christian like about serving the King of princes?

Chapter 8 Daniel Defoe and Jonathan Swift
第8章 丹尼尔·笛福和乔纳森·斯威夫特

Among the many other famous British writers of the time was John Dryden (1631-1700) who was a poet and a playwright. He was made Poet Laureate in 1668. A popular quote from the prologue of his heroic drama called *All for Love* (1677) is:

'Errows [Errors], like straws, upon the surface flow;
He who would search for pearls must dive below.'

This play was a tragedy written in blank verse in imitation of Shakespeare's *Antony and Cleopatra*.

A very important diarist was Samuel Pepys (1633-1703). From the diary that he kept between 1660 and 1669, we can see many detailed descriptions of seventeenth century disasters in England.

A little later we have William Congreve (1670-1729), an English playwright and poet. He is famous for his comedies, such as *Love for Love* (1695) and *The Way of the World* (1700). The commonly heard saying, 'Hell hath no fury like a woman scorned', can be traced back to William Congreve's 1697 play called *The Mourning Bride*, misquoted from the following:

'Heav' n has no rage like love to hatred turn' d
Nor Hell a fury, like a woman scorn' d'

Another famous writer that we cannot ignore was Daniel Defoe (1660-1731). He is seen by many as the originator of the English novel, but as we have seen already, John Bunyan's *Pilgrim's Progress* was written in 1678, much earlier than Daniel Defoe's novels, which include *Robinson Crusoe* (1719) and *Moll Flanders* (1722). Like Ian Fleming later, Daniel Defoe worked in British Intelligence. In

Robinson Crusoe, Defoe explores the concept of an island as a microcosm of the world, like Shakespeare before him in *The Tempest* and William Golding's *Lord of the Flies* much later.

Daniel Defoe's *Robinson Crusoe*

Robinson Crusoe is a very believable account of a young man called Robinson who sets out to sea on a voyage that is interrupted by a terrible storm. He is shipwrecked off the coast of an uninhabited island. He is the only human survivor. However, he eventually discovers he is not alone, as cannibals visit the island to eat their prisoners. Robinson Crusoe saves one of them who is a native of the area. Robinson names him Friday, as he was rescued on a Friday. Friday and Robinson later rescue some more prisoners, one of whom is Friday's father. Eventually, an English ship anchors beside the island and the captain takes Robinson and Friday to England.

The story begins with a description of Robinson Crusoe as follows:

'*I was born in the year 1632, in the city of York, of a good family, though not of that country, my father being a foreigner of Bremen who settled first at Hull. He got a good estate by merchandise and, leaving off his trade, lived afterward at York, from whence he had married my mother, whose relations were named Robinson, a very good family in the country, and from whom I was called Robinson Kreutznaer; but by the usual corruption of words in England we are now called, nay, we call ourselves, and write our name "Crusoe," and so my companions always called me.*'

Glossary

of a good family ... not of that country ... a foreigner of Bremen   from a good family... not from that country... a foreigner from Bremen (in Germany)

leaving off his trade   giving up his trade

from whence from where

we are now called, nay, we call ourselves we are now called, actually, we call ourselves

According to the story, the fictional character of Robinson Crusoe was said to have lived in the mid-seventeenth century, but of course the story was written at the beginning of the eighteenth century, and reflects the grammar and vocabulary of that time. You can see some examples in the glossary of how the English language of the time has changed today.

In the story, Robinson Crusoe's father wants him to go into law, but he goes against his father's wishes and the advice of his mother and friends, in his desire to go to sea.

In the following extract, Robinson has already been on the island for a long time and wakes up to the sound of a gun in the distance.

Extract 29

The perturbation of my mind, during this fifteen or sixteen months' interval, was very great; I slept unquiet, dreamed always frightful dreams, and often started out of my sleep in the night. In the day great troubles overwhelmed my mind, and in the night I dreamed often of killing the savages, and of the reasons why I might justify the doing of it; but to waive all this for a while; it was in the middle of May, on the sixteenth day, I think, as well as my poor wooden calendar would reckon; for I marked all upon the post still; I say, it was the sixteenth day of May that it blew a very great storm of wind all day, with a great deal of lightning and thunder, and a very foul night it was after it; I know not what was the particular occasion of it; but as I was reading in the Bible, and taken up with very serious thoughts about my present condition, I was surprised with a noise of a gun, as I thought, fired at sea.

This was, to be sure, a surprise of a quite different nature from any I had met with before; for the notions this put into my thoughts were quite of another kind.

I started up in the greatest haste imaginable, and in a trice clapped my ladder to the middle place of the rock, and pulled it after me, and mounting it the second time, got to the top of the hill the very moment that a flash of fire bade me listen for a second gun, which accordingly, in about half a minute I heard, and by the sound I knew that it was from that part of the sea where I was driven down the current in my boat.

I immediately considered that this must be some ship in distress ...

Task 29a

Again, we can see the elements of Early Modern English that are not used in today's writing and speech. Underline or list all the phrases that are not used this way in today's English.

Task 29b

Now change your list of phrases into today's modern English, and compare them with the answers at the back of the book.

Shortly after this, Robinson Crusoe describes 'Friday,' the native that he saved from cannibals. A small section has been removed for ease of reading.

Extract 30a

He was a comely, handsome fellow, perfectly well made, with straight strong limbs, not too large, tall and well-shaped, and, as I reckon, about twenty-six years of age. He had a very good countenance, not a fierce and surly aspect, but seemed to have something very manly in his face, and yet he had all the sweetness and softness of an European in his countenance too, especially when he smiled. His hair was long and black, not curled like wool; his forehead very high and large; and a great vivacity and sparkling sharpness in his eyes. The colour of his skin was not quite black, but very tawny ...

I led him up to the top of the hill, to see if his enemies were gone; and pulling out my glass, I looked, and saw plainly the place where they had been, but no appearance of them or of their canoes; so that it was plain that they were gone, and had left their two comrades behind them, without any search after them.

But I was not content with this discovery, but having now more courage, and consequently more curiosity, I took my man Friday with me, giving him the sword in his hand, with the bow and arrows at his back, which I found he could use very dextrously, making him carry one gun for me, and I two for myself, and away we marched to the place where these creatures had been; for I had a mind now to get some fuller intelligence of them. When I came to the place, my very blood ran chill in my veins, and my heart sunk within me at the horror of the spectacle. Indeed, it was a dreadful sight, at least it was so to me, though Friday made nothing of it. The place was covered with human bones, the ground dyed with their blood, great pieces of flesh left here and there, half eaten, mangled and scorched; and in short, all the tokens of the triumphant feast they had been making there, after a victory over their enemies. I saw three skulls, five hands, and the bones of three or four legs and feet, and abundance of other parts of the bodies; and Friday, by his signs, made me understand that they brought over four prisoners to feast upon; that three of them were eaten up, and that he, pointing to himself, was the fourth; that there had been a great battle between them and their next king, whose subjects it seems he had been one of; and that they had taken a great number of prisoners, all of which were carried to several places by those that had taken them in the fight, in order to feast upon them, as was done here by these wretches upon those they brought hither.

I caused Friday to gather all the skulls, bones, flesh, and whatever remained, and lay them together on a heap, and make a great fire upon it and burn them all to ashes. I found Friday had still a hankering stomach after some of the flesh, and was still a cannibal in his nature ...

This extract can be easily understood by the modern reader, but the use of language is in many ways strange and old fashioned. Most English Literature enthusiasts would prefer to read such works in their original form, and in fact most updated versions will be for children, to introduce them to historical works of fiction. However, those who use English as a second language need to be aware that Early Modern English is not suitable for communication in English today, whether that be in speech or writing. In view of this, I have updated the extract below. Read both the original and the updated version carefully. Do not concern yourself with the underlined areas for now.

Extract 30b

He was a <u>good looking, handsome young man, fit and healthy</u>, with straight strong limbs, not too large, tall and <u>well-formed</u>, and, <u>I estimate</u>, about twenty-six years of age. He had a very <u>pleasing face</u>, not a fierce and surly <u>look</u>, but seemed to have something very manly in his <u>facial features</u>, and yet he had all the sweetness and softness of <u>a European</u> in his <u>expression</u> too, especially when he smiled. His hair was long and black, not curled like wool; his forehead very high and large; and a great vivacity and sparkling sharpness in his eyes. The colour of his skin was not quite black, but very tawny ...

I led him up to the top of the hill, to see if his enemies were gone; and pulling out my <u>telescope</u>, I looked, and <u>could clearly see</u> the place where they had been, but no <u>sight of them or</u> their canoes; so <u>it was obvious</u> that they <u>had</u> gone, and had left their two <u>companions</u> behind them, without <u>caring to look for</u> them.

But I was not content with this discovery, <u>so</u> having now more courage, and consequently more curiosity, I took my man Friday with me, giving him the sword <u>to hold</u>, with the bow and arrows <u>on</u> his back, which I found he could use very <u>skilfully</u>, making him carry one gun for me, and I two for myself, and away we marched to the place where these creatures had been; for I had a mind now to get some <u>more information about</u> them. When I came to the place, my very blood ran <u>cold</u> in my veins, and my heart <u>sank</u> within me at the horror of the spectacle. Indeed, it was a dreadful sight, at least it <u>was to</u> me, <u>although</u> Friday made nothing of it. The place was covered with human bones, the ground dyed with their blood, great pieces of flesh left here and there, half eaten, mangled and scorched; and in short, all the tokens of the triumphant feast they had been <u>having</u> there, after a victory over their enemies. I saw three skulls, five hands, and the bones of three or four legs and feet, <u>and an abundance</u> of other parts of the bodies; and Friday, by <u>making</u> signs, made me understand that they brought over four prisoners to feast <u>on</u>; that three of them were eaten up, and that he, pointing to himself, was the fourth; that there had been a great battle between them and their next king, whose subjects it seems <u>had included him</u>; and that they had taken a <u>lot</u> of prisoners, all of which were carried to several places by those that had taken them in the fight, <u>to</u> feast <u>on</u> them, as was done here by these wretches <u>on the ones they brought here</u>.

I <u>got</u> Friday to gather all the skulls, bones, flesh, and whatever remained, and lay them together <u>in</u> a heap, <u>set them all on fire</u> and burn them all to ashes. I found Friday had still a hankering <u>appetite for</u> some of the flesh, and was still a cannibal in his nature ...

Task 30

Analyse the underlined areas of **Extract 30b** and compare them carefully with the original text in **Extract 30a**. Then, explain to a partner why you think the corresponding original sections are not representative of today's modern English.

Gulliver's Travels by Jonathan Swift

Jonathan Swift (1667–1745) was an <u>Anglo-Irish</u> poet, writer and clergyman. He is most famous for his work *Gulliver's Travels* which was published in 1726, and amended before being published again in 1735. Although it is enjoyed by all ages, it is more like a children's book than Defoe's *Robinson Crusoe*. Having said that, Swift wrote *Gulliver's Travels* as a satire of human nature, which gives appeal to adult readers.

Gulliver's Travels involves several voyages undertaken by Lemuel Gulliver. On his first voyage, he is shipwrecked and only he survives. After swimming to shore, he falls asleep during which time he is tied up by the tiny inhabitants of that place called Lilliputians. They shoot at him with their arrows, but they feel like nothing more than pinpricks. Eventually, Gulliver is accepted and he even helps the Lilliputians to win a war. But he has to escape in a boat due to a conspiracy against him after he rises to power in the land.

Gulliver's next voyage takes him to Brobdingnag where he is captured by giants. His third voyage brings him to the flying island of Laputa. Finally, on his last voyage, Gulliver is set ashore in a strange land inhabited by Houyhnhnms, who are horses with human intelligence, yet completely ignorant of human vices. The rest of the population is made up of Yahoos which look like human beings, but they are appalling in their behaviour, reminding Gulliver of the society in England of which he is a part.

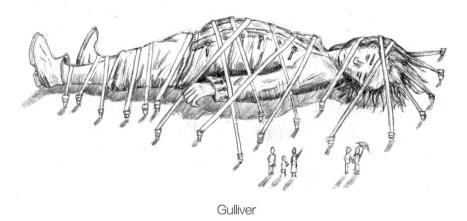

Gulliver

In the following extract, the Emperor of Lilliput, his Imperial Majesty, visits Gulliver who is in confinement.

Read the extract carefully, ignoring the underlined areas for now.

Extract 31

When I found myself on my feet, <u>I looked about me</u>, and must confess I never beheld a more entertaining prospect. <u>The country round appeared like a continued garden</u>; and the <u>inclosed fields</u>, which were generally forty foot square, resembled so many beds of flowers. These fields were intermingled with <u>woods of half a stang</u>, <u>and the tallest trees, as I could judge, appeared to be seven foot high</u>. I viewed the town on my left hand, which looked like the painted scene of a city in a theatre ...

<u>For the better convenience of beholding him</u>, I lay on my side, so that my face was parallel to his, and he stood <u>but three yards off</u>: However, I <u>have had him since many times in my hand</u>, and therefore <u>cannot be deceived in the description</u>. <u>His dress was very plain</u> and simple, <u>the fashion of it between the Asiatick and the European</u>; but he had on his head a light helmet of gold, adorned with jewels, and a plume on the crest. He held his sword drawn in his hand, to defend himself, <u>if I should happen to break loose</u>; it was almost three inches long, the hilt and scabbard were gold enriched with diamonds. His voice was shrill, but very clear and articulate, and I could distinctly hear it when I stood up. The ladies and courtiers were all <u>most magnificently clad</u>, so that the spot they stood upon seemed to resemble a petticoat spread on the ground, embroidered with figures of gold and silver. His Imperial Majesty spoke often to me, and I returned answers, but neither of us could understand a syllable. There were several of his priests and lawyers present (as I conjectured by their habits) who were commanded to <u>address themselves to me</u>, and I spoke to them in as many languages as I had the least smattering of, which were High and Low Dutch, Latin, French, Spanish, Italian, and Lingua Franca; but all <u>to no purpose</u>. After about two hours the court retired, and I was left with a strong guard, to prevent <u>the impertinence, and probably the malice of the rabble, who were very impatient to croud about me as near as they durst</u>; and some of them had the impudence to shoot their arrows at

me as I <u>sate</u> on the ground by the door of my house; <u>whereof one</u> very narrowly missed my left eye. But the Colonel ordered six of the ringleaders to be seized, and <u>thought no punishment so proper as to deliver them bound</u> into my hands, which some of his soldiers <u>accordingly did</u>, pushing them forwards with the but-ends of their pikes into my reach: I took them all in my right hand, put five of them into my coat-pocket; <u>and as to the sixth, I made a countenance as if I would eat him alive</u>. The poor man <u>squalled terribly</u>, and the Colonel and his officers <u>were in much pain</u>, especially when they saw me take out my penknife: But I soon <u>put them out of fear; for, looking mildly</u>, and immediately cutting the strings he was bound with, I set him gently on the ground, and away he ran. I treated the rest in the same manner, taking them one by one out of my pocket; and I observed, both the soldiers and people were <u>highly obliged at this mark of my clemency</u>, which was represented very much to my advantage at court.

Task 31

Read the above extract a couple of times to understand it fully, looking up in a dictionary any words you do not understand. Then study the underlined areas and rewrite them in today's modern English.

From the answers to Task 31, you can see that in spite of the fact that seventeenth century English language can be easily understood by today's English speakers, there are many changes in phrasal structure and vocabulary. I will address a handful of examples from Extract 31 below.

There are changes in the conventional use of the words 'around' 'round' and 'about':

<u>I looked about me</u>

I looked around me

<u>The country round appeared like a continued garden</u>

The countryside around me appeared like a continuous garden

croud about me

crowd around me

There are changes in word order (although in poetry we can still use word order that 'breaks the rules' to express a variety of connotations or inspire our imagination):

I have had him since many times in my hand

Since then I have had him in my hand many times

accordingly did

did accordingly

Changes in the meaning of vocabulary:

His dress was very plain

His form of dress was very plain

Using the word 'dress' on its own implies the emperor was wearing women's clothes. So we need to say 'form of dress', meaning style of clothing.

Different conventions in phrasal structures:

if I should happen to break loose

in case I managed to break loose

to address themselves to me

to address me directly

to no purpose

to no avail

thought no punishment so proper as to

thought there was no better punishment than to

Words no longer used:

stang

pole

durst

dare

sate

sat

Additional Notes for Unit 4
第4单元附加注释

Synonyms

When comparing Extract 23 with Extract 16, we found that the two versions of the same text used a different English synonym to translate the same Hebrew word. They were the verbs 'to separate' and 'to divide.' Either synonym was and still is perfectly acceptable. You can also see from the respective sentences below that the sentence structure does not need to change to accommodate the alternative synonyms.

Extract 16

God separated the light from the darkness
... let it separate the waters from the waters

Extract 23

God divided the light from the darkness
... let it divide the waters from the waters

So let's consider some other synonyms of 'separate' and 'divide', such as: **part, split** and **divorce**. The question is, can they all be slotted into the sentence in the same way that 'separate' and 'divide' can?

The synonym 'part' can be used in exactly the same way, and so can 'split' except for one thing: 'split' cannot receive the suffix '-ed'; the word 'split' can be used for the present and the past tense without adding a suffix. So far, so good. But when it comes to 'divorce' it is nonsense to say here that the light was divorced from the darkness. The word 'divorce' is primarily used to mean that two people have ceased to be married. Using the word in the second sentence ('let it divorce the waters from the waters') would be even more ridiculous.

When two people are 'divorced', they could say they have 'separated', but they would not say they had 'divided,' although they may say they have 'split up'. However, 'separated' could mean they are still married but they just no longer consider themselves to be a couple. The synonyms 'separated' and 'split up' are less precise than 'divorced'. Added to this complication, people divorce when they have no intention of being a couple again, whereas 'separated' couples may decide to be a couple again in the future.

Consider the following long sentence and how the synonyms are used correctly:

Additional Extract A

*We decided not to get **divorced**, we just **separated** for a while to think about things on our own; we did not **divide** our possessions either because we haven't actually **split up**.*

The synonyms are in the following order:

divorced, separated, divide, split up

Additional Task A

Using the extract above, replace the synonyms with the same synonyms in the following orders. I have slightly altered the synonyms where necessary to make them fit as closely as possible with the grammatical structure of the sentence. Does the sentence make sense in each case?

separated, divided, split up, divorced

divided, split up, divorce, separated

split up, divorced, separate, divided

Every word has its own unique nuance of meaning, so we must remember not to randomly pick synonyms from a dictionary to insert into any given sentence. Using different synonyms for a given sentence is of course acceptable on many occasions, but we must remember that the structure of the sentence may need to be adapted to accommodate it.

The first clause of Additional Extract A can be used to illustrate this. We have:

*We decided not to get **divorced***

This clause is in the past tense, so we need to retain this when we insert the synonyms: *'to separate'* *'to divide'* and *'to split up'*. The following extract lists the results after inserting the alternative synonyms into the same clause.

Additional Extract B

*We decided not to get **divorced** (original)*
*We decided not to **separate***
*We decided not to **divide up** our possessions [an object is necessary]*
*We decided not to **split up***

I have tried to keep the three alternative clauses as accurate as possible to the original. These skills are important for translators.

Additional Task B

Consider each of the three alternative clauses in turn and explain the changes to the sentence structure that have been necessary to keep the original meaning as accurate as possible.

Within the same context, the above synonyms also have varying strengths and nuances of meaning. 'To divorce' is very strong as it has a permanence to the division. 'To split up' implies permanence, so it is the next degree of division, yet not as complex and strong as 'to divorce'. 'To separate' is more general in meaning, and in this context it implies there is a possibility of reconciliation later, so the meaning is weaker. However, unlike the word 'divorce', the synonyms 'to separate' and 'to split up' have a broader quantity of meanings. They are not restricted to the subject of two people.

To illustrate and reinforce this phenomenon of diversity of meaning among synonyms, I have devised what I call 'Synonym Ladders'.

<u>Synonym Ladders</u>
(Taken from *The Mark of the Beast* by Andrew Harrison.
Copyright 2018)

Synonym Ladders show the extent to which synonyms intersect. Using Synonym Ladders helps to confirm the fact that you cannot simply replace a word in a sentence with a synonym from the dictionary. For example, in the first Synonym Ladder, we have the verbs: **to know, to understand, to comprehend, to see, to get it** and **to discern**. The subject of the ladder is **KNOWING**.

Additional Extract Ci

K N O W
U N D E R S T A N D
C O M P R E H E N D
S E E
GET IT
D I S C E R N

The Ladder shows that in some contexts, all of the words can mean the same thing, because they all overlap in the diagram. 'To know' is a very general term so it is often replaced by others when the context needs to be more specific. 'To understand' indicates a deep knowledge, not just a state of having acquired head-knowledge. 'To understand' can also mean to know how to act upon that knowledge.

However, 'to comprehend' is even more specific, emphasising a thorough and deep understanding, so in the diagram, it extends further to the left of 'know' than 'understand' does.

'To see' and 'to get it' are very non-specific verbal indications that some kind of information or instruction has simply been received, so on the diagram, 'know' is broader.

'To discern' is to have a knowledge and understanding with the aid of instinct or inspiration. So it has a unique meaning, but it also intersects with the other terms.

In the second Synonym Ladder, we have 6 adjectives: **sad, unhappy, disillusioned, anxious, depressed** and **miserable.** The subject of the ladder is **UNHAPPINESS**.

Additional Extract Cii

<pre>
              S A D
            U N H A P P Y
         DISILLUSIONED
           A N X I O U S
         D E P R E S S E D
             M I S E R A B L E
</pre>

The words 'sad' and 'unhappy' are general words to mean the same thing, and can be mild or extreme, depending on the context.

Being 'disillusioned' is in some ways similar to being 'confused', but being 'confused' is not as strongly linked to being 'sad' or 'unhappy' as being 'disillusioned' is, so we have not included it on the Synonym Ladder. Being 'disillusioned' can involve unhappiness, but not always, so it only partly overlaps with 'sad' and 'unhappy'.

Being 'anxious' intersects with being 'disillusioned', but being 'anxious' is more extreme and linked more closely with being 'depressed'. However, being 'depressed' can express an experience far more acute than anxiety, so the word 'depressed' extends beyond 'anxious'. In regard to 'anxious' and 'depressed,' they are more likely to involve unhappiness than 'disillusioned,' so 'disillusioned' intersects 'sad' and 'unhappy' less; however, 'depressed' completely intersects 'sad' and 'unhappy' as being depressed is almost always associated with being 'sad.'

All 'miserable' people are 'sad'/'unhappy', but the word can also be used uniquely as an insult, therefore making 'miserable' extend in the opposite direction to the other words.

Additional Task C

Now design your own Synonym Ladder using the following words: *happy, ecstatic, thrilled, delighted, pleased* and *content*. The subject of the ladder is HAPPINESS. Then analyse it and discuss it with a partner.

Glossary for Unit 4

Native American 美国原住民

This refers to 'Native American Indians', the indigenous peoples of North America where the United States of America was later established as an independent nation. Many people today refuse to use the word 'Indian' and especially the phrase 'Red Indian' in reference to the original inhabitants of the US, as it is deemed to be inappropriate or offensive, although most Native Americans do not consider it offensive to be called 'Indians', although that is not because they consider themselves to be from Asia.

loanwords 外借词

A loanword is a word that is taken from one language and added into another.

Psalm《圣经》诗篇

A song or poem in *the Bible* that praises God.

allegory 寓言

Here an allegory is a symbolic story with a moral teaching. In this case, each character's name represents a certain type of person.

coined the phrase 创造新词

invented the phrase

satirical novel 讽刺小说

This is a novel that exposes human folly to ridicule.

British Intelligence 英国情报局

An intelligence agency is a unit for gathering and interpreting information about an enemy. So this phrase refers to the British Government's primary intelligence agency.

Anglo-Irish 居爱尔兰的英格兰人

Jonathan Swift's parents were from England, but he was born in Southern Ireland. 'Anglo' means 'from England'.

Unit 5

Literature from the Romantic Period
浪漫主义时期文学

Chapter 9   The Modern English Period
第9章   现代英语时期

Chapter 10   Romantic Novelists
第10章   浪漫主义小说家

Chapter 11   Romance Poets
第11章   浪漫主义诗人

Additional Notes for Unit 5
第5单元附加注释

Chapter 9　The Modern English Period
第9章　现代英语时期

This Unit covers the first hundred years of what is termed the Modern English Period (following after Early Modern English), representative of the English language during the 200 years from 1750 to 1950. Although we can call the English language of today 'modern English', in fact, for linguistical research purposes, today's English is labelled as 'Late Modern English,' dating from 1950 onwards.

The Modern English Period (1750–1950) saw the <u>British Industrial Revolution</u> (from the latter half of the 18th century to the first half of the 19th century), and the introduction of the use of English as the medium of education in many parts of the World. English also became the international language of advertising and consumerism. By the 18th century, English punctuation as we know and use it today in our writing was also already in place.

The settlement of Australia by the people of England took place nearly two centuries after the settlement in America. It was Captain James Cook (1728–1779) from England who sailed to Australia and claimed the east coast of Australia for Britain. <u>Penal colonies</u> were established on the south-east coast of Australia in 1788. Many of the convicts established their own smallholdings after they had served their sentences, and thus began the development of Australia as we have it today.

At the same time as the penal colonies were being set up in Australia, there were different kinds of settlement set up in West Africa. For example, after 1807 (the date when the slave trade was officially ended), freed and escaped African slaves who had come to share a common language in English, settled in Sierra Leone. Although the slave trade was a dreadful thing, these events had a very positive influence upon the English language. Through the continuing link between the Americas and Africa, these factors gave rise to Black English in the Caribbean and the United States. This in turn had an immense effect upon the younger English speakers of the world, partly through music. Black English has also led to the development of Pidgins and Creoles.

Creoles arise through the contact between speakers of different languages, in this case the clash between English language and various African languages. The first stage is the formation of an English Pidgin. But when that English Pidgin becomes the language of a whole community, it becomes a Creole. For example, the Creole spoken in Jamaica is called 'Jamaican Creole English.' There are also many English-based Creoles in West Africa.

现代英语时期代表了从1750年到1950年之间的200年中使用的英语，本单元涵盖了现代英语时期（在早期现代英语之后）的前100年。尽管我们也可以把今天的英语称为"现代英语"，但实际上，从语言学的研究角度出发，1950年之后到现在的英语被称为"现代英语晚期"。

现代英语时期（1750—1950）见证了英国工业革命（从18世纪下半叶到19世纪上半叶），以及英语作为教育媒介被世界许多地方引入的历史。英语也成为广告和消费主义的国际语言。到18世纪，我们如今在写作中所了解和使用的英语标点符号也已经出现。

英格兰人在美洲定居近两个世纪后才开始殖民澳大利亚。詹姆斯·库克船长（1728—1779）从英格兰航行到澳大利亚，宣称澳大利亚东海岸为英国所有。1788年，英格兰在澳大利亚东南海岸建立了流放殖民地。许多罪犯在服刑后建立了自己的小农场，从而开始了今天澳大利亚的发展。

在澳大利亚建立流放殖民地的同时，在西非也建立了各种各样的殖民点。例如，在1807年（奴隶贸易正式结束的日期）之后，获得自由和逃跑的非洲奴隶来到塞拉利昂定居，他们使用相同的语言——英语。虽然奴隶贸易是一件可怕的事情，但这些事件对英语语言产生了非常积极的影响。美洲和非洲之间持续的联系等因素使加勒比和美国产生了黑人英语。这对世界上说英语的年轻人产生了巨大的影响，这种影响一部分是通过音乐带来的。黑人英语也促进了皮钦语（又称洋泾浜）和克里奥尔语的发展。

克里奥尔语是通过讲不同语言的人之间的接触而产生的，这里所说的是英语和各种非洲语言之间的碰撞。第一阶段是洋泾浜英语的形成。但是当洋泾浜英语成为整个社区的语言时，它就变成了克里奥尔语。例如，在牙买加说的克里奥尔语被称为"牙买加克里奥尔英语"。在西非也存在许多从英语衍化而来的克里奥尔语。

The Romantic Period Emerges

Just before the Romantic Period was established, Scotland, Ireland and England continued to produce excellent writers of English, including the famous novelist and dramatist Henry Fielding (1707-1754) who was born in Somerset in England. He wrote the comic novel *The History of Tom Jones, a Foundling* published in 1749, in which Tom Jones pursued and won the heart of Sophia Western in an elaborate plot.

An Irish poet and novelist of the time was Oliver Goldsmith (1730-1774). He is very well-known for his novel *The Vicar of Wakefield* published in 1766.

Robert Burns

A Scottish nationalist poet who had a profound impact on the peoples of Scotland at this time was Robert Burns (1759-1796). Considered to be the greatest of the Scottish poets, Robert Burns is remembered throughout Scotland and Northern Ireland every year on what is often referred to as Burns Night. Suppers are usually held on or near the poet's birthday on the 25th January, when his life and poetry are remembered. The celebrations invariably include haggis, a Scottish dish, as Burns wrote the poem *Address to a Haggis*; and of course Scotch whisky will be drunk too, but the key feature will be the recitation of Burns' poetry. The majority of Burns' poetry is in the Scottish dialect (Scots English), and this encourages the people of Scotland to continue to take pride in their dialect.

The poem Burns is most famous for internationally is *Auld Lang Syne* (1788), which is sung throughout the world during the transition from one solar year to another. The <u>refrain</u> 'Auld Lang Syne,' literally 'old-long-since,' means 'Times long past' 'Time(s) gone by' 'Old times sake' or 'Old times past' in today's Standard English. It is sung on New Year's Eve to say goodbye to the old year and welcome the New Year.

Read the extract below containing the original poem *Auld Lang Syne* which is sung internationally to a Scottish folk melody.

Extract 32

<u>Auld Lang Syne</u>
Should auld acquaintance be forgot,
And never brought to min'?
Should auld acquaintance be forgot,
And auld lang syne!
Chorus:
For auld lang syne, my jo,
For auld lang syne,
We'll tak a cup o' kindness yet
For auld lang syne.
And surely ye'll be your pint-stowp!
And surely I'll be mine!
And we'll tak a cup o' kindness yet,
For auld lang syne.
Repeat Chorus
We twa hae run about the braes,
And pou'd the gowans fine;
But we've wander'd mony a weary fitt,
Sin auld lang syne.

Repeat Chorus

We twa hae paidl' d in the burn
Frae morning sun till dine;
But seas between us braid hae roar' d,
Sin auld lang syne.

Repeat Chorus

And there' s a hand, my trusty fiere!
And gie' s a hand o' thine!
And we' ll tak a right gude-willie-waught,
For auld lang syne.

Repeat Chorus

This poem is in late eighteenth century Scots English. The first verse and the chorus are very well known internationally, and the original words are retained out of respect for the old original poem; this is not surprising as the song is symbolic of the past that we are saying goodbye to. However, it is very common to hear people sing 'dear' instead of 'jo'. This is because 'jo,' like many other words in Scots English, are unfamiliar to the rest of the English-speaking world.

Task 32

Search through the poem and make a list or underline all the words and phrases that you think are unique to Scots English. Incidentally, min' means mind; the Scottish will often treat the final 'd' as a silent letter.

When you have highlighted the unique words and phrases, see if you can identify the meanings.

The next extract is Robert Burn' s poem, *My Heart' s in the Highlands* (1789).

Extract 33

My Heart's in the Highlands

My heart's in the Highlands, my heart is not here;
My heart's in the Highlands, a-chasing the deer;
Chasing the wild deer, and following the roe—
My heart's in the Highlands wherever I go.
Farewell to the Highlands, farewell to the North!
The birthplace of valour, the country of worth;
Wherever I wander, wherever I rove.
The hills of the Highlands for ever I love.

Farewell to the mountains high covered with snow!
Farewell to the straths and green valleys below!
Farewell to the forests and wild-hanging woods!
Farewell to the torrents and loud-pouring floods!
My heart's in the Highlands, my heart is not here;
My heart's in the Highlands, a-chasing the deer;
Chasing the wild deer, and following the roe—
My heart's in the Highlands wherever I go.

Glossary

Highlands	the mountainous part of northern Scotland
a-chasing	The additional 'a' is common in poetic English. The meaning is 'chasing.'
roe	A roe deer is a small species of deer.
rove	To rove is to wander around places.

Task 33

Interestingly, the English of this poem is the same as today's poetic Standard English. There is only one word that is uniquely Scots. Can you find it? Look up the word in a dictionary or online and find out its meaning.

William Blake

Another writer to remember at the beginning of the Romantic Period is William Blake (1757–1827). He was a painter, poet and printmaker from England, who spent almost his entire life in London. His earliest poems were published in *Poetical Sketches*, in 1783. He then engraved and published *Songs of Innocence* in 1789.

In the extract below, you can read Blake's poem called *The Tyger* (*The Tiger*), which was published as part of his *Songs of Experience* collection in 1794.

Extract 34

The Tyger

Tyger Tyger, burning bright,
In the forests of the night;
What immortal hand or eye,
Could frame thy fearful symmetry?

In what distant deeps or skies,
Burnt the fire of thine eyes?
On what wings dare he aspire?
What the hand, dare seize the fire?

And what shoulder, and what art,
Could twist the sinews of thy heart?
And when thy heart began to beat,
What dread hand? And what dread feet?

What the hammer? What the chain?,
In what furnace was thy brain?
What the anvil? What dread grasp,
Dare its deadly terrors clasp?

When the stars threw down their spears
And water'd heaven with their tears;
Did he smile his work to see?
Did he who made the lamb make thee?

Tyger Tyger, burning bright,
In the forests of the night;
What immortal hand or eye,
Dare frame thy fearful symmetry?

Task 34a

As you can see, this poem has six stanzas. The first and the last are identical except for one word. Can you find the word? Why exactly has Blake changed the word in the final stanza?

Task 34b

If you read the poem carefully, you will see that the poem is as much about the Creator of the tiger as it is about the tiger itself. Write out the

words and phrases that directly refer to the 'Creator' in one list, and the words and phrases that refer to the 'tiger' in another. Then do a final list noting down the words and phrases that describe the 'creative process'.

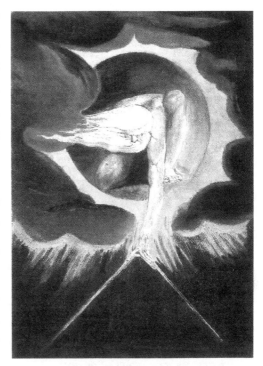

The Creator depicted as the great architect, by William Blake

You will see from the above task that it is sometimes very difficult to be certain which word or phrase belongs in which list. This is the beauty of poetry. On reading it one more time, you will be in a better position to enjoy exploring the connection between all three aspects of the poem (The Creator, the tiger, and the creative process); you will see that the Creator and his creation have features and attributes in common, and that the created creature itself (the tiger) displays the marks of the Creator's craftsmanship.

William Blake was largely unrecognised in his days as he was considered to be mad, but he is regarded highly today for his contribution to visual art as well as his unique 'prophetic poetry.' One such prophetic poem is *Jerusalem* (and did those feet in ancient time), published in 1804. It is now well-known as a hymn, with music written by Sir Hubert Parry in 1916. It is by many adored as a kind of unofficial national anthem for England.

Each stanza of the poem is a quatrain. The poetic devices used include alliteration, rhyme and personification. See the poem below.

Extract 35

Jerusalem

And did those feet in ancient time
Walk upon England's mountains green:
And was the holy Lamb of God,
On England's pleasant pastures seen!

And did the Countenance Divine,
Shine forth upon our clouded hills?
And was Jerusalem builded here,
Among these dark Satanic mills?

Bring me my bow of burning gold:
Bring me my arrows of desire:
Bring me my spear: O clouds unfold!
Bring me my chariot of fire!

I will not cease from mental flight,
Nor shall my sword sleep in my hand:
Till we have built Jerusalem,
In England's green and pleasant land.

Glossary

feet	the feet of Jesus Christ
the holy Lamb of God	This is another name for Jesus Christ who was sacrificed on a cross, as innocent as a lamb.
Countenance Divine	This means 'divine countenance.' The poem asks if the face of God looked favourably upon the landscape of

	England.
Jerusalem	This is literally the capital city of Israel, but in the poem it represents Heaven on Earth in England.
builded	built
dark Satanic mills	Blake had great sympathy for those who worked in terrible conditions during the Industrial Revolution. The adjective 'satanic' is very strong. Satan is the embodiment of evil, the Devil, the opponent of all things good, and the very enemy of God himself. Blake clearly saw the origin of child labour, unhealthy working conditions and ensuing pollution as intensely evil.
my chariot of fire	This is a heavenly mode of transport.
mental flight	imagining

In this poem, Blake is expressing his desire for God to create Paradise on earth, specifically in England, hoping that in the past, Jesus Christ (the holy Lamb of God), had visited England and looked upon the land of green pastures with divine favour. The weapons he refers to are spiritual weapons rather than weapons of human war.

Task 35a

Note down every example of personification in the poem and discuss with a partner what you think they are personifying. My notes on this poem above will help you.

Task 35b

How many lines end in a word that rhymes with another in the same quatrain? List each rhyming word with its partner.

Chapter 10 Romantic Novelists
第10章 浪漫主义小说家

Sir Walter Scott (1771–1832) was born in Edinburgh, Scotland. He was a Scottish historical novelist, playwright and poet in the Romantic Period. His poems included works such as *The Lady of the Lake* (1810), set in the Trossachs in Scotland. His first *Waverley* novel was published in 1812; he is also well-known for his novel called *Rob Roy* (1817), about the Scottish clan leader and outlaw. However, his famous novel *Ivanhoe* (1819) was not about Scotland, but rather a historical romance set in twelfth century England.

Jane Austen

Jane Austen (1775–1817), the seventh of eight children, was a major novelist in the Romantic Period. Among her works are the novels *Sense and Sensibility* (1811), *Pride and Prejudice* (1813), *Mansfield Park* (1814), and *Emma* (1815). Jane Austen is depicted and quoted on the back of the British ten pound note. The quotation reads:

'I declare after all there is no enjoyment like reading!'

Other popular Jane Austen quotations are:

'A lady's imagination is very rapid; it jumps from admiration to love, from love to matrimony in a moment.'

'A woman, especially, if she have the misfortune of knowing anything, should conceal it as well as she can.'

The following extract is from her novel, *Pride and Prejudice*. The heroine is Elizabeth Bennet, and her proud romantic interest is Mr Darcy. Elizabeth's mother Mrs Bennet tries to find husbands for all five of her daughters, and the first time Elizabeth meets Mr Darcy is at a ball. Mr Darcy attends the ball with Elizabeth's new neighbour Mr Bingley and Mr Bingley's two sisters.

The Bennets' oldest daughter Jane and Mr Bingley become attracted to each other, whereas Mr Darcy is a cold and very proud guest. Mr Darcy refuses to dance with Elizabeth, which offends her father as Elizabeth is Mr Bennet's favourite daughter. But Darcy gradually begins to admire Elizabeth, who declines the opportunity to dance with him on a later occasion.

One of Mr Bingley's sisters, Caroline, is very critical of the Bennet family because she herself wants to marry Darcy and is aware of his developing interest in Elizabeth. But eventually, after many challenges, Elizabeth and Darcy get engaged, humbling pride and overcoming prejudice.

Below is an extract from the beginning of *Pride and Prejudice*.

Extract 36

It is a truth universally acknowledged that a single man in possession of a good fortune must be in want of a wife.

However little known the feelings or views of such a man may be on his first entering a neighbourhood, this truth is so well fixed in the minds of the surrounding families, that he is considered as the rightful property of some one or other of their daughters.

'My dear Mr Bennet,' said his lady to him one day, 'have you heard that Netherfield Park is let at last?'

Mr Bennet replied that he had not.

'But it is,' returned she; 'for Mrs Long has just been here, and she told me all about it.'

Mr Bennet made no answer.

'Do not you want to know who has taken it?' cried his wife impatiently.

'You want to tell me, and I have no objection to hearing it.'

This was information enough.

'Why, my dear, you must know, Mrs Long says that Netherfield is taken by a young man of large fortune from the north of England; that he came down on Monday in a chaise and four to see the place, and was so much delighted with it that he agreed with Mr Morris immediately; that he is to take possession before Michaelmas, and some of his servants are to be in the house by the end of next week.'

'What is his name?'

'Bingley.'

'Is he married or single?'

'Oh! single, my dear, to be sure! A single man of large fortune; four or five thousand a year. What a fine thing for our girls!'

'How so? How can it affect them?'

'My dear Mr Bennet,' replied his wife, 'how can you be so tiresome! You must know that I am thinking of his marrying one of them.'

'Is that his design in settling here?'

'Design! nonsense, how can you talk so! But it is very likely that he may fall in love with one of them, and therefore you must visit him as soon as he comes.'

'I see no occasion for that. You and the girls may go, or you may send them by themselves, which perhaps will be still better, for as you are as handsome as any of them, Mr Bingley might like you the best of the party.'

'My dear, you flatter me. I certainly have had my share of beauty, but I do not pretend to be any thing extraordinary now. When a woman has five grown up daughters, she ought to give over thinking of her own beauty.'

Glossary

chaise and four This is a carriage that seated three people, pulled by four horses.

Michaelmas This is a Christian holy day in honour of Saint Michael in September each year.

Task 36

The language in *Pride and Prejudice*, representative of early 19th century English, is quite different to today's English in writing and speech. I have given some examples below:

A single man in possession of a good fortune must be in want of a wife.
'Oh! single, my dear, to be sure!'
'What a fine thing for our girls!'
'How can you be so tiresome! You must know that I am thinking of his marrying one of them.'
'Is that his design in settling here?'
'How can you talk so!'
'I see no occasion for that.'
'... for as you are as handsome as any of them, Mr Bingley might like you the best of the party.'

Rewrite the sentences above, converting them into today's Standard English.

The following extract is also taken from *Pride and Prejudice* when Elizabeth Bennet refuses to dance with Darcy. It begins with Sir William suggesting that Darcy and Elizabeth should dance together.

Extract 37

'My dear Miss Eliza, why are you not dancing? — Mr Darcy, you must allow me to present this young lady to you as a very desirable dancing partner. — You cannot refuse to dance I am sure, when so much beauty is before you. And taking her hand, he would have given it to Mr Darcy, who, though extremely surprised,

was not unwilling to receive it, when she instantly drew back, and said with some discomposure to Sir William,

'Indeed, Sir, I have not the least intention of dancing. — I entreat you not to suppose that I moved this way in order to beg for a partner.'

Mr Darcy with grave propriety requested to be allowed the honour of her hand; but in vain. Elizabeth was determined; nor did Sir William at all shake her purpose by his attempt at persuasion.

'You excel so much in the dance, Miss Eliza, that it is cruel to deny me the happiness of seeing you; and though this gentleman dislikes the amusement in general, he can have no objection, I am sure, to oblige us for one half hour.'

'Mr Darcy is all politeness,' said Elizabeth, smiling.

'He is indeed — but considering the inducement, my dear Eliza, we cannot wonder at his complaisance; for who would object to such a partner?'

Elizabeth looked archly, and turned away.

Glossary

inducement	positive expectation
complaisance	willingness
Elizabeth looked archly	Elizabeth gave a condescending look

Task 37

Read and study the extract above and then rewrite it in today's English, keeping as close as possible to the original.

The next extract is also from one of Jane Austen's books, called *Emma*, which was the fourth of Austen's six completed novels. It has recently been made into a new BBC (British Broadcasting Corporation) drama.

In the novel, Emma Woodhouse, the heroine, is rich and intelligent. She befriends Harriet Smith who is from unknown parentage. Emma seeks to find Harriet the ideal husband.

Below is an extract from the beginning of the novel.

Extract 38

Emma Woodhouse, handsome, clever, and rich, with a comfortable home and happy disposition, seemed to unite some of the best blessings of existence; and had lived nearly twenty-one years in the world with very little to distress or vex her.

She was the youngest of the two daughters of a most affectionate, indulgent father, and had, in consequence of her sister's marriage, been mistress of his house from a very early period. Her mother had died too long ago for her to have more than an indistinct remembrance of her caresses, and her place had been supplied by an excellent woman as governess, who had fallen little short of a mother in affection.

Sixteen years had Miss Taylor been in Mr Woodhouse's family, less as a governess than a friend, very fond of both daughters, but particularly of Emma.

We do not call women 'handsome' these days; the word is reserved for male children and men. The word 'attractive' would be more appropriate here.

Task 38

As this extract is representative of Standard English 200 years ago, it is good for you to consider how it should be expressed in today's Standard English. Consider the phrases and sentences below and rewrite them in today's English, staying as close as possible to the original.

Emma Woodhouse, handsome, clever, and rich.

She had, in consequence of her sister's marriage ...

Her mother had died too long ago for her to have more than an indistinct remembrance of her caresses.

Next, we see what Mr Knightley, Emma's love interest, thinks about Emma's friendship with Harriet.

Extract 39

'I do not know what your opinion may be, Mrs Weston,' said Mr Knightley, 'of this great intimacy between Emma and Harriet Smith, but I think it a bad thing.'

'A bad thing! Do you really think it a bad thing? — why so?'

'I think they will neither of them do the other any good.'

'You surprise me! Emma must do Harriet good: and by supplying her with a new object of interest, Harriet may be said to do Emma good. I have been seeing their intimacy with the greatest pleasure. How very differently we feel! — Not think they will do each other any good! This will certainly be the beginning of one of our quarrels about Emma, Mr Knightley.'

'Perhaps you think I am come on purpose to quarrel with you, knowing Weston to be out, and that you must still fight your own battle.'

'Mr Weston would undoubtedly support me, if he were here, for he thinks exactly as I do on the subject. We were speaking of it only yesterday, and agreeing how fortunate it was for Emma, that there should be such a girl in Highbury for her to associate with ...'

Task 39

Again consider the phrases and sentences below and rewrite them in today's English, staying as close as possible to the original.

'... but I think it a bad thing.'

'Emma must do Harriet good.'

'I have been seeing their intimacy with the greatest pleasure.'

'How very differently we feel!'

'Perhaps you think I am come on purpose to quarrel with you, knowing Weston to be out.'

'... for he thinks exactly as I do on the subject.'

'We were speaking of it only yesterday.'

Mary Shelley

Mary Shelley (1797-1851) from the Romantic Period introduced a new genre, that of Science Fiction, in her Gothic (Horror fiction with romantic elements) novel *Frankenstein* (1818). It is like a pre-runner to Bram Stoker's *Dracula*.

Mary Shelley was married to Percy Shelley (the Romantic poet who wrote *To a Sky-Lark*). Mary was born in England and began writing *Frankenstein; or, The Modern Prometheus* when she was only 18 years old; the novel was published in 1818. The story is about a young scientist called Victor Frankenstein who creates a human monster (made out of the parts of dead human bodies); this brings tragedy to his life. The main part of the story takes place in Geneva in Switzerland.

The monster in Shelley's novel reads the poem *Paradise Lost* by John Milton and then says to its own creator, Victor Frankenstein:

'I ought to be thy Adam, but I am rather the fallen angel.'

Lucifer in *Paradise Lost*, by John Milton, is referred to as the 'fallen angel,' so the monster considers himself to be the evil Satan, the Devil from the Garden of Eden rather than the first man Adam. However, it is the scientist Frankenstein himself who is seeking forbidden knowledge by attempting to take over God's role as Creator and Master of the universe.

In the novel's title, Victor Frankenstein is also likened to Prometheus from

Greek mythology. Prometheus was the Titan who stole fire from Olympus to give it to humankind. Zeus (the mythical god of the Greeks) punished *Prometheus* by chaining him to a rock where an eagle gnawed at his liver until Hercules finally rescued him.

The following extract is taken from chapter 4 of Mary Shelley's *Frankenstein*. The text has some sections removed for ease of reading. Victor Frankenstein is speaking.

Extract 40

From this day natural philosophy, and particularly chemistry, in the most comprehensive sense of the term, became nearly my sole occupation. I read with ardour those works, so full of genius and discrimination, which modern inquirers have written on these subjects. I attended the lectures and cultivated the acquaintance of the men of science of the university, and I found even in M. Krempe a great deal of sound sense and real information, combined, it is true, with a repulsive physiognomy and manners, but not on that account the less valuable. In M. Waldman I found a true friend ...

In other studies you go as far as others have gone before you, and there is nothing more to know; but in a scientific pursuit there is continual food for discovery and wonder. A mind of moderate capacity which closely pursues one study must infallibly arrive at great proficiency in that study; and I, who continually sought the attainment of one object of pursuit and was solely wrapped up in this, improved so rapidly that at the end of two years I made some new discoveries in the improvement of some chemical instruments, which procured me great esteem and admiration at the university ...

After days and nights of incredible labour and fatigue, I succeeded in discovering the cause of generation and life; nay, more, I became myself capable of bestowing animation upon lifeless matter ... I see by your eagerness and the wonder and hope which your eyes express, my friend, that you expect to be informed of the secret with which I am acquainted; that cannot be; listen patiently until the end of my story, and you will easily perceive why I am reserved upon that subject ... Learn from me, if not by my precepts, at least by my example, how dangerous is the acquirement of knowledge and how much happier that man is who believes his native town to be the world, than he who aspires to become greater than his nature will allow.

Task 40

After studying the whole extract, answer the following questions in full, clear sentences.

    a What subjects did Victor Frankenstein study?

    b In your own words, according to Frankenstein, how does scientific pursuit differ from studying other subjects?

    c What did Frankenstein do to acquire the knowledge he needed?

    d What was the result of his hard work?

    e The author says that the 'acquirement of knowledge' is dangerous, and 'how much happier that man is who believes his native town to be the world, than he who aspires to become greater than his nature will allow.'

    i In your opinion, how and when is the acquirement of knowledge sometimes dangerous? Discuss it with your partner before you share it with others.

    ii What does 'how much happier that man is who believes his native town to be the world' mean? Discuss. Do you agree? Why? Why not?

    iii What does the author mean by 'he who aspires to become greater than his nature will allow'?

Frankenstein has been adapted to film on many occasions, and more recently, a TV series has been created called *The Frankenstein Chronicles*, in which you can also see samples of William Blake's artwork.

The following extract is taken from chapter 5 of Mary Shelley's *Frankenstein*, and describes the first moment when the human-creature, formed from old body parts, moves.

Extract 41

It was on a dreary night of November that I beheld the accomplishment of my toils. With an anxiety that almost amounted to agony, I collected the instruments of life around me, that I might infuse a spark of being into the lifeless thing that lay at my feet. It was already one in the morning; the rain pattered dismally against the panes, and my candle was nearly burnt out, when, by the glimmer of the half-extinguished light, I saw the dull yellow eye of the creature open; it breathed hard, and a convulsive motion agitated its limbs. How can I describe my emotions at this catastrophe, or how delineate the wretch whom with such infinite pains and care I had endeavoured to form?

... His yellow skin scarcely covered the work of muscles and arteries beneath; his hair was of a lustrous black, and flowing; his teeth of a pearly whiteness; but these luxuriances only formed a more horrid contrast with his watery eyes, that seemed almost of the same colour as the dun-white sockets in which they were set, his shrivelled complexion and straight black lips ... but now that I had finished, the beauty of the dream vanished, and breathless horror and disgust filled my heart. Unable to endure the aspect of the being I had created, I rushed out of the room and continued a long time traversing my bed-chamber, unable to compose my mind to sleep.

Task 41

After studying the whole extract, answer the following questions in full, clear sentences.

a Why was Frankenstein so anxious to the point of agony?

b Why did the author call the human corpse a 'thing'?

c Why do you think the author set this event on a late, dreary, rainy night, with his candle dim?

d Why does he call his creation a wretch?

e What does the following quotation mean and why did he say it?:

'the beauty of the dream vanished, and breathless horror and disgust filled my heart'

Chapter 11　Romance Poets

第11章　浪漫主义诗人

In this chapter, we will focus on Romantic poets from England, such as Lord Byron, Percy Bysshe Shelley, John Keats and William Wordsworth.

William Wordsworth is the best known of the Lake Poets which included Samuel Coleridge and Robert Southey. Wordsworth did not become Poet Laureate until late in life in 1843, after the death of Southey.

Before we look at the works of the poets mentioned above, we are going to look at an example of children's poetry from the time. Jane Taylor (1783–1824) wrote the poem called *The Star*. This poem was the basis of the song *Twinkle, Twinkle Little Star*, a popular <u>lullaby</u> that dates from 1806.

The next extract contains the original poem, *The Star*.

Extract 42

The Star

Twinkle, twinkle, little star,
How I wonder what you are!
Up above the world so high,
Like a diamond in the sky.

When the blazing sun is gone,
When he nothing shines upon,
Then you show your little light,

Twinkle, twinkle, all the night.

Then the trav'ller in the dark,
Thanks you for your tiny spark,
He could not see which way to go,
If you did not twinkle so.

In the dark blue sky you keep,
And often thro' my curtains peep,
For you never shut your eye,
Till the sun is in the sky.

'Tis your bright and tiny spark,
Lights the trav'ller in the dark:
Tho' I know not what you are,
Twinkle, twinkle, little star.

In the lullaby, the first two lines of the first verse are repeated at the end of the verse, giving:

Twinkle, twinkle, little star,
How I wonder what you are!
Up above the world so high,
Like a diamond in the sky.
Twinkle, twinkle, little star,
How I wonder what you are!

Task 42

The above lyrics to the lullaby are known well to English speakers.

Memorise the six lines of the song if you do not already know them.

William Wordsworth

Back to the Lake Poets now, with some quotations from William Wordsworth (1770–1850):

Fill your paper with the breathings of your heart.

Come forth into the light of things, let nature be your teacher.

How does the meadow flower its bloom unfold? Because the lovely little flower is free down to its root, and in that freedom is bold.

The extract below contains the first two verses of Wordsworth's famous poem called *I Wandered Lonely as a Cloud*, published in 1807.

Extract 43

I Wandered Lonely as a Cloud

I wandered lonely as a cloud
That floats on high o' er vales and hills,
When all at once I saw a crowd,
A host, of golden daffodils;
Beside the lake, beneath the trees,
Fluttering and dancing in the breeze.

Continuous as the stars that shine
And twinkle on the milky way,
They stretched in never-ending line
Along the margin of a bay:
Ten thousand saw I at a glance,
Tossing their heads in sprightly dance.

Golden daffodils

Task 43

Memorise these two verses as they are very well-known in English-speaking countries. As you memorise the lines, take note of how grammatical structure can change in the creation of poetry.

Lord Byron/George Gordon Byron (1788–1824), also a poet from England, was a leading figure in the Romantic Movement. Read the popular quote from his *Mazeppa's Ride*:

With flowing tail and a flying mane ...
A thousand horse — the wild — the free —
Like waves that follow o' er the sea,
Came thickly thundering on.

Byron is well-known for his poem *Don Juan* (1819). The poem is set in the latter quarter of the eighteenth century, and begins with scenes from Don Juan's childhood. Don Juan was from an aristocratic Spanish family. He falls in love several times, travels to various countries, is sold as a slave, and ends up in England.

Percy Shelley

Percy Bysshe Shelley (1792–1822) became the husband of Mary Shelley (1797–1851) who is known for her novel *Frankenstein*. Percy Shelley is also one of the major Romantic poets from England. Below are the first five verses of his poem *To a Sky-Lark* (1820).

The skylark

Extract 44

Hail to thee, blithe Spirit!
Bird thou never wert —
That from Heaven, or near it,
Pourest thy full heart
In profuse strains of unpremeditated art.

Higher still and higher
From the earth thou springest
Like a cloud of fire;
The blue deep thou wingest,
And singing still dost soar, and soaring ever singest.

In the golden lightning
Of the sunken Sun —
O' er which clouds are brightning,
Thou dost float and run;
Like an unbodied joy whose race is just begun.

The pale purple even
Melts around thy flight,
Like a star of Heaven
In the broad day-light
Thou art unseen, — but yet I hear thy shrill delight.

Keen as are the arrows
Of that silver sphere,
Whose intense lamp narrows
In the white dawn clear
Until we hardly see — we feel that it is there.

Glossary

Hail to thee	(I/We) praise you
blithe Spirit	carefree and happy being
wert	were
profuse strains	abundant energy
unpremeditated	unplanned
The blue deep thou wingest	You fly high in the sky
dost	do
And singing still dost soar	(You) sing as you fly, remaining in a fixed position (in the sky)
O' er	Over

pale purple even	pale purple evening
Thou dost float and run	You (do) float and run
silver sphere	morning star

Task 44

Using the poem as your source, describe the bird (the skylark) in your own words in today's English. Write the description in a flowing paragraph.

Keats

John Keats (1795–1821), another Romantic poet from England, abandoned a career in medicine to write poetry. He died of tuberculosis at 25 years of age after publishing three volumes of verse.

The extract below contains the first three stanzas of Keats' *Ode to a Nightingale* (1819).

The nightingale

Extract 45

Ode to a Nightingale

My heart aches, and a drowsy numbness pains
My sense, as though of hemlock I had drunk,
Or emptied some dull opiate to the drains
One minute past, and Lethe-wards had sunk:
' Tis not through envy of thy happy lot,
But being too happy in thine happiness, —
That thou, light-winged Dryad of the trees,
In some melodious plot
Of beechen green, and shadows numberless,
Singest of summer in full-throated ease.

O, for a draught of vintage! that hath been
Cool' d a long age in the deep-delved earth,
Tasting of Flora and the country green,
Dance, a Provencal song, and sunburnt mirth!
O for a breaker full of the warm South,
Full of the true, the blushful Hippocrene,
With beaded bubbles winking at the brim,
And purple-stained mouth;
That I might drink, and leave the world unseen,
And with thee fade away into the forest dim:

Fade far away, dissolve, and quite forget
What thou among the leaves hast never known,
The weariness, the fever, and the fret
Here, where men sit and hear each other groan;

Where palsy shakes a few, sad last gray hairs,
Where youth grows pale, and spectre-thin, and dies;
Where but to think is to be full of sorrow
And leaden-eyed despairs,
Where Beauty cannot keep her lustrous eyes,
Or new Love pine at them beyond to-morrow.

Glossary

hemlock	Hemlock is a poisonous herb.
dull opiate	a drug/drink that dulls the senses
to the drains	to the dregs
Lethe-wards	This means 'towards Lethe.' Lethe is a river in Hades and when you drink form this river, you forget your past life.
'Tis	It is
thy happy lot	your happy life
Dryad of the trees	A dryad is a female spirit, a nymph, who lives in a tree.
beechen green	beechwood green
draught of vintage	drink of wine
deep-delved earth	deeply-dug ground
Flora	Flora is the Roman goddess of flowers, so here the name implies the flowers themselves.
country green	green countryside
Provencal song	A song of Provence. Provence is in southern France.
breaker	wave
blushful Hippocrene	Hippocrene was the name of a sacred fountain in Greece, believed to have been formed by the hooves of Pegasus, a mythical horse with wings. The fountain was supposed to inspire poetry. The fountain ran with wine instead of water, hence the word 'blushful.'
spectre-thin	like a ghost

leaden-eyed despairs	grief over loss of opportunity due to age and lack of energy
lustrous eyes	healthy, bright eyes

Task 45

Just like you did with *To a Sky-Lark* in the previous task, describe the bird (the nightingale) in *Ode to a Nightingale* in your own words in today's English. Write the description in a flowing paragraph.

If you compare your answer from Task 44 with that of Task 45, you will see a different style of description. In *To a Sky-Lark*, the bird's movements are described directly; even its song is described as 'shrill.' However, in *Ode to a Nightingale*, the bird is not described so directly, but rather the effects of its singing on humankind is of paramount significance.

Robert Southey

The historian, biographer and essayist Robert Southey (1774–1843), was also one of the Lake Poets. He was in fact England's Poet Laureate for the last thirty years of his life. But it is his, *The Story of the Three Bears* that has had the greatest impact on people's imagination over the last 200 years since it was written. It is a children's story in narrative form and was first published in 1837.

Originally, the story featured a dirty, badly behaved, old woman who invaded the home of three male bears while they went for a walk to wait for their porridge to cool down. She sat down in their chairs, ate some of their porridge and slept in the small bear's bed. When the three bears returned, she jumped out of the window. The bears are described as good-natured and trusting.

However, the story has undergone some adaptions, as many stories do when they are popular with children, ensuring they are child-friendly (suitable for children and not too disturbing). The first change was the removal of the naughty old woman, who was replaced by a curious girl called Goldilocks. The next change concerned the three male bears. The big bear became the daddy bear, the middle-sized bear became the mummy bear, and the small bear became baby bear. These changes made the story more friendly for children, and made it more inclusive, having a female bear instead of three male bears. Originally, the story only had one female who happened to be bad.

The extract below contains the whole of the original story.

Extract 46

The Story of the Three Bears

Once upon a time there were three bears, who lived together in a house of their own, in a wood. One of them was a little, small, wee bear; and one was a middle-sized bear, and the other was a great, huge bear. They each had a pot for their porridge, a little pot for the little, small, wee bear, and a middle-sized pot for the middle bear, and a great pot for the great, huge bear. And they each had a chair to sit in; a little chair for the little, small, wee bear; and a middle-sized chair for the middle bear; and a great chair for the great, huge bear. And they each had a bed to sleep in; a little bed for the little, small, wee bear; and a middle-sized bed for the middle bear; and a great bed for the great, huge bear.

One day, after they had made the porridge for their breakfast, and poured it into their porridge pots, they walked out into the woods while the porridge cooling, that they might not burn their mouths, by beginning too soon to eat it. And while they were walking, a little old woman came to the house. She could not have been a good, honest old woman; for first she looked in at the window, and then she peeped in at the keyhole; and seeing nobody in the house, she lifted the latch. The door was not fastened, because the bears were good bears, who did nobody any harm, and never suspected that anybody would harm them. So the little old woman opened the door, and went in; and well pleased she was when she saw the porridge on the table. If she had been a good little old woman, she would have waited till the bears came home, and then, perhaps, they would have asked her to breakfast; for they were good bears — a little rough or so, as the manner of bears is, but for all that very good-natured and hospitable. But she was an impudent, bad old woman, and set about helping herself.

So first she tasted the porridge of the great, huge bear, and that was too cold for her; and she said a bad word about that. And then she tasted the porridge of the middle bear, and that was too cold for her; and she said a bad word about that too. And then she went to the porridge of the little, small, wee bear, and tasted that; and that was neither too hot nor too cold, but just right; and she liked it so well that she ate it all up: but the naughty old woman said a bad word about the little porridge-pot, because it did not hold enough for her.

Then the little old woman sate down in the chair of the great, huge bear, and that was too hard for her. And then she sate down in the chair of the middle bear, and that was too soft for her. And then she sate down in the chair of the little, small, wee bear, and that was neither too hard, nor too soft, but just right. So she seated herself in it, and there she sate till the bottom of the chair came out and down she came, plump upon the ground. And the naughty old woman said a wicked word about that too.

Then the little old woman went upstairs into the bed-chamber in which the three bears slept. And first she lay down upon the bed of the great, huge bear; but that was too high at the foot of her. And then she lay down upon the bed of the middle bear, and that was too high at the foot of her. And then she lay down upon the bed of the little, small, wee bear, and that was neither too high at the head nor at the foot, but just right. So she covered herself up comfortably, and lay there till she fell fast asleep.

By this time the three bears thought their porridge would be cool enough, so they came home to breakfast. Now the little old woman had left the spoon of the great, huge bear, standing in his porridge.

'Somebody has been at my porridge!' said the great, huge bear, in his great, rough, gruff voice. And when the middle bear looked at his, he saw that the spoon

was standing in it too. They were wooden spoons; if they had been silver ones, the naughty old woman would have put them in her pocket.

'Somebody has been at my porridge!' said the middle bear in his middle voice. Then the little, small, wee bear looked at his, and there was the spoon in the porridge-pot, but the porridge was all gone.

'Somebody has been at my porridge, and has eaten it all up!' said the little, small, wee bear, in his little, small, wee voice.

Upon this the three bears, seeing that someone had entered their house, and eaten up the little, small, wee bear's breakfast, began to look about them. Now the little old woman had not put the hard cushion straight when she rose from the chair of the great, huge bear.

'Somebody has been sitting in my chair!' said the great, huge bear, in his great, rough, gruff voice.

And the little old woman had squatted down the soft cushion of the middle bear.

'Somebody has been sitting in my chair!' said the middle bear, in his middle voice. And you know what the little old woman had done to the third chair.

'Somebody has been sitting in my chair and has sate the bottom out of it!' said the little, small, wee bear in his little, small, wee voice.

Then the three bears thought it necessary that they should make further search; so they went upstairs into their bed-chamber. Now the little old woman had pulled the pillow of the great, huge bear out of its place.

'Somebody has been lying in my bed!' said the great, huge bear, in his great, rough, gruff voice. And the little old woman had pulled the bolster of the middle bear out of its place.

'Somebody has been lying in my bed!' said the middle bear, in his middle voice. And when the little, small, wee bear came to look at his bed, there was the bolster in its right place, and the pillow in its place upon the bolster; and upon the pillow was the little old woman's ugly, dirty head — which was not in its place, for she had no business there.

'Somebody has been lying in my bed — and here she is!' said the little, *small, wee bear, in his little, small, wee voice.*

The little old woman had heard in her sleep the great, rough, gruff voice of the great, huge bear; but she was so fast asleep that it was no more to her than the roaring of wind or the rumbling of thunder. And she had heard the middle voice of the middle bear, but it was only as if she had heard someone speaking in a dream. But when she heard the little, small, wee voice of the little, small, wee bear, it was so sharp, and so shrill, that it awakened her at once. Up she started; and when she saw the three bears on one side of the bed, she tumbled herself out at the other, and ran to the window.

Now the window was open, because the bears, like good, tidy bears as they were, always opened their bed-chamber window when they got up in the morning. Out the little old woman jumped; and whether she broke her neck in the fall; or ran into the wood and was lost there; or found her way out of the wood, and was taken up by the constable and sent to the House of Correction for a vagrant as she was, I cannot tell. But the three bears never saw anything more of her.

Glossary

wee bear	Wee means small, but it is mostly heard in Scottish English.
by beginning too soon to eat it	by beginning to eat it too soon
she liked it so well	she liked it so much
sate down	sat down
plump upon the ground	straight down onto the ground
bed-chamber	bedroom
Somebody has been at my porridge!	Somebody has been eating my porridge!
began to look about them	began to look around them
squatted down the cushion	squashed down the cushion
sate the bottom out of it	knocked the bottom out of it
that they should make further search	to investigate further
taken up by the constable	arrested by the police

for a vagrant　　　　　　　　　for vagrancy

The glossary above converts most of the phrases that may be considered to be old fashioned into today's Standard English.

Not only are there examples of English that are no longer used today, but there are also old fashioned attitudes expressed. For example, the old woman is criticised for being a vagrant, but these days, English society helps people in these circumstances because they consider them to be in serious need. The word 'vagrant' is not commonly used these days (although 'vagrancy' is an official term still in use), but the word 'homeless' is used in its place.

There are also descriptions of furniture typical of the days in which Southey lived, including the descriptions of the chairs and beds. For example, in regard to the little bear's bed, we are told that the pillow was in its place upon the bolster.

In regard to grammar, we have examples (from the original) of the precision typical of today in the following use of auxiliary verbs:

'*If she **had been** a good little old woman ...*'

'*...they **would have asked** her to breakfast*'

'*And she **had heard** the middle voice ...*'

Western children's stories often have a repetitive element to them and the number three is common too. Other examples are *The Three Little Pigs* in which there is a big, bad wolf who *huffs*, *puffs* and *blows* their house down; and *The Three Billy Goats Gruff* who cross a bridge that is controlled by a troll, one by one, until all three have passed over. These features are very evident in *The Story of the Three Bears*. This repetitive structure is one reason why children's stories are remembered so vividly by so many people throughout their lives.

Task 46

Make a note of all the examples of repeated threes in the story above.

Additional Notes for Unit 5
第5单元附加注释

Standard Nigerian English

Although the term 'Standard English' originally refers to the Standard English of England, other standard varieties have developed, such as in Africa.

The morphology and syntax of Standard Nigerian English is generally the same as Standard English English (i.e. the Standard English of England), but there are some exceptions. One example is the presence of strange plural forms, such as 'aircrafts' or 'equipments' where we would expect the singular form to indicate both singular and plural meanings. Another example is in the formation of antonyms, such as 'indisciplined' instead of 'undisciplined.'

In Standard Nigerian English, they may leave out the word 'to' from the Infinitive, for example in '... enable him (to) do it'. They will also use prepositions differently; for example, they will 'discuss about the issue,' whereas we would just 'discuss the issue.' They will say 'I congratulate you for...,' whereas we would say, 'I congratulate you on....'

Strong and Weak Verbs

Old English had a lot of strong-verb forms (irregular verbs), but many of them were lost during the development of the English language. The remaining strong verb system was simplified before the eighteenth century in both formal and informal usage, but after this, the use of strong verbs gradually increased again in Standard English, leaving the simpler form for <u>vernacular</u> usage. A good example of a 'strong' (irregular) verb used in today's Standard English is: *I sing, I sang, I sung*.

As I mentioned, Standard English had simplified the verb-system before it was strengthened again, and an example of this temporary reduction in the use of Strong Verbs can be found in Jane Austen. The Strong (irregular) verb 'to go' today has the following forms: *I go, I went, I have gone*. But in *Sense and Sensibility* (1811), instead of '... the troubles we **had gone** through,' she wrote:

'... *the troubles we* **had went** *through*'

In today's Standard English, it should be '... the troubles we **had gone** through,' and any teacher of English grammar in England would frown upon Jane Austen's usage; however, in Ireland, you would commonly hear 'went' instead of 'gone' for the Past Participle.

Present Perfective Aspect

Standard English differs, among the different varieties of English, in the use of the Present Perfective, which consists of the word *have* plus the Past Participle, for example, *I have bitten*. This phrase ('I have bitten') as a consequence relates to the past event with significance remaining up until the present. This can be illustrated more clearly by the sentence: *'My friend has been single for a long time.'* So up until the time of making this statement, 'my friend' has been single. This usage is typical of today's Standard English. However, in the case of the Standard English English sentence, *'I went to the show last week,'* using the simple past form, the Standard English of some other countries (i.e. Scotland, Ireland, the US, the Caribbean and India) would prefer the present perfective form. Conversely, Irish English would prefer the sentence, *'I know him all my life'*, whereas the other varieties of English, including Standard English English, would prefer, *'I have known him all my life.'*

Progressive Aspect

The Progressive Aspect indicates something is in progress at a given time. Using an example in the present tense, we have:

Simple form: *She runs fast.*

Progressive form: *She is running fast.*

The first sentence refers to her general ability, whereas the second sentence (progressive aspect) refers to what she is doing at the time.

These progressive aspect forms were rare in Middle English, but throughout the Middle English period they became more and more common.

Passives

Passive forms (using 'is being' or 'was being') typical of today's Standard English, began to develop from the end of the eighteenth century. An example of the origins of this usage can be found in something Robert Southey wrote (1795):

'*a fellow, whose uppermost upper grinder* **is being torn out by** *a mutton-fisted barber*'

Even today, this construction is generally only used for the Present or the Simple Past.

Glossary for Unit 5

British Industrial Revolution 英国工业革命

From about 1760-1820, manufacturing processes changed dramatically, from hand production to the use of machines and the use of iron.

Penal colonies 流放殖民地

A penal colony is a settlement where prisoners are sent far away from the general population.

Black English 黑人英语

African-American vernacular English (see vernacular below)

haggis 羊杂布丁

This is a Scottish dish, made from the sheep's internal organs, minced with suet and oatmeal. It is boiled inside a skin made from the sheep's stomach.

refrain 叠句

This is the regularly repeated part of a song.

prophetic poetry 预言诗

This refers to poetry that has the character of being inspired.

quatrain 四行诗

This is a stanza (verse/unit of a poem) with four lines.

personification 拟人

Personification is the representation of a quality or an idea as a person or a creature.

lullaby 摇篮曲

a song that helps a child to get to sleep, by lulling them

Ode 颂

An Ode is a poem or a song written to praise something or someone.

vernacular 白话

the non-standard dialect of a specific group, or the everyday usage of a language

Unit 6

Literature from the Victorian Period
维多利亚时期文学

Chapter 12　Charles Dickens and the Bronte Sisters
　　第12章　查尔斯·狄更斯与勃朗特姐妹

Chapter 13　Poetry from the 1840s
　　第13章　19世纪40年代的诗歌

Chapter 14　More Novels from the 1840s to the 1860s
　　第14章　19世纪40—60年代的小说

Chapter 15　Nonsense Writing
　　第15章　荒诞文学

Chapter 16　The 1870s and 1880s
　　第16章　19世纪70与80年代

Chapter 17　The 1890s
　　第17章　19世纪90年代

Additional Notes for Unit 6
　　第6单元附加注释

Chapter 12 Charles Dickens and the Bronte Sisters

第12章 查尔斯·狄更斯与勃朗特姐妹

This Unit covers the third quarter of the Modern English Period (1750-1950), which roughly corresponds with the Victorian period (1837-1901). The nineteenth century was a time of great change, including technological progress. British technological inventions led the world at this time, and private enterprises created wealth which benefited every aspect of society.

本单元涵盖了现代英语时期（1750—1950）并重点介绍了1850—1900年的文学，这大致与维多利亚时期（1837—1901）相对应。19世纪是一个技术进步的巨变时代。当时，英国的技术发明引领着世界，私营企业创造的财富造福于社会的方方面面。

Dickens

Charles Dickens (1812-1870) is an exceedingly important author from this period. He wrote in great detail about life in London for the poor, a constant reminder to our society to ensure we continue to meet the needs of those who are in difficulties today. Dickens' works include *Oliver* (1838), *The Old Curiosity Shop* (1840), *A Christmas Carol* (1842), *David Copperfield* (1850), *Bleak House* (1853), *A Tale of Two Cities* (1859) and *Great Expectations* (1861).

Great Expectations opens with a scene on the eerie marshes of Kent, a southern County in England. Pip, an orphan, meets an escaped convict and gives him food. Thereafter, Pip goes through misfortune and suffering until he eventually matures. *Oliver* likewise starts with an orphan, Oliver Twist, who was born in a workhouse not far from London. The workhouse official, Bumble, was responsible for him.

Oliver left for London after being released from his imprisonment in a cellar during his time working for Mrs Sowerberry the casket maker. In London, Oliver met Jack Dawkins, known as the Artful Dodger, who offered him a place to stay, Oliver not knowing he would be living with a gang of thieves. The gang's boss was known as Fagin. Oliver was taught the skills of a pickpocket.

Later in the story, Oliver ended up being part of a trio of thieves, including the gang's evil co-leader Bill Sykes. The trio were assigned to rob a house, against Oliver's wishes, and Oliver was shot and wounded. But after many tragedies, Oliver was eventually happily adopted by Mr Brownlow.

Here is an extract from the second chapter of the novel, while Oliver is in the workhouse.

Extract 47

A council was held; lots were cast who should walk up to the master after supper that evening and ask for more; and it fell to Oliver Twist.

The evening arrived; the boys took their places. The master, in his cook's uniform, stationed himself at the copper; his pauper assistants ranged themselves behind him; the gruel was served out, and a long grace was said over the short commons. The gruel disappeared; the boys whispered each other, and winked at Oliver, while his next neighbours nudged him. Child as he was, he was desperate with hunger, and reckless with misery. He rose from the table, and advancing to the master, basin and spoon in hand, said, somewhat alarmed at his own temerity.

"Please, sir, I want some more."

The master was a fat, healthy man, but he turned very pale. He gazed in stupefied astonishment on the small rebel for some seconds, and then clung for support to the copper. The assistants were paralysed with wonder, the boys with fear.

"What!" said the master at length, in a faint voice.

"Please, sir," replied Oliver, "I want some more."

The master aimed a blow at Oliver's head with the ladle, pinioned him in his arms, and shrieked aloud for the beadle.

The board were sitting in solemn conclave when Mr. Bumble rushed into the room in great excitement, and addressing the gentleman in the high chair, said:

"Mr. Limbkins, I beg your pardon, sir! Oliver Twist has asked for more!"

There was a general start. Horror was depicted on every countenance.

"For more!" said Mr. Limbkins. "Compose yourself, Bumble, and answer me distinctly. Do I understand that he asked for more, after he had eaten the supper allotted by the dietary?"

"He did, sir," replied Bumble.

"That boy will be hung," said the gentleman in the white waistcoat. "I know that boy will be hung."

Please sir, I want some more

Nobody controverted the prophetic gentleman's opinion. An animated discussion took place. Oliver was ordered into instant confinement; and a bill *was next morning pasted on the outside of the gate, ordering a reward of five pounds to anybody who would take Oliver Twist off the hands of the parish. In other words, five pounds and Oliver Twist were offered to any man or woman who wanted an apprentice to any trade, business or calling.*

....

For a week after the commission of the impious and profane offence of asking for more, Oliver remained a close prisoner in the dark and solitary room to which he had been consigned by the wisdom and mercy of the board.

Glossary

stationed himself at the copper	positioned himself beside the vessel from which the gruel would be ladled
pauper assistants	very poor assistants
gruel	This is a type of cereal such as oats boiled in water or milk.
a long grace was said over the short commons	a long prayer of thanksgiving to God was said for the meagre quantity of food
whispered each other	whispered to each other
at length	eventually
beadle	A beadle is a minor parish official. Mr Bumble was the wicked parish beadle who put Oliver into the terrible workhouse.
The board were sitting in solemn conclave	The board were having a solemn, private meeting
There was a general start.	There was a general sense of surprise.
countenance	face
dietary	regulated daily food allowance
hung	hanged
controverted	contradicted

and Oliver Twist were offered to …   and Oliver Twist would be offered to …

Task 47a

Look at the last paragraph rewritten below. You can see the author's sarcasm, that is, knowingly stating the opposite of what he and the readers would believe to be true.

Read the paragraph again below, then note down or underline the phrases that are clearly sarcastic.

'For a week after the commission of the impious and profane offence of asking for more, Oliver remained a close prisoner in the dark and solitary room to which he had been consigned by the wisdom and mercy of the board.'

Now rewrite your selected phrases in a way that is not sarcastic, to clearly express the author's meaning, and explain to your partner why you believe the author feels this way.

Task 47b

Using the information in the extract and my commentary, discuss with a partner whether a similar kind of unjust situation occurs in the world today. If not, why not? If you can think of similar situations today, discuss how you think society can deal with these things fairly.

The following extract is taken from *A Christmas Carol*. Ebenezer Scrooge, a miserly money-lender, has received a visit from the ghost of Jacob Marley, his late business partner, and now another ghost is due. He will in fact receive visits from four spirits in total, who will lead him to the realisation that he must stop being a greedy, selfish miser. The four ghosts are Jacob Marley, Ghost of Christmas Past, Ghost of Christmas Present and Ghost of Christmas Future. A section has been removed for ease of reading.

Extract 48a

Marley's Ghost bothered him exceedingly. Every time he resolved within himself, after mature inquiry, that it was all a dream, his mind flew back again, like a strong spring released, to its first position, and presented the same problem to be worked all through, "Was it a dream or not?"

Scrooge lay in this state until the chime had gone three quarters more, when he remembered, on a sudden, that the Ghost had warned him of a visitation when the bell tolled one. He resolved to lie awake until the hour was passed; and, considering that he could no more go to sleep than go to Heaven, this was perhaps the wisest resolution in his power.

The quarter was so long, that he was more than once convinced he must have sunk into a doze unconsciously, and missed the clock. At length it broke upon his listening ear.

"Ding, dong!"

"A quarter past," said Scrooge, counting.

"Ding, dong!"

"Half-past!" said Scrooge.

"Ding, dong!"

"A quarter to it," said Scrooge.

"Ding, dong!"

"The hour itself," said Scrooge, triumphantly, "and nothing else!"

He spoke before the hour bell sounded, which it now did with a deep, dull, hollow, melancholy ONE. Light flashed up in the room upon the instant, and the curtains of his bed were drawn.

The curtains of his bed were drawn aside, I tell you, by a hand. Not the curtains at his feet, nor the curtains at his back, but those to which his face was addressed. The curtains of his bed were drawn aside; and Scrooge, starting up into a half-recumbent attitude, found himself face to face with the unearthly visitor who drew them: as close to it as I am now to you, and I am standing in the spirit at your elbow.

It was a strange figure — like a child: yet not so like a child as like an old man, viewed through some supernatural medium, which gave him the appearance of having receded from the view, and being diminished to a child's proportions.

"Are you the Spirit, sir, whose coming was foretold to me?" asked Scrooge:

"I am!"

The voice was soft and gentle. Singularly low, as if instead of being so close beside him, it were at a distance.

"Who, and what are you?" Scrooge demanded.

"I am the Ghost of Christmas Past."

"Long past?" inquired Scrooge: observant of its dwarfish stature.

"No. Your past."

...

He then made bold to inquire what business brought him there.

"Your welfare!" said the Ghost.

Scrooge expressed himself much obliged, but could not help thinking that a night of unbroken rest would have been more conducive to that end. The Spirit must have heard him thinking, for it said immediately:

"Your reclamation, then. Take heed!"

It put out its strong hand as it spoke, and clasped him gently by the arm.

"Rise! and walk with me!"

It would have been in vain for Scrooge to plead that the weather and the hour were not adapted to pedestrian purposes; that bed was warm, and the thermometer a long way below freezing; that he was clad but lightly in his slippers, dressing-gown, and nightcap; and that he had a cold upon him at that time. The grasp, though gentle as a woman's hand, was not to be resisted. He rose: but finding that the Spirit made towards the window, clasped his robe in supplication.

"I am a mortal," Scrooge remonstrated, "and liable to fall."

"Bear but a touch of my hand there," said the Spirit, laying it upon his heart, "and you shall be upheld in more than this!"

As the words were spoken, they passed through the wall, and stood upon an open country road, with fields on either hand. The city had entirely vanished. Not a vestige of it was to be seen. The darkness and the mist had vanished with it, for it was a clear, cold, winter day, with snow upon the ground.

"Good Heaven!" said Scrooge, clasping his hands together, as he looked about him. "I was bred in this place. I was a boy here!"

Even though the extract can be easily understood, the language conventions have changed considerably. Have a look at the adapted version below and compare it to the original above. I have underlined the areas where I have made changes to adapt it into today's English.

Extract 48b

Marley's Ghost bothered him <u>intensely.</u> Every time he <u>tried to convince himself, after much soul-searching</u>, that it was all a dream, his mind <u>sprang</u> back again, like a strong spring <u>being</u> released, to its first position, and presented the same problem <u>for him to work through again</u>, "Was it a dream or not?"

Scrooge lay in this state until the chime had gone <u>another three quarters</u>, when he remembered, <u>all of</u> a sudden, that the Ghost had warned him of a <u>visit</u> when the <u>clock struck</u> one. He <u>decided</u> to lie awake until the hour was passed; and, <u>realising</u> that he <u>was as likely to</u> go to sleep <u>as he was to</u> go to Heaven, this was perhaps the <u>only decision he could realistically make</u>.

The <u>final</u> quarter was so long, that he <u>thought, several times, that he must have unconsciously sunk into a doze</u>, and missed the clock. <u>Eventually</u>, it <u>rang loudly in his</u> ear.

"Ding, dong!"

"<u>Quarter</u> past," said Scrooge, counting.

"Ding, dong!"

"Half-past!" said Scrooge.

"Ding, dong!"

"Quarter to," said Scrooge.

"Ding, dong!"

"On the hour," said Scrooge, triumphantly, "and nothing else!"

He spoke before the hour bell sounded, which it now did with a deep, dull, hollow, melancholy ONE. Light flashed in the room at that moment, and the curtains of his bed were drawn aside.

It's true, the curtains of his bed were drawn aside - by a hand! Not the curtains at his feet, nor the curtains at the back, but those to which his face was looking. The curtains of his bed were drawn aside; and Scrooge, jolting up into a half-reclining position, found himself face to face with the unearthly visitor who drew them: as close to it as I am now to you, and I am standing in the spirit at your elbow.

It was a strange figure — like a child: yet not so like a child as like an old man, viewed through some supernatural medium, which gave him the appearance of having receded from view, and being diminished to a child's proportions.

"Are you the Spirit, sir, who I was told was coming?" asked Scrooge:

"I am!"

The voice was soft and gentle; unusually low, as if instead of being close beside him, it was at a distance.

"Who, and what are you?" Scrooge demanded.

"I am the Ghost of Christmas Past."

"Long past?" inquired Scrooge, observant of its dwarfish stature.

"No. Your past."

...

He then boldly inquired as to what business brought him there.

"Your welfare!" said the Ghost.

Scrooge expressed his gratitude, but could not help thinking that a night of unbroken rest would have been more conducive to that end. The Spirit must have heard him thinking, <u>because it immediately said</u>:

"Your <u>restoration</u>, then. Take <u>note</u>!"

It put out its strong hand as it spoke, and clasped him gently by the arm.

"<u>Get up</u>! and walk with me!"

It would have been in vain for Scrooge to plead that the weather and the hour were not <u>suitable for going for a walk</u>; that bed was warm, and the thermometer a long way below freezing; that he was <u>only dressed</u> in his slippers, dressing-gown, and nightcap; and that he had a <u>cold at</u> that time. The grasp <u>was not easy to get away from</u>, even though it was as gentle as a woman's hand. He got up, but when <u>the Spirit headed</u> towards the window, he clasped his robe in supplication.

"I am a mortal," Scrooge remonstrated, "and liable to fall."

"<u>Allow just</u> a touch of my hand there," said the Spirit, laying it <u>on</u> his heart, "and you shall be upheld in more than this!"

As the words were spoken, they passed through the wall, and stood <u>on</u> an open country road, with fields on either <u>side</u>. The city had entirely vanished. Not <u>even a trace of it could</u> be seen. The darkness and the mist had vanished <u>along</u> with it, <u>as</u> it was a clear, cold, <u>winter's</u> day, with snow <u>on</u> the ground.

"Good <u>Heavens</u>!" said Scrooge, clasping his hands together, as he looked <u>around</u> him. "I was <u>brought up</u> in this place. I was a boy here!"

Task 48

As you can see, there are lots of underlined sections in the extract from *A Christmas Carol*. All of the changes are necessary to bring the English up-to-date. Most avid readers of English Literature would prefer to read the original text, especially as native English speakers today can understand it. But students who are studying English as a second or foreign language would benefit from an updated version alongside the original so that they do not get confused between old fashioned English and the correct use of English today for both writing and speaking.

Independently, or as a group, carefully compare the two versions of the extract and try to understand why the changes are necessary, and then, try to apply a similar logic to other old works of English Literature as you progress through this book.

The Bronte Sisters

The Bronte Sisters, Charlotte Bronte (1816–1855), Emily Bronte (1818–1848), and Anne Bronte (1820–1849) were born in Yorkshire, England. Their mother was from Cornwall, a County in southwest England, and their father was from Ireland.

The three sisters published a novel each at the same time: Charlotte's *Jane Eyre* (1847), Emily's *Wuthering Heights* (1847), and Anne's *Agnes Grey* (1847).

Charlotte's novel *Jane Eyre*, which was dedicated to Thackery, is basically about the love between a young governess Jane and her married employer Mr Rochester. It begins with Jane as an orphan, whose parents died when she was a baby. She was looked after by her relative Mrs Reed of Gateshead Hall where Jane experienced 10 years of neglect. She was eventually sent to Lowood School where she studied hard. When her studies finished, she became a teacher. When she needed a change in her life, she acquired the role of a governess at Thornfield, near Millcote, in a beautiful old house surrounded by exquisite gardens. Her job was to teach Adele Varens, a ward of Jane's employer, Mr Edward Rochester.

The first time Jane met Mr Rochester was when he was thrown from his horse, and she came to his aid. He did not have much of a friendly disposition.

One night, Jane heard a strange noise and found Mr Rochester's bedroom door open and his bed on fire. She was led to believe this was connected to a mad tenant at Thornfield who lived on the third floor.

Later on in the story, Edward Rochester actually proposed marriage to Jane, who accepted, but shortly before the marriage ceremony was due to take place, Jane was awakened to find a terrifying woman in her room who tried on her wedding veil before tearing it up. Mr Rochester tried to ignore it and acted as though he thought Jane had imagined it. But, at the wedding ceremony, someone declared there to be an impediment to their marriage, as Edward Rochester was already married; he had married Bertha Mason fifteen years before.

Jane left Thornfield the next morning, but she fell on hard times. However, she was picked up and cared for by Reverend St. John Rivers and his sisters. Rev St. John Rivers found Jane a job in a school. St. John eventually decided to go to India as a missionary, and wanted Jane to go with him as his wife, even though he was not in love with her. She felt she owed him for all that he had done for her, but she hesitated, to St. John's great disappointment.

At this time, Jane had a dream about Mr Rochester calling her name, so the following day she returned to Thornfield to find the mansion had been burnt to the ground. She was told that the mansion had been set on fire by the mad resident, and that she died while Mr Rochester was trying to save her. Mr Rochester was blinded in the incident and was living on a farm called Ferndean. Jane went to him and they married.

In the following extract, Jane is talking to St. John about their friendship. St. John wants Jane to go to India with him. I have omitted some parts for ease of reading.

Extract 49a

"Must we part this way, St. John? And when you go to India, will you leave me so, without a kinder word than you have yet spoken?"

He now turned quite from the moon, and faced me.

"When I go to India, Jane, will I leave you? What! Do you not go to India?"

"You said I could not, unless I married you."

"And you will not marry me? You adhere to that resolution?"

...

"No, St. John, I will not marry you. I adhere to my resolution."

"Once more, why this refusal?" he asked.

"Formerly," I answered, "because you did not love me now, I reply, because you almost hate me. If I were to marry you, you would kill me. You are killing me now."

His lips and cheeks turned white — quite white.

"I should kill — I am killing you? Your words are such that ought not to be used; violent, unfeminine, and untrue. They betray an unfortunate state of mind; they merit severe reproof. They would seem inexcusable, but that it is the duty of man to forgive his fellow, even until seventy-and-seven times."

...

"Now you will indeed hate me," I said. "It is useless to attempt to conciliate you; I see I have made an eternal enemy of you."

A fresh wrong did these words inflict; the worse, because they touched on the truth. That bloodless lip quivered to a temporary spasm. I knew the steely ire I had whetted. I was heart-wrung.

"You utterly misinterpret my words," I said, at once seizing his hand; "I have no intention to grieve or pain you — indeed I have not."

Most bitterly he smiled — most decidedly he withdrew his hand from mine. "And now you will recall your promise, and will not go to India at all, I presume?" said he, after a considerable pause.

"Yes I will, as your assistant," I answered.

Although this novel is a classic, and the extract is easy to understand, the language is quite old fashioned, and many parts are not typical of speech or writing today. Therefore, I have rewritten the passage below. The underlined sections indicate where changes have been necessary to update the language into today's English.

Extract 49b

"<u>Do we have to</u> part this way, St. John? And when you go to India, <u>are you</u>

going to leave me like this, without a kinder word than you've already spoken?"

He now turned away from the moon, and faced me.

"Will I leave you when I go to India? What! Aren't you going to India, Jane?"

"You said I couldn't, unless I married you."

"And you're not going to marry me? So, have you decided that for certain?"

...

"No, St. John, I will not marry you. I am sticking to my decision."

"Again, why have you decided not to marry me?" he asked.

"Before," I answered, "it was because you didn't love me anymore, and now it's because you almost hate me. If I married you, you'd kill me. You're killing me now."

His lips and cheeks turned white — very white.

"I'd kill — I'm killing you? You shouldn't say such things, you're being too aggressive and unfeminine; and you're wrong! It just shows that you're not thinking straight. I should be really angry with you for accusing me like that, but it's our duty to forgive, even until seventy-seven times."

...

"Now you'll definitely hate me," I said. "It's useless trying to appease you; I can see I've made you my enemy forever."

These words hurt him even more, partly because they actually touched on the truth. That bloodless lip quivered and twitched. I realised I had stirred up deep, painful feelings in him. I felt so guilty.

"You have completely misinterpreted my words," I said, quickly seizing his hand; "I have no intention of upsetting you or causing you pain — absolutely not."

He smiled a bitter smile, and snatched his hand away from mine. "And now you'll break your promise, and not go to India at all, I presume?" he said, after a considerable pause.

"Yes I will, as your assistant," I answered.

Even though the text has been correctly updated, the language still seems old fashioned due to its cultural background; Jane and St. John are still speaking a little too formally. So, to be completely up-to-date, the historical background would need to be changed. Many films that are adapted from English Classics do this — they are set in modern times along with modern verbal expressions.

Task 49

Study the two versions of the extract from *Jane Eyre* and consider why the changes are necessary to be clearly understood in today's English.

Consider the cultural and historical background of the dialogue in the original text (using the modernised version to help your understanding). Write a list of formal aspects of the language used in the original text, and alongside each point explain what historical or cultural factors would require such language.

Now we come to Emily's *Wuthering Heights*. In this novel, Cathy and Heathcliff were childhood friends, and their love grew stronger and stronger as time went by. The backdrop to the story is the Yorkshire Moors with which Emily Bronte was very familiar.

In the following extract, Cathy cannot understand Heathcliff's strange mood.

Extract 50

'Why, Master Heathcliff, you are not fit for enjoying a ramble, this morning. How ill you do look!'

Catherine surveyed him with grief and astonishment; and changed the ejaculation of joy on her lips, to one of alarm; and the congratulation on their long postponed meeting to an anxious inquiry, whether he were worse than usual?

'No—better—better!' he panted, trembling, and retaining her hand as if he needed its support, while his large blue eyes wandered timidly over her; the hollowness round them transforming to haggard wildness the languid expression they once possessed.

'But you have been worse,' persisted his cousin; 'worse than when I saw you last—you are thinner, and—'

'I'm tired,' he interrupted, hurriedly, 'It is too hot for walking; let us rest here. And, in the morning, I often feel sick—papa says I grow so fast.'

Badly satisfied, Cathy sat down, and he reclined beside her.

'This is something like your paradise,' said she, making an effort at cheerfulness. 'You recollect the two days we agreed to spend in the place and way each thought pleasantest? This is nearly yours, only there are clouds; but then they are so soft and mellow, it is nicer than sunshine. Next week, if you can, we'll ride down to the Grange Park, and try mine.'

Glossary

Why, Master Heathcliff, you are not fit for enjoying a ramble, this morning. Master Heathcliff, you don't look like you're up to a ramble, this morning.

How ill you do look! You look really ill!

Catherine surveyed him Catherine studied him

changed the ejaculation of joy on her lips, to one of alarm changed her joyful words to ones of alarm

and the congratulation on their long postponed meeting and her enthusiastic greeting over their long postponed meeting

retaining her hand as if he needed its support keeping her hand as if he needed its support

transforming to haggard wildness the languid expression they once possessed transforming from the languid expression they once had into haggard wildness

But you have been worse	But you look worse ['have been worse' would imply the opposite meaning today, suggesting he looks a little better now]
let us rest here	let's rest here
Badly satisfied	Not satisfied
This is something like your paradise	This is a bit like your paradise
You recollect the two days we agreed to spend in the place and way each thought pleasantest?	Do you recollect the two days we agreed to spend in whatever place and way we wanted?
This is nearly yours, only there are clouds	This is almost like yours, except there are clouds
but then they are so soft and mellow	but they are soft and gentle
it is nicer than sunshine	it's better than sunshine

The use of language in this extract is quite strange to us today, hence the need for so many phrases to be interpreted in the glossary. In the glossary, I have brought the language up-to-date while keeping the formal style in line with the original historical and cultural context.

Task 50

Carefully study the extract alongside the glossary entries, to understand how English has changed over the last 70 to 80 years. You may find it helpful to rewrite the extract, replacing the original phrases in the extract with the updated ones in the glossary.

Try to remain aware of these developments in English as a language, so that you can understand Victorian English Literature better.

Feeling their conversation was ineffective, Cathy considered leaving, but the idea of her leaving suddenly agitated Heathcliff:

Extract 51a

He glanced fearfully towards the Heights, begging she would remain another half-hour, at least.

'But I think,' said Cathy, 'you'd be more comfortable at home than sitting here; and I cannot amuse you to-day, I see, by my tales, and songs, and chatter: you have grown wiser than I, in these six months; you have little taste for my diversions now; or else, if I could amuse you, I'd willingly stay.'

'Stay to rest yourself,' he replied. 'And, Catherine, don't think, or say that I'm very unwell: it is the heavy weather and heat that make me dull; and I walked about, before you came, a great deal, for me. Tell uncle, I'm in tolerable health, will you?'

'I'll tell him that you say so, Linton. I couldn't affirm that you are,' observed my young lady, wondering at his pertinacious assertion of what was evidently an untruth.

'And be here again next Thursday,' continued he, shunning her puzzled gaze. 'And give him my thanks for permitting you to come — my best thanks, Catherine. And — and, if you did meet my father, and he asked you about me, don't lead him to suppose that I've been extremely silent and stupid: don't look sad and downcast, as you are doing — he'll be angry.'

'I care nothing for his anger,' exclaimed Cathy, imagining she would be its object.

'But I do,' said her cousin, shuddering. 'Don't provoke him against me, Catherine, for he is very hard.'

Below, I have written a version in today's English, remaining faithful to the historical and cultural background.

Extract 51b

He glanced towards the Heights with a sense of fear, begging her to remain *for another half an hour, at least.*

'But I think,' said Cathy, 'you'd be more comfortable at home than sitting here; and I don't seem to be able to amuse you today with my tales, my songs, and chatter: you've grown wiser than I, in these last six months; you don't have much interest in my diversions now; if you did, and I could amuse you, I'd willingly stay.'

'Stay to have a rest,' he replied. 'And, Catherine, don't think, or say that I'm really ill: it's just the heavy weather and the heat that're making me depressed; and I had a walk around before you came, a long walk, for me. Please tell uncle that I'm in good health!'

'I'll tell him that you say so, Linton, but I won't try to convince him that you are,' she observed, puzzled as to why he was so stubbornly sticking to his assertion, even though it was obviously a lie.

'And come here again next Thursday,' he continued, shunning her puzzled gaze. 'And give him my thanks for allowing you to come — my best thanks, Catherine. And — and, if you do meet my father, and he asks you about me, don't let him know I've been extremely silent and stupid: don't look sad and downcast, as you are doing now, or he'll be angry.'

'I couldn't care less about his anger,' exclaimed Cathy, imagining being in that situation.

'But I could,' said her cousin, shuddering. 'Don't provoke him against me, Catherine — he's really cold.'

Task 51

Write down ALL the changes I have made to the original. Write the original phrase with its newer version (in the same style as my glossary for Extract 50). This can be used as a glossary for Extract 51a.

Chapter 13 Poetry from the 1840s
第13章　19世纪40年代的诗歌

The poet, Alfred Tennyson (1809-1892), was born in Lincolnshire in England, and his father was a Vicar in the Church of England. In 1830, he studied as an undergraduate at Cambridge University.

When William Wordsworth died in 1850, Tennyson became Poet Laureate of Great Britain and Ireland (Wordsworth had become Poet Laureate after his associate Southey died).

Among his poems were the well-known *Ulysses* (1842) and *In Memoriam A.H.H.* (1850) from where we get the famous words:

'Tis better to have loved and lost,

Than never to have loved at all.'

In Memoriam A.H.H. (1850) established Tennyson's reputation. The poem was about the immortality of the soul, and written in memory of his friend Arthur Hallam. After this came *Maud* (1855), and at his peak, *Idylls of the King* (1859), in which he developed a picture of King Arthur as the first national hero of England. Tennyson's 'Arthur' had done everything possible to bring civilisation to his realm through his knights, but his attempts failed due to sins that Tennyson believed were also typical of his own times.

Ulysses

Here is an extract from Tennyson's poem *Ulysses*. Ulysses is another name for Odysseus, the crafty Greek soldier who devised the plan of the Trojan Horse of ancient historical writings, which defeated the great citadel of Troy. This poem is based on an account in Dante's *Inferno*, stating that Ulysses set out on an additional voyage from his home and kingdom (the Island of Ithaca) in his old age.

Extract 52

Ulysses
It little profits that an idle king,
By this still hearth, among these barren crags,
Matched with an aged wife, I mete and dole
Unequal laws unto a savage race,
That hoard, and sleep, and feed, and know not me.
I cannot rest from travel: I will drink
Life to the lees: all times I have enjoyed
Greatly, have suffered greatly, both with those
That loved me, and alone; on shore, and when
Through scudding drifts the rainy Hyades
Vext the dim sea: I am become a name;
For always roaming with a hungry heart
Much have I seen and known; cities of men
And manners, climates, councils, governments,
Myself not least, but honoured of them all;
And drunk delight of battle with my peers,
Far on the ringing plains of windy Troy.
I am a part of all that I have met;
Yet all experience is an arch wherethrough
Gleams that untravelled world, whose margin fades
For ever and for ever when I move.
How dull it is to pause, to make an end,
To rust unburnished, not to shine in use!

Glossary

I mete and dole unequal laws	I measure out justice
know not me	do not know me
lees	dregs
scudding drifts	wind-blown rain
the rainy Hyades	The 'Hyades' is a group of stars which was believed to signal rain was coming.
Vext	Vexed
I am become a name	I have become famous
Troy	An ancient city in what is now modern Turkey
margin	border

Task 52

Use this extract from *Ulysses* to practice recitation (but you do not have to commit it to memory). Stand in front of your partner or group, and recite the poem several times, focusing on verbal expression. Ask your audience for feedback after each recitation.

In Memoriam A.H.H.

The next extract consists of the first four introductory verses of *In Memoriam A.H.H.*

Extract 53

Strong Son of God, immortal Love,
Whom we, that have not seen thy face,
By faith, and faith alone, embrace,
Believing where we cannot prove;

Thine are these orbs of light and shade;
Thou madest Life in man and brute;
Thou madest Death; and lo, Thy foot
Is on the skull which thou hast made.

Thou wilt not leave us in the dust:
Thou madest man, he knows not why,
He thinks he was not made to die;
And thou hast made him: Thou art just.

Thou seemest human and divine,
The highest, holiest manhood, Thou:
Our wills are ours, we know not how;
Our wills are ours, to make them Thine.

Glossary

orbs	Orbs are ball-shaped objects.
and lo, Thy foot	and behold (look), Your foot
Thou art just.	You are just ('just' here indicates that he is a being of justice, and always acts with justice)
Thou seemest human and divine	You seem to be human AND divine (The Son of God, Jesus Christ, was God and human at the same time)

Task 53

In your opinion, what do the following quotations from the poem mean?
'Thy foot is on the skull which thou hast made'
'Thou wilt not leave us in the dust'

'He thinks he was not made to die'
'The highest, holiest manhood, Thou'
'Our wills are ours, we know not how'
'Our wills are ours, to make them Thine'

Robert Browning

Robert Browning (1812–1889) was a poet born in London in England, and famous for his dramatic monologues. Among his works were *Dramatic Lyrics* (1842), *The Laboratory* (1845) and *My Last Duchess* (1845). Not every poem he wrote was for adults. For example, in *Dramatic Lyrics*, he wrote the poem called *The Pied Piper of Hamelin* (1842), based on an old German story set in the German town of Hamelin, which was expecting an infestation of rats. A colourfully dressed piper appeared and promised to get rid of the rats for money, and the town agreed. So, the piper succeeded in leading the rats away with his music, but the town refused to pay him. That was when the piper decided to take revenge, and he did so the same year by leading away all the children of the town (except for a couple who remained), never to be seen again, in the same way that he had made the rats disappear.

The story is based on a historical event that was, in the Lueneburg manuscript, recorded to have taken place on the 26th June in 1284. It says that a piper, clothed in many kinds of colours, deceived 130 children born in Hamelin, and as a result they were lost. Today, nobody knows what happened to those children. Here is a section of Robert Browning's poem *The Pied Piper of Hamelin: A Child's Story*:

'When, lo! as they reached the mountain-side,
A wondrous portal opened wide,
As if a cavern was suddenly hollowed;
And the Piper advanced and the children followed,
And when all were in to the very last,
The door in the mountain-side shut fast.

Below, is an extract from the first half of Browning's poem *The Laboratory*. This poem is based on a true event that took place in France in the seventeenth century in which Madame de Brinvilliers poisoned several members of her family before she was executed by guillotine in Paris. The poem is a monologue, featuring a vengeful wife who is watching an apothecary (now called a pharmacist — a medical practitioner who makes and dispenses medicines) while he creates a poison which she wants to use to kill her husband's lover. It is written in a gleeful style as the vengeful wife becomes more and more excited about the process.

Extract 54

Now that I, tying thy glass mask tightly,
May gaze thro' these faint smokes curling whitely,
As thou pliest thy trade in this devil's smithy —
Which is the poison to poison her, prithee?

He is with her, and they know that I know
Where they are, what they do: they believe my tears flow
While they laugh, laugh at me, at me fled to the drear
Empty church, to pray God in, for them! — I am here.

Grind away, moisten and mash up they paste,
Pound at thy powder, — I am not in haste!
Better sit thus, and observe thy strange things,
Than go where men wait me and dance at the King's.

That in the mortar — you call it a gum?
Ah, the brave tree whence such gold oozings come!
And yonder soft phial, the exquisite blue,
Sure to taste sweetly, — is that poison too?

Had I but all of them, thee and thy treasures,
What a wild crowd of invisible pleasures!
To carry pure death in an earring, a casket,
A signet, a fan-mount, a filigree basket!

Soon, at the King's, a mere lozenge to give,
And Pauline should have just thirty minutes to live!
But to light a pastille, and Elise, with her head
And her breast and her arms and her hands, should drop dead!

Glossary

prithee	This comes from the old fashioned phrase 'pray thee' ('I beg you'), which later formed into an interjection 'prithee,' meaning, 'If you please.' According to the Oxford English Dictionary, the form 'prithee' is first found in 1577, and last found in 1875. It was most commonly used in the seventeenth century, the historical time on which this poem is based.
drear	dreary
the King's	the King's court where dances would take place

Task 54a

In your own words, write a short paragraph, one for each of the 6 verses, describing what this poem is telling us.

Task 54b

The poem has many rhyming words. Read the poem out loud, paying close attention to the rhyming patterns. Is there a regular pattern? What is it?

Chapter 14 More Novels from the 1840s to the 1860s
第14章 19世纪40—60年代的小说

William Makepeace Thackery (1811-1863), a novelist from England, was famous for his satirical works. For example, he wrote *Vanity Fair* (1848), which is now a major TV series. The term 'Vanity Fair' and the meaning it conveys was taken from John Bunyan's seventeenth century allegorical *Pilgrim's Progress*; Thackery associates the title of his book with the aristocracy of his day, which he believed to be uncontrollably hypocritical, full of immorality and the worship of money.

Thackery's *Vanity Fair*

The story is set in the first half of the nineteenth century, where Becky Sharp, a perfect example of Vanity Fair society, will stop at nothing to rise to a much higher position in society. She is the exact opposite of her naive schoolmate Amelia Sedley who is from a wealthy family. The story is set against the background of the Napoleonic Wars, and England's corrupt society of the day.

The extract below is taken from *Vanity Fair*.

Extract 55a

Poor Joe's panic lasted for two or three days; during which he did not visit the house, nor during that period did Miss Rebecca ever mention his name. She was all respectful gratitude to Mrs. Sedley: delighted beyond measure at the Bazaars; and in a whirl of wonder at the theatre, whither the good-natured lady took her. One day, Amelia had a headache, and could not go upon some party of pleasure to which the two young people were invited: nothing could induce her friend to go without her. "What! you who have shown the poor orphan what happiness and love are for the first time in her life — quit you? never!" and the green eyes looked up to Heaven and filled with tears; and Mrs. Sedley could not but own that her daughter's friend had a charming kind heart of her own.

Here is a version of the same extract in today's English:

Extract 55b

Poor Joe's panic lasted for two or three days; during which he did not visit the house; neither did Rebecca ever mention his name during that period. She was full of respectful gratitude to Mrs. Sedley: extremely delighted at the Bazaars; and in a whirl of wonder at the theatre, wherever the good-natured lady took her. One day, Amelia had a headache, and could not go to a certain party of pleasure to which the two young people were invited: nothing could induce her friend, Rebecca, to go without her: "What! You who have shown me, a poor orphan, what happiness and love are for the first time in my life; you can't stop now, surely!" and her green eyes looked up to Heaven and filled with tears; and Mrs. Sedley could not forget that her daughter's friend had a charming, kind heart too.

Task 55

I have not underlined the phrases that I have altered. That is your job for this task. Underline every word, phrase or sentence that has been changed, and assess why you think these underlined sections are so different in today's English.

Share your conclusions with your partner.

Trolloppe and Hughes

Anthony Trolloppe (1815-1882), a writer from England, portrayed landowners of early Victorian England in novels. The Chronicles of Barsetshire (or, The Barchester Chronicles) are a series of 6 novels. The first of the Barchester novels is called *The Warden* (1855).

Thomas Hughes (1822-1896) was an English lawyer, judge and author, who is famous for his novel, *Tom Brown's Schooldays* (1857), a children's story that inspired Enid Blyton and J.K. Rowling, among others. This novel is based at Rugby School, where Tom experiences boarding school life. Tom rises from being frightened on his first day at Rugby, to becoming the Captain of the School. During that time he goes through joys and sorrows, and the bullying received at the hands of Flashman.

Tom Brown's Schooldays

The following is an extract from *Tom Brown's Schooldays*.

Extract 56

When Tom came back into the school after a couple of days in the sick-room, he found matters much changed for the better, as East had led him to expect. Flashman's brutality had disgusted most even of his intimate friends, and his cowardice had once more been made plain to the House; for Diggs had encountered him on the morning after the lottery, and after high words on both sides had struck him, and the blow was not returned. However, Flashey was not unused to this sort of thing, and had lived through as awkward affairs before, and, as Diggs had said, fed and toadied himself back into favour again. Two or three of the boys who had helped to roast Tom came up and begged his pardon, and thanked him for not telling anything. Morgan sent for him, and was inclined to take the matter up warmly, but Tom begged him not to do it; to which he agreed, on Tom's promising to come to him at once in future — a promise which I regret to say he didn't keep. Tom kept Harkaway all to himself, and won the second prize in the lottery, some thirty shillings, which he and East contrived to spend in about three days, in the purchase of pictures for the study, two new bats and a cricket-ball, all the best that could be got, and a supper of sausages, kidneys, and beef-steak pies to all the rebels.

Glossary

matters much changed for the better	things had changed much for the better
had disgusted most even of his intimate friends	had even disgusted most of his close friends
plain	clear
for	because
high words	strong words
the blow	the attack
as awkward affairs	such awkward difficulties
toadied	crept
begged his pardon	apologised
telling anything	telling anyone
warmly	sensitively
some thirty shillings	thirty shillings. A shilling (a shilling coin) is a unit of currency, formerly used in the UK and other British Commonwealth countries.
contrived	planned
in the purchase of pictures	on pictures
two new bats and a cricket-ball	Cricket, invented in England, is a world-famous sport, in which there are two teams of 11 players each. Team members score points by hitting a hard cricket-ball with a cricket-bat and running

	between two sets of wickets.
be got	be bought
to all the rebels	for all the rebels

Task 56

Answer the following comprehension questions on the extract.
a Why do you think Tom had been in the sick-room?
b What kind of person was Flashey?
c What does 'toadied himself back into favour again' mean?
d Why did Flashey have to 'toady himself back into favour'?
e Two or three boys helped to 'roast' Tom. What do you think this means?

The Water Babies

The Reverend Charles Kingsley (1819–1875) was a priest in the Church of England, a university professor, a historian and novelist. *The Water Babies, A Fairy Tale for a Land Baby* (1863) has been made into film. Although the novel is a satire, it is classified as children's literature.

The novel is in the form of a moral <u>fable</u>. The protagonist is Tom, a young <u>chimney sweep</u> who falls into a river and drowns. He is then transformed into a 'water-baby' who has adventures that help to make him into a moral creature.

In his novel, Kingsley argues that nobody is qualified to say that something that they have never seen (like the human soul or even a water-baby) does not exist, as we can see from the following extract.

Extract 57

'How do you know that? Have you been there to see? And if you had been *there to see, and had seen none, that would not prove that there were none ... And no one has the right to say that no water babies exist till they have seen no water babies existing, which is quite a different thing, mind, from not seeing water babies.'*

This sounds a little contradictory to an English speaker today, so let's examine the meaning of this statement:

The extract refers to going to a place to find out if certain specified things really exist. If the result is that you have *'seen none,'* that is not proof that those things do not exist, as Kingsley says: *'that would not prove that there were none.'* This is quite clear.

Then Kingsley says that nobody has the right to assume that those things do not exist, until ...

'they have seen no water babies existing'

But this appears to have the same meaning as *'seen none,'* so it does not make sense for Kingsley to go on to say:

'which is quite a different thing ... from not seeing water babies'

How do we make sense of this? The answer lies in the different interpretations of the phrase:

'they have seen no water babies existing'

Today, we would not say this, we would say:

'they have seen [i.e. seen clear evidence] that water babies do NOT EXIST'

In this updated clause, the word 'seen' refers to an informed knowledge, obtained by thorough investigation, that it is impossible for water babies to exist.

Task 57

Now we know the meaning of the passage, discuss the following topic in a group or with a partner.

Do you agree that just because you cannot see the human soul, you cannot assume it does not exist?

Chapter 15　Nonsense Writing
第15章　荒诞文学

Lewis Carroll (Charles Lutwidge Dodgson) (1832-1898), from England, was the writer of the extremely popular books *Alice's Adventures in Wonderland* (1865), and *Through the Looking Glass and What Alice Found There* (1871), the latter being a sequel to the first. These books are full of fantasy, humour and what is called 'Literary Nonsense'. The next two extracts will demonstrate this. The stories are filled with talking animals, such as the Cheshire Cat, and dream-like events. Alice's adventures begin when she follows a white rabbit, resulting in her falling deep into a hole in the ground. In that underground world, Alice eats and drinks substances which immediately make her big or small.

Alice's Adventures in Wonderland

The following extract is taken from chapter 7 of *Alice's Adventures in Wonderland*. The scene is the Mad Tea-Party. A small section has been omitted in the middle.

Extract 58

There was a table set out under a tree in front of the house, and the March Hare and the Hatter were having tea at it: a Dormouse was sitting between them, fast asleep, and the other two were using it as a cushion, resting their elbows on it, and talking over its head. "Very uncomfortable for the Dormouse," thought Alice; "only as it's asleep, I suppose it doesn't mind."

The table was a large one, but the three were all crowded together at one corner of it. "No room! No room!" they cried out when they saw Alice coming. "There's plenty of room!" said Alice indignantly, and she sat down in a large arm-chair at one end of the table.

"Have some wine," the March Hare said in an encouraging tone.

Alice looked all round the table, but there was nothing on it but tea. "I don't see any wine," she remarked.

"There isn't any," said the March Hare.

"Then it wasn't very civil of you to offer it," said Alice angrily.

"It wasn't very civil of you to sit down without being invited," said the March Hare.

"I didn't know it was your table," said Alice: "it's laid for a great many more than three."

"Your hair wants cutting," said the Hatter. He had been looking at Alice for some time with great curiosity, and this was his first speech.

"You should learn not to make personal remarks," Alice said with some severity: "it's very rude."

The Hatter opened his eyes very wide on hearing this; but all he said was "Why is a raven like a writing-desk?"

"Come, we shall have some fun now!" thought Alice. "I'm glad they've begun asking riddles — I believe I can guess that," she added aloud.

"Do you mean that you think you can find out the answer to it?" said the March Hare.

"Exactly so," said Alice.

"Then you should say what you mean," the March Hare went on.

"I do," Alice hastily replied: "at least — at least I mean what I say — that's the same thing, you know."

"Not the same thing a bit!" said the Hatter. "Why, you might just as well say that 'I see what I eat' is the same thing as 'I eat what I see'!"

"You might just as well say," added the March Hare, "that 'I like what I get'

is the same thing as 'I get what I like'!"

"You might just as well say," added the Dormouse, which seemed to be talking in its sleep, "that 'I breathe when I sleep' is the same thing as 'I sleep when I breathe'!"

"It is the same thing with you," said the Hatter, and here the conversation dropped, and the party sat silent for a minute, while Alice thought over all she could remember about ravens and writing-desks, which wasn't much.

...

"Have you guessed the riddle yet?" the Hatter said, turning to Alice again.

"No, I give it up," Alice replied. "What's the answer?"

"I haven't the slightest idea," said the Hatter.

"Nor I," said the March Hare.

Alice sighed wearily. "I think you might do something better with the time," she said, "than wasting it in asking riddles that have no answers."

"If you knew Time as well as I do," said the Hatter, "you wouldn't talk about wasting it. It's him."

"I don't know what you mean," said Alice.

"Of course you don't!" the Hatter said, tossing his head contemptuously. "I dare say you never even spoke to Time!"

"Perhaps not," Alice cautiously replied; "but I know I have to beat time when I learn music."

"Ah! That accounts for it," said the Hatter. "He won't stand beating. Now, if you only kept on good terms with him, he'd do almost anything you liked with the clock. For instance, suppose it were nine o'clock in the morning, just time to begin lessons: you'd only have to whisper a hint to Time, and round goes the clock in a twinkling! Half past one, time for dinner!"

("I only wish it was," the March Hare said to itself in a whisper.)

"That would be grand, certainly," said Alice thoughtfully; "but then — I shouldn't be hungry for it, you know."

"Not at first, perhaps," said the Hatter: but you could keep it to half-past one as long as you liked."

"Is that the way you manage?" Alice asked.

The Hatter shook his head mournfully. "Not I!" he replied. "We quarrelled last March — just before he went mad, you know —" (pointing with his teaspoon at the March Hare,) " — it was at the great concert given by the Queen of Hearts, and I had to sing

'Twinkle, twinkle, little bat!

How I wonder what you're at!'

You know the song, perhaps?"

"I've heard something like it," said Alice.

"It goes on, you know," the Hatter continued, "in this way: —

'Up above the world you fly,

Like a tea-tray in the sky.

Twinkle, twinkle —'"

Here the Dormouse shook itself, and began singing in its sleep "Twinkle, twinkle, twinkle, twinkle —" and went on so long that they had to pinch it to make it stop.

"Well, I'd hardly finished the first verse," said the Hatter, "when the Queen bawled out 'He's murdering the time! Off with his head!'"

"How dreadfully savage!" exclaimed Alice.

"And ever since that," the Hatter went on in a mournful tone, "he wo'n't do a thing I ask! It's always six o'clock now."

Glossary

Twinkle, twinkle	Jane Taylor's *Twinkle, Twinkle Little Star* of 1806, which she wrote in Lavenham, Suffolk, England, is parodied in the extract; it is inaccurately recited by the Hatter, 60 years after the lullaby was composed.
wo'n't	won't. This form of the word with two apostrophes was common in nineteenth century English. The same applied to *ca'n't* (*can't*) and *sha'n't* (*shan't*). So, in

nineteenth century English, there were two apostrophes instead of one. For example, *shan't* means *shall not*; an apostrophe replaces 'll' and another replaces the 'o'. Originally, this would give *sha'n't*, but to make it easier to write, the first apostrophe has been dropped over time.

For the word *cannot*, the first 'n' and the 'o' are replaced with apostrophes. The same principle applies to the word *won't*. This is formed from the two words *will* (originally *woll*, an old form of the word *will*) plus not.

Task 58

There are several <u>puns</u> in the above extract, along with other types of humour. Can you identify and understand them all? Read the passage several times until you begin to grasp the various forms of word play, then answer the questions below.

a Does *'I see what I eat,'* mean the same as *'I eat what I see.'* ?

b Does *'I like what I get'* mean the same as *'I get what I like'* ?

c Does *'I breathe when I sleep'* mean the same as *'I sleep when I breathe'* ?

d Alice says, "*I think you might do something better with the time … than wasting it in asking riddles that have no answers.*" This is almost identical to today's English. Today, we might say, "I think you should do something better with the time … than waste it by asking riddles that have no answers."

The Hatter replies, "*If you knew Time as well as I do … you wouldn't talk about wasting it.*"

Explain why 'time' has an initial capital letter in the Hatter's speech, but not in Alice's.

e Alice says, "*I have to beat time when I learn music.*" This means she has to clap her hands when she listens to music to become familiar with the rhythm. But the Hatter understands (or pretends to understand) Alice to mean 'beat Time;' Alice's spoken words and meaning require a small 't' for time. The Hatter's words and meaning require a capital 'T' for time.

With the information above, explain why the Hatter then says, "He won't stand beating."

f What did the Queen mean when she shouted, "*He's murdering time!*"?

g What did the Hatter understand the Queen's words to mean?

Through the Looking Glass

In 'Through the Looking Glass and What Alice Found There,' Alice opened a book lying beside her. She could not read it properly, but then she realised that it was because the words were inverted, so she referred to it as a 'Looking-glass book.' When she held it up to the looking-glass, she read what follows. It is a poem.

Extract 59

JABBERWOCKY

'Twas brillig, and the slithy toves
Did gyre and gimble in the wabe:
All mimsy were the borogoves,
And the mome raths outgrabe.

"Beware the Jabberwock, my son!
The jaws that bite, the claws that catch!
Beware the Jubjub bird, and shun
The frumious Bandersnatch!"

He took his vorpal sword in hand:
Long time the manxome foe he sought—
So rested he by the Tumtum tree,
And stood awhile in thought.

And as in uffish thought he stood,
The Jabberwock, with eyes of flame,
Came whiffling through the tulgey wood,
And burbled as it came!

One, two! One, two! and through and through
The vorpal blade went snicker-snack!
He left it dead, and with its head
He went galumphing back.

"And hast thou slain the Jabberwock?
Come to my arms, my beamish boy!
O frabjous day! Callooh! Callay!"
He chortled in his joy.

'Twas brillig, and the slithy toves
Did gyre and gimble in the wabe:
All mimsy were the borogoves,
And the mome raths outgrabe.

"It seems very pretty," she said when she had finished it, "but it's rather hard to understand!" (You see she didn't like to confess, even to herself, that she couldn't make it out at all.) "Somehow it seems to fill my head with ideas — only I don't exactly know what they are! However, somebody killed something: that's clear, at any rate — "

You can immediately see that a lot of the words do not make sense as they are not real English words; they are words invented by Lewis Carroll. However, the subject matter of the poem is fairly obvious. This poem is used by many educational institutions as a fun exercise for appreciating grammatical structure (also see Extract 115 and Task 115). The 'Jabberwock' is identified as a dragon by readers, in films, music and other forms of art. This dragon is depicted as being defeated by a young knight with a sword.

Task 59

This is the first and last verse of the poem:

> 'Twas brillig, and the slithy toves
> Did gyre and gimble in the wabe;
> All mimsy were the borogoves,
> And the mome raths outgrabe.

a List the words from this poetic verse that you think must be nouns.

b List the words that you think must be adjectives.

c List the words that you think are verbs.

Now replace the words you have identified with your own nouns, adjectives and verbs to create your own poetic verse. Try to make the last word in both line 1 and 3, and the last word in both line 2 and 4, rhyme.

Note: Your own version of the verse must make sense, but it can be serious or funny. You can also replace the word 'brillig' with anything you want as long as it makes sense.

Share your version of the verse with your partner.

Edward Lear

Edward Lear (1812–1888) was an English artist, illustrator, musician, author and poet. He is well-known for his poem called *The Owl and the Pussycat*, which was published in 1871.

Extract 60

The Owl and the Pussycat went to sea
In a beautiful pea green boat.
They took some honey, and plenty of money
Wrapped up in a five pound note.
The Owl looked up to the stars above,
And sang to a small guitar,
'O lovely Pussy! O Pussy, my love,
What a beautiful Pussy you are,
You are, You are!
What a beautiful Pussy you are!'

Pussy said to Owl, 'You elegant fowl!
How charmingly sweet you sing!
O let us be married! Too long we have tarried,
But what shall we do for a ring?'
They sailed away, for a year and a day,
To the land where the Bong-Tree grows,
And there in a wood a Piggy-wig stood,
With a ring at the end of his nose,
His nose, His nose!
With a ring at the end of his nose.

'Dear Pig, are you willing to sell for one shilling
Your ring?' Said the Piggy, 'I will.'
So they took it away, and were married next day
By the Turkey who lives on the hill.

They dined on mince, and slices of quince,
Which they ate with a runcible spoon;
And hand in hand, on the edge of the sand
They danced by the light of the moon,
The moon, The moon,
They danced by the light of the moon.

The owl and the pussycat

Glossary

runcible spoon The word 'runcible' is a nonsense word, invented by Edward Lear himself.

Task 60

Study this poem well, until you fully understand the story. Then write the story in prose and read it to your partner.

Chapter 16　The 1870s and 1880s
第16章　19世纪70与80年代

Robert Louis Stevenson (1850-1894) was a Scottish novelist, born in Edinburgh. He studied engineering at Edinburgh University in 1867, and then changed to Law and was called to the Scottish Bar in 1875. His book, *Treasure Island* (1883) is an adventure fiction for young adults, with buccaneers, treasure maps, buried gold, schooners and pirates, and not forgetting a one-legged seaman with a parrot on his shoulder.

The hero is called Jim Hawkins, who went hunting for buried treasure, but he had to face the villainous pirate Long John Silver.

Treasure Island

The extract below is taken from *Treasure Island*.

Extract 61

I was so pleased at having given the slip to Long John, that I began to enjoy myself and look around me with some interest on the strange land that I was in.

I had crossed a marshy tract full of willows, bulrushes, and odd, outlandish, swampy trees; and I had now come out upon the skirts of an open piece of undulating, sandy country, about a mile long, dotted with a few pines, and a great number of contorted trees, not unlike the oak in growth, but pale in the foliage, like willows. On the far side of the open stood one of the hills, with two quaint, craggy peaks, shining vividly in the sun.

I now felt for the first time the joy of exploration. The isle was uninhabited; my shipmates I had left behind, and nothing lived in front of me but dumb brutes and fowls. I turned hither and thither among the trees. Here and there were flowering plants, unknown to me; here and there I saw snakes, and one raised his head from a ledge of rock and hissed at me with a noise not unlike the spinning of a top. Little did I suppose that he was a deadly enemy, and that the noise was the famous rattle.

Then I came to a long thicket of these oak-like trees — live, or evergreen, oaks, I heard afterwards they should be called — which grew low along the sand like brambles, the boughs curiously twisted, the foliage compact, like thatch. The thicket stretched down from the top of one of the sandy knolls, spreading and growing taller as it went, until it reached the margin of the broad, reedy fen, through which the nearest of the little rivers soaked its way into the anchorage. The marsh was steaming in the strong sun, and the outline of the Spy-glass trembled through the haze.

All at once there began to go a sort of bustle among the bulrushes; a wild duck flew up with a quack, another followed, and soon over the whole surface of the marsh a great cloud of birds hung screaming and circling in the air. I judged at once that some of my shipmates must be drawing near along the borders of the fen. Nor was I deceived; for soon I heard the very distant and low tones of a human voice, which, as I continued to give ear, grew steadily louder and nearer.

This put me in a great fear, and I crawled under cover of the nearest live-oak, and squatted there, hearkening, as silent as a mouse.

Another voice answered; and then the first voice, which I now recognised to be Silver's, once more took up the story, and ran on for a long while in a stream, only now and again interrupted by the other. By the sound they must have been talking earnestly, and almost fiercely; but no distinct word came to my hearing.

At last the speakers seemed to have paused, and perhaps to have sat down; for not only did they cease to draw any nearer, but the birds themselves began to grow more quiet, and to settle again to their places in the swamp.

And now I began to feel that I was neglecting my business; that since I had been so foolhardy as to come ashore with these desperadoes, the least I could do was to overhear them at their councils; and that my plain and obvious duty was to draw as close as I could manage, under the favourable ambush of the crouching trees.

I could tell the direction of the speakers pretty exactly, not only by the sound of their voices, but by the behaviour of the few birds that still hung in alarm above the heads of the intruders.

Crawling on all-fours, I made steadily but slowly towards them; till at last, raising my head to an aperture among the leaves, I could see clear down into a little green dell beside the marsh, and closely set about with trees, where Long John Silver and another of the crew stood face to face in conversation.

The sun beat full upon them. Silver had thrown his hat beside him on the ground, and his great, smooth, blond face, all shining with heat, was lifted to the other man's in a kind of appeal.

'Mate,' he was saying, 'it's because I thinks gold dust of you — gold dust, and you may lay to that! If I hadn't took to you like pitch, do you think I'd have been here a-warning of you? All's up — you can't make nor mend; it's to save your neck that I'm a-speaking, and if one of the wild' uns knew it, where' ud I be, Tom — now, tell me, where' ud I be?'

'Silver,' said the other man — and I observed he was not only red in the face, but spoke as hoarse as a crow, and his voice shook, too, like a taut rope — 'Silver,' says he, 'you're old, and you're honest, or has the name for it; and you've money, too, which lots of poor sailors hasn't; and you're brave, or I'm mistook. And will you tell me you'll let yourself be led away with that kind of a mess of swabs? not you! As sure as God sees me, I'd sooner lose my hand....'

Glossary

I had now come out upon sandy country	I had now reached sandy land

pale in the foliage	with pale leaves
of the open	of the opening
my shipmates I had left behind	I had left my shipmates behind
brutes and fowls	wild animals and birds
a ledge of rock	the ledge of a rock
Little did I suppose	Little did I realise
boughs curiously twisted	branches twisted in an interesting way
Spy-glass	Telescope
All at once there began to go a sort of bustle	All of a sudden there was a bustling
give ear	listen carefully
This put me in a great fear	This terrified me
hearkening	listening intensely
ran on	continued
long while in a stream	long time without stopping
By the sound they must have been talking earnestly, and almost fiercely	They sounded like they were having a very serious and even angry conversation
but no distinct word came to my hearing	but I could not hear any word clearly
and to settle again to their places	and settle into their places again
business	purpose
… that since I had been so foolhardy as to come ashore with these desperadoes, the least I could do was to overhear them at their councils; and that my plain …	I had been so foolish coming ashore with these desperadoes, that the least I could do was listen in on their discussion, and my plain ...
I could tell the direction of the speakers	I could tell where the speakers were
Crawling on all-fours, I made steadily but slowly towards them	I crawled steadily and slowly towards them on all-fours
till at last	until at last
to an aperture	through an aperture

clear	clearly
closely set about with trees	closely surrounded by trees
blond face	pale face
says he	he says

This glossary is extremely important when making a distinction between today's English and the English of 1883 (137 years ago).

Task 61a

Spend some time reading the lengthy visual description of the island, checking in a dictionary when the words are unfamiliar.

Task 61b

The pirate, Long John Silver, and a member of the ship's crew to whom he is speaking, use a strange vernacular language! Hawkins can see them in a dell (a small valley with grass and trees), and is secretly listening to their conversation.

Change the following spoken words into today's English.

Long John Silver:

'Mate, it's because I thinks gold dust of you — gold dust, and you may lay to that! If I hadn't took to you like pitch, do you think I'd have been here a-warning of you? All's up — you can't make nor mend; it's to save your neck that I'm a-speaking, and if one of the wild' uns knew it, where' ud I be, Tom — now, tell me, where' ud I be?'

Crew Member:

'Silver, you're old, and you're honest, or has the name for it; and you've money, too, which lots of poor sailors hasn't; and you're brave, or I'm mistook.

And will you tell me you'll let yourself be led away with that kind of a mess of swabs? not you! As sure as God sees me, I'd sooner lose my hand....'

Strange Case of Dr. Jekyll and Mr. Hyde

Robert Louis Stevenson is also well-known for his adult novel *Strange Case of Dr. Jekyll and Mr. Hyde* (1886), a psychological thriller. It can also be categorised as Gothic Horror or Science Fiction. It explores the dual nature of the human soul. Dr. Jekyll kept turning into evil Mr. Hyde whenever he drank a certain concoction, until Mr. Hyde was determined to take complete control of the doctor.

Here is an extract from the novel.

Extract 62a

Nearly a year later, in the month of October 1884, London was startled by a crime of singular ferocity and rendered all the more notable by the high position of the victim. The details were few and startling. A maid servant living alone in a house not far from the river, had gone upstairs to bed about eleven. Although a fog rolled over the city in the small hours, the early part of the night was cloudless, and the lane, which the maid's window overlooked, was brilliantly lit by the full moon. It seems she was romantically given, for she sat down upon her box, which stood immediately under the window, and fell into a dream of musing. Never (she used to say, with streaming tears, when she narrated that experience) never had she felt more at peace with all men or thought more kindly of the world. And as she so sat she became aware of an aged and beautiful gentleman with white hair, drawing near along the lane; and advancing to meet him, another and very small gentleman, to whom at first she paid less attention. When they had come within speech (which was just under the maid's eyes) the older man bowed and accosted the other with a very pretty manner of politeness. It did not seem as if the subject of his address were of great importance; indeed, from his pointing, it sometimes appeared as if he were only inquiring his way; but the moon shone on his face as he spoke, and the girl was pleased to watch it, it seemed to breathe such an innocent and old-world kindness of disposition, yet with something high too, as of a well-founded self-content. Presently her eye wondered to the other, and she was surprised to recognise in him a certain Mr. Hyde, who had once visited her master and for whom she had conceived a dislike. He had in his hand a heavy cane, with which he was trifling; but he answered never a word, and seemed to listen with an ill-contained impatience. And then all of a sudden he broke out in a great flame of anger, stamping with his foot, brandishing the cane, and carrying on (as the maid described it) like a madman. The old gentleman took a step back, with the air of one very much surprised and a trifle hurt; and at that Mr. Hyde broke out of all bounds and clubbed him to the earth. And next moment, with ape-like fury, he was trampling his victim under foot, and hailing down a storm of blows, under which the bones were audibly shattered and the body jumped upon the roadway. At the horror of these sights and sounds, the maid fainted.

Below is the same passage rewritten in today's English. Every part that has been changed has been underlined.

Extract 62b

Nearly a year later, in the month of October 1884, London was startled by a crime of <u>great</u> ferocity <u>which was considered</u> all the more <u>astonishing because of the high standing</u> of the victim. The details were <u>vague but disturbing</u>. A maid servant living alone in a house not far from the river, had gone upstairs to bed about eleven. Although a fog rolled over the city in the small hours, the early part of the night was cloudless, and the lane, which the maid's window overlooked, was brilliantly lit by the full moon. <u>Perhaps she was having romantic fantasies at the time, because</u> she <u>was sitting down on</u> her box, which <u>was situated</u> under the window, and <u>daydreaming</u>. Never (she used to say, with streaming tears, when she narrated that experience) never had she felt more at peace with all men or <u>felt more at ease with the world</u>. And as she <u>was sat there</u> she <u>saw</u> an <u>elderly</u> and <u>handsome</u> gentleman with white hair, drawing near along the lane; and <u>coming to meet him <u>was another very short</u> gentleman, to whom <u>she paid little attention at first</u>. When they had come within <u>speaking distance</u> (which was just under the maid's eyes) the older man bowed and <u>addressed</u> the other <u>one in a very polite manner</u>. It did not <u>look like he said anything particularly important; and by the way he kept pointing, it looked like he was only asking for directions</u>. The moon shone on his face as he spoke, and the girl <u>enjoyed watching him because it seemed to give an air of innocent, old fashioned manners, and he looked dignified, with a sense of</u> well-founded self-content. <u>Then her eyes</u> wondered to the other <u>man</u>, and she was surprised to recognise <u>him as</u> Mr. Hyde, who had <u>visited her master once</u> and for whom she <u>had a particular dislike</u>. He had <u>a heavy cane in his hand, and he was fiddling around with it</u>; but he <u>did not speak a word</u>, and seemed to <u>be only listening with a noticeable impatience</u>. And then all of a sudden he broke out in a great <u>rage, stamping</u> his foot, brandishing the cane, and carrying on (as the maid described it) like a madman. The old gentleman took a step back, <u>very shocked and a bit offended</u>; and <u>then Mr. Hyde went berserk</u> and clubbed him to the <u>ground</u>. And next moment, with ape-like fury, he <u>started stamping on his victim</u>, and <u>hitting him again and again until she could hear the bones shattering and see his body jerking about on</u> the roadway. At the horror of these sights and sounds, the maid fainted.

Task 62

Read the updated version very carefully, and consider how senseless this violent attack was. Discuss with your partner what the dual nature of the soul is. For example, do you believe everyone is capable of such irrational behaviour? If so, how can we help people to focus more on the better side of their nature?

Later on in the account, a connection with Dr. Jekyll is found, as we can see from the following short extract.

Extract 63

Mr. Utterson had already quailed at the name of Hyde; but when the stick was laid before him, he could doubt no longer; broken and battered as it was, he recognised it for one that he had himself presented many years before to Henry Jekyll.

"Is this Mr. Hyde a person of small stature?" he inquired.

"Particularly small and particularly wicked-looking, is what the maid calls him," said the officer.

Task 63

Read and study this short extract very closely and rewrite it in today's English before you check my version at the back of the book.

As Mr Utterson travels to Mr. Hyde's premises to investigate, the author describes the pollution in London at the time. It is referred to as 'fog,' but the word used today is 'smog,' to express the mixture of smoke and fog.

Extract 64

It was by this time about nine in the morning, and the first fog of the season. A great chocolate-coloured pall lowered over heaven, but the wind was continually charging and routing these embattled vapours; so that as the cab crawled from street to street, Mr. Utterson beheld a marvellous number of degrees and hues of twilight; for here it would be dark like the back-end of evening; and there would be a glow of rich, lurid brown, like the light of some strange *conflagration; and here, for a moment, the fog would be quite broken up, and a haggard shaft of daylight would glance in between the swirling wreaths. The dismal quarter of Soho seen under these changing glimpses, with its muddy ways, and slatternly passengers, and its lamps, which had never been extinguished or had been kindled afresh to combat this mournful reinvasion of darkness, seemed, in the lawyer's eyes, like a district of some city in a nightmare. The thoughts of his mind, besides, were of the gloomiest dye; and when he glanced at the companion of his drive, he was conscious of some touch of that terror of the law and the law's officers, which may at times assail the most honest.*

As the cab drew up before the address indicated, the fog lifted a little and showed him a dingy street, a gin palace, a low French eating house, a shop for the retail of penny numbers and twopenny salads, many ragged children huddled in the doorways, and many women of many different nationalities passing out, key in hand, to have a morning glass.

Glossary

pall	numbing dread
lowered	hovered threateningly
heaven	the sky
charging and routing	chasing away
embattled vapours	deadly gases
cab	This was a small horse-drawn carriage with a hood.
degrees and hues	varied light-intensity and colours
rich, lurid brown	dense, foreboding brown
conflagration	This is a very large fire that destroys a wide area.
quite broken up	dispersed a little
haggard shaft of daylight	weak and fragmented beam of daylight
quarter of Soho	district of Soho
slatternly passengers	sexually promiscuous female companions
gloomiest dye	gloomiest nature

the companion of his drive	fellow-passenger in the cab
some touch of that terror of the law	a sense of fear of the law
gin palace	a derogatory way to describe the cheapest type of drinking (of alcohol) establishment
low French eating house	distasteful French eating house
penny numbers	Also called 'penny dreadfuls.' These were popular serials of sensational fiction. There is a fairly recent British TV horror series called *Penny Dreadful*.
twopenny	The cost is two pennies. A penny was an old currency in England. Today's currency includes 'pennies' but they are officially referred to as 'pence,' therefore 'two pence.'

Task 64

In the above extract, there are many phrases describing the smog of London. List all of the phrases. You should have at least 8 phrases in your list. Note: The glossary will help you to understand some of these phrases.

This dismal atmosphere of Victorian London is ideal for a horror story or a murder mystery. Actually, it was not long after the publication of this novel that a terrible unidentified serial-killer killed and mutilated prostitutes in the Whitechapel district of London in 1888.

Thomas Hardy

Thomas Hardy (1840–1928), a novelist and poet from England, is well known for his works *Under the Greenwood Tree* (1872), *Far from the Madding Crowd* (1874), *The Mayor of Casterbridge* (1886), *Tess of the d'Urbervilles*

(1891), *Jude the Obscure* (1895), *Wessex Poems and Other Verses* (1898), and the poem called *The Man He Killed* (1902). In his poetry, he was heavily influenced by the Romantic Movement, especially the works of William Wordsworth.

The following extract is taken from his novel *Far From the Madding Crowd*.

Extract 65

It was the first day of June, and the sheep-shearing season culminated, the landscape, even to the leanest pasture, being all health and colour. Every green was young, every pore was open, and every stalk was swollen with crowding currents of juice. God was palpably present in the country, and the devil had gone with the world to town. Flossy catkins of the later kinds, fern-fronds like bishops' crosiers, the square headed moschatelle, the odd cuckoo-pint — like an apoplectic saint in a niche of malachite — clean white lady's-smocks, the toothwort, approximating to human flesh, the enchanter's nightshade, and the black-petaled doleful-bells were among the quainter objects of the vegetable world in and about Weatherbury at this teeming time, and of the animal, the metamorphosed figures of Mr Jan Coggan, the master shearer, the second and third shearers who travelled in the exercise of their calling and do not require definition by name, Henry Fray the fourth shearer, Susan Tall's husband the fifth, Joseph Poorgrass the sixth, young Cain Ball as assistant shearer, and Gabriel Oak as general supervisor. None of these were clothed to any extent worth mentioning, each appearing to have hit in the manner of raiment the decent mean between high and low caste Hindu. An angularity of lineament and a fixity of facial machinery in general, proclaimed that serious work was the order of the day.

They sheared in the great barn, called for the nonce the Shearing Barn ...

....

To-day the large side doors were thrown open towards the sun to admit a beautiful light to the immediate spot of the shearers' operations, which was the wood threshing-floor in the centre, formed of thick oak, black with age and polished by the beating of flails for many generations till it had grown as slippery and as rich in hue as the state-room floors of an Elizabethan mansion. Here the shearers knelt, the sun slanting in upon their bleached shirts, tanned arms, and the polished shears they flourished, causing these to bristle with a thousand rays, strong enough to blind a weak-eyed man. Beneath them a captive sheep lay panting, increasing the rapidity of its pants as misgiving merged in terror, till it quivered like the hot landscape outside.

Glossary

culminated	arrived
being all health and colour	being full of health and colour
Every green	All greenery
the devil had gone with the world to town	This implies that the countryside is innocent and pure, and life in the countryside is therefore closer to God.
moschatelle	A type of small pale green plant
figures	A 'figure' is a human shape or form.
who travelled in the exercise of their calling	who travelled around to do their job
appearing to have hit in the manner of raiment the decent mean between high and low caste Hindu	appearing to have dressed in apparel similar to a decently-dressed Hindu between high and low caste
An angularity of lineament and a fixity of facial machinery	A fixed, angular expression on their faces
proclaimed	showed
the nonce	that particular occasion
To-day	Today
flails	threshing tools
flourished	wielded
bristle	glisten

rays	rays of light from the sun
in terror	into terror

Setting the scene was very important to the Victorian period novelists, and this feature of Victorian novels is very helpful for historians and filmmakers, and of course for readers of later generations who want to accurately visualise what they are reading.

Task 65

Read the extract very carefully, and then answer the following comprehension questions.

a Name all of the plants that Thomas Hardy refers to when setting the scene.

b List all of the shearers. There should be 7 shearers and one Supervisor.

c What was the great barn called on this occasion?

d Quote all the clauses and phrases that describe the way the LIGHT of nature is acting.

Thomas Hardy believed his society had <u>double standards,</u> and this is exemplified in *Tess of the D'Urbervilles*. Tess Durbeyfield, a virtuous woman, claims her family is connected with the aristocratic D'Urbervilles, but Alec D'Urberville causes her great pain in this story that leaves Tess with a difficult moral dilemma.

The extract below has been taken from *Tess of the D'Urbervilles*.

Extract 66

Her mother bore Tess no ill-will for leaving the house-work to her single-

handed efforts for so long: indeed, Joan seldom upbraided her thereon at any time, feeling but slightly the lack of Tess's assistance whilst her instinctive plan for relieving herself of her labours lay in postponing them. To-night, however, she was even in a blither mood than usual. There was a dreaminess, a preoccupation, an exaltation, in the maternal look which the girl could not understand.

"Well I'm glad you've come," her mother said as soon as the last note had passed out of her. "I want to go and fetch your father; but what's more'n that, I want to tell'ee what have happened. Y'll be fess enough, my poppet, when th'st know!" (Mrs Durbeyfield habitually spoke the dialect: her daughter, who had passed the sixth standard in the National school under a London-trained mistress, spoke two languages; the dialect at home, more or less; ordinary English abroad and to persons of quality.)

"Since I've been away?" Tess asked.

"Ay!"

"Had it anything to do with father's making such a mommet of himself in thik carriage this afternoon? — Why did'er? I felt inclined to sink into the ground with shame!"

"That wer all a part of the larry! We've been found to be the greatest gentlefolk in the whole county — reaching all back long before Oliver Grumble's time — to the days of the Pagan Turks — with monuments and vaults and crests and 'scutcheons, and the Lord knows what-all. In Saint Charles's days we was made Knights o' the Royal Oak, our real name being d'Urberville ... Don't that make your bosom plim?"

Glossary

Joan seldom upbraided her thereon at any time

                        Joan very rarely criticised her about this at all

feeling but slightly   barely noticing

To-night   Tonight

blither mood   happier

fess	proud
poppet	This is a term of endearment, like 'darling' 'sweety', etc.
Ay!	Yes!
mommet	fool
thik	that
larry	excitement
the greatest gentlefolk	from the best family breeding
Oliver Grumble	Oliver Cromwell
'scutcheons	shields
bosom plim	chest swell

It is interesting to note aspects of the development of writing in these two extracts, by comparing them to today's English. For example, in Extract 65 we have 'to-day,' and in this extract (Extract 66), we have 'to-night.' The hyphen (-) has been dropped over time. We noticed a similar process from the *Alice's Adventures in Wonderland* extract (Extract 58), with the form 'wo'n't'; this form gradually lost the first apostrophe, changing it to 'won't,' as we know it today. Another example of this type of development in writing can also be found in this extract (Extract 66) regarding the possessive form of a name, in this case, the name Charles in the following phrase: 'In Saint Charles's days.' Today, the additional 's' after the apostrophe (when the name of the person or place already has a final consonant 's'), is dropped, leaving instead 'In Saint Charles' days.'

Task 66

Tess (to some extent), and her mother Joan, are speaking a localised form of English. Analyse the samples of speech from the passage below and then rewrite them in today's English, checking the extract's glossary to help you with some of the unfamiliar words.

Joan:

"I want to go and fetch your father; but what's more'n that, I want to tell'ee what have happened. Y'll be fess enough, my poppet, when th'st know!"

Tess:

"Had it anything to do with father's making such a mommet of himself in thik carriage this afternoon? — Why did'er? I felt inclined to sink into the ground with shame!"

Joan:

"That wer all a part of the larry! We've been found to be the greatest gentlefolk in the whole county — reaching all back long before Oliver Grumble's time — to the days of the Pagan Turks — with monuments and vaults and crests and 'scutcheons …"

"In Saint Charles's days we was made Knights o' the Royal Oak, our real name being d'Urberville … Don't that make your bosom plim?"

Arthur Conan Doyle

Sir Arthur Conan Doyle (1859–1930) was a Scottish writer and physician. He was born in Edinburgh, Scotland. *Sherlock Holmes: A Study in Scarlet* (1887) was his first novel to include the private detective Sherlock Holmes. His stories have been televised time and time again, and the black and white Hammer Films production of *The Hound of the Baskervilles* (from his book published in 1901) is regarded as a classic, set on Dartmoor in Devon, England. As well as his Sherlock Holmes series, he is known for his science fiction tale *The Lost World* (1912).

Sherlock Holmes' deductive skills makes him such a popular fictional detective that people are tempted to believe he was a real person. Holmes was a private detective who lived in Baker Street, London in Victorian England. His friend Dr Watson recorded his cases, including the deadly mystery of The Speckled Band.

The following is an extract from The Speckled Band, one of Doyle's 56 short stories. The Speckled Band was published in *The Adventures of Sherlock Holmes* (1892).

Extract 67

In glancing over my notes of the seventy odd cases in which I have during the last eight years studied the methods of my friend Sherlock Holmes, I find many tragic, some comic, a large number merely strange, but none commonplace; for, working as he did rather for the love of his art than for the acquirement of wealth, he refused to associate himself with any investigation which did not tend towards the unusual, and even the fantastic. Of all these varied cases, however, I cannot recall any which presented more singular features than that which was associated with the well-known Surrey family of the Roylotts of Stoke Moran. The events in question occurred in the early days of my association with Holmes, when we were sharing rooms as bachelors, in Baker Street. It is possible that I might have placed them upon record before, but a promise of secrecy was made at the time, from which I have only been freed during the last month by the untimely death of the lady to whom the pledge was given. It is perhaps as well that the facts should now come to light, for I have reasons to know there are widespread rumours as to the death of Dr Grimesby Roylott which tend to make the matter even more terrible than the truth.

It was early in April, in the year '83, that I woke one morning to find Sherlock Holmes standing, fully dressed, by the side of my bed. He was a late riser as a rule, and, as the clock on the mantelpiece showed me that it was only a quarter past seven, I blinked up at him in some surprise, and perhaps just a little resentment, for I was myself regular in my habits.

'Very sorry to knock you up, Watson,' said he, 'but it's the common lot this morning. Mrs Hudson has been knocked up, she retorted upon me, and I on you.'

'What is it, then? A fire?'

'No, a client. It seems that a young lady has arrived in a considerable state of excitement, who insists upon seeing me. She is waiting now in the sitting-room.'

Glossary

singular features	unusual features
placed them upon record before	recorded them before
as well	appropriate
a quarter past seven	quarter past seven
in some surprise, and perhaps just a little resentment	surprised, and perhaps with a little resentment
said he	he said
it's the common lot	it seems to be the norm
excitement	distress

The English used in the narrative of this extract is almost typical of today's very formal language. The formality seems a little extreme, but it is to be expected from a well-educated doctor writing a scientific document in a society where respect for class and position is strong.

Task 67a

You might have noticed that the first sentence of the extract is very long. Count the words in this sentence. How many are there?

Now write your own very long sentence about any subject you like, using basically the same grammatical structure and punctuation. Share your long sentence with your partner.

Task 67b

The speech of Sherlock Holmes in this extract is quite different to today.

Rewrite the following samples of speech in today's English. Note: Check the glossary for any helpful information.

'but it's the common lot this morning. Mrs Hudson has been knocked up, she retorted upon me, and I on you.'

'It seems that a young lady has arrived in a considerable state of excitement, who insists upon seeing me. She is waiting now in the sitting-room.'

As we continue with the story, we can see that Sherlock immediately impresses his visitor with his deductive skills:

Extract 68

'... You have come in by train this morning, I see.'

'You know me, then?'

'No, but I observe the second half of a return ticket in the palm of your left glove. You must have started early and yet you have had a good drive in a dog-cart, along heavy roads, before you reached the station.'

The lady gave a violent start, and stared in bewilderment at my companion.

'There is no mystery, my dear madam,' said he, smiling. 'The left arm of your jacket is spattered with mud in no less than seven places. The marks are perfectly fresh. There is no vehicle save a dog-cart which throws up mud in that way, and then only when you sit on the left-hand side of the driver.'

'Whatever your reasons may be, you are perfectly correct,' said she.

Task 68

Keeping the extreme formality of the extract, rewrite it in today's English.

Chapter 17   The 1890s
第17章   19世纪90年代

Rudyard Kipling (1865-1936) was an English poet and story writer, born in Bombay in India, but educated in England. He won the Nobel Prize for Literature in 1907. 'The Jungle Books' include *The Jungle Book*, published in Great Britain in 1894 and *The Second Jungle Book*, published in Great Britain in 1895.

The story is reminiscent of the story of Romulus and Remus concerning the founding of the city of Rome in Italy three thousand years before, as Mowgli, from *The Jungle Book*, was also raised by wolves. Mowgli must face Shere Khan the tiger with the help of Baloo the bear and Bagheera the panther.

The Jungle Book

Read the extract below, where Mowgli is facing humans and struggling to adapt.

Extract 69

The priest came to the gate, and with him at least a hundred people, who stared and talked and shouted and pointed at Mowgli.

'They have no manners, these Men Folk,' said Mowgli to himself. 'Only the gray ape would behave as they do.' So he threw back his long hair and frowned at the crowd.

'What is there to be afraid of?' said the priest. 'Look at the marks on his arms and legs. They are the bites of wolves. He is but a wolf-child run away from *the jungle.'*

Of course, in playing together, the cubs had often nipped Mowgli harder than they intended, and there were white scars all over his arms and legs. But he would have been the last person in the world to call these bites, for he knew what real biting meant.

'Arre! Arre!' said two or three women together. 'To be bitten by wolves, poor child! He is a handsome boy. He has eyes like red fire. By my honour, Messua, he is not unlike thy boy that was taken by the tiger.'

'Let me look,' said a woman with heavy copper rings on her wrists and ankles, and she peered at Mowgli under the palm of her hand. 'Indeed he is not. He is thinner, but he has the very look of my boy.' ...

' ... all this talking is like another looking over by the Pack! Well, if I am a man, a man I must be.'

Task 69

Mowgli was shocked at the poor manners of humans, as it says in the first two paragraphs of the extract. Mowgli could not communicate with the humans as he had been raised by wolves, but he could think clearly, and thought to himself: *'They have no manners, these Men Folk.'*

Mowgli felt this way because about a hundred people stared, shouted and pointed at him, and talked to each other about him while they did so. Mowgli thought to himself: *'Only the gray ape would behave as they do.'*

Discuss in a group or with your partner how you think Mowgli felt. Also discuss whether you sympathise with Mowgli; why or why not?

Oscar Wilde

Oscar Wilde (1854–1900) was an Irish writer and playwright. He wrote *The Picture of Dorian Gray* (1890), a Gothic Horror fiction novel about a young man (Dorian Gray), who had a painting done of himself by an artist called Basil Hallward. Hallward's friend Henry Wotton stated that the only thing worth painting was beauty. As a result, Dorian wished his portrait would age instead of himself. His wish came true, but this led to Dorian's behaviour becoming debauched. Every time he did something sinful, his painting would display his corruption by the visual aging of his image. As such, this novel can be described as a Faustian novel, meaning the story involves a person making a pact with the Devil, exchanging their soul for worldly pleasures, riches or unlimited knowledge.

Oscar Wilde became one of London's most popular playwrights in the early 1890's. He wrote *A Woman of No Importance* (1893), *The Importance of Being Earnest* (1895), and a wonderful children's story called *The Selfish Giant*. A famous quotation from Oscar Wilde is:

'*Be yourself, everyone else is already taken.*'

Task 70a

What does Oscar Wilde's quotation mean? Discuss it in a group or with a partner. You should refer to issues such as:

Your own value as an individual with unique characteristics.

The value of every other person in the world, regardless of whether they are your friend or not.

The <u>pros and cons</u> of following other people's example.

Below is an extract from Oscar Wilde's *The Picture of Dorian Gray*.

Extract 70

"How sad it is!" murmured Dorian Gray, with his eyes still fixed upon his own portrait. "How sad it is! I shall grow old, and horrible, and dreadful. But *this picture will remain always young. It will never be older than this particular day of June ... If it were only the other way! If it were I who was to be always young, and the picture that was to grow old! For that — for that — I would give everything! Yes, there is nothing in the whole world I would not give! I would give my soul for that!"*

Glossary

How sad it is!	It's so sad!
remain always young	always remain young
If it were only the other way!	If it were only the other way round!

You will see from the glossary that 'How sad it is!' has been corrected to 'It's so sad!' This change is due to the fact that this structure is not used in the same way today. Exclamations such as 'How beautiful you are!' 'How happy he is!' and 'How sad I am!' are very unusual now, but in the days of Oscar Wilde, they were quite normal.

Task 70b

Using the glossary to help you, rewrite this extract in today's English.

The next extract is taken from the last chapter of the novel. A section has been removed for ease of reading.

The picture of Dorian Gray

Extract 71a

He looked round and saw the knife that had stabbed Basil Hallward. He had cleaned it many times, till there was no stain left upon it. It was bright, and glistened. As it had killed the painter, so it would kill the painter's work, and all that that meant. It would kill the past, and when that was dead he would be free... He seized the thing, and stabbed the picture with it.

There was a cry heard, and a crash. The cry was so horrible in its agony that the frightened servants woke, and crept out of their rooms.

....

When they entered they found, hanging upon the wall, a splendid portrait of their master as they had last seen him, in all the wonder of his exquisite youth and beauty. Lying on the floor was a dead man, in evening dress, with a knife in his heart. He was withered, wrinkled, and loathsome of visage. It was not till they had examined the rings that they recognised who it was.

I have rewritten the extract below in today's English and underlined the areas where adaptions have been necessary.

Extract 71b

He looked round and saw the knife that had stabbed Basil Hallward. He had cleaned it many times, <u>until</u> there was no stain left <u>on</u> it. It was bright, and glistened. As it had killed the painter, so it would kill the painter's work, and all that that meant. It would kill the past, and when that was dead he would be free ... He seized the thing, and stabbed the picture with it.
<u>A cry was</u> heard, and a crash. The cry was so horrible in its agony that the frightened servants woke <u>up</u>, and crept out of their rooms.
....
When they entered they found, hanging <u>on</u> the wall, a <u>beautiful</u> portrait of their master as they had last seen him, in all the <u>glory</u> of his exquisite youth and beauty. Lying on the floor was a dead man, in evening dress, with a knife in his heart. He <u>looked</u> withered, wrinkled, and <u>loathsome</u>. It was not <u>until</u> they had examined the rings that they recognised who it was.

Note: The phrase *'and all that that meant,'* looks strange due to the double 'that.' However, this is perfectly normal in today's English too.

Task 71

Spend some time analysing the two versions of the same extract and discuss with your partner why the changes are necessary.

You will notice that the changes are not hugely significant, and any average reader of English should understand the passage well. Why do you think today's version is almost identical to the original?

H.G. Wells

H.G. Wells (1866–1946), a writer from England famous for his Science Fiction novels, wrote *The Time Machine* (1895), *The Invisible Man* (1897) and *War of the Worlds* (1897).

Here is an extract from *The Time Machine*, which is the inspiration for countless films. On one of his time-travelling journeys, the hero is confronted by monstrous creatures called Morlocks. I have underlined sections that would need to be altered if an updated version of the text were required.

Extract 72

'<u>Presently</u> I noticed how dry <u>was some of the foliage above me, for</u> since my arrival on the Time Machine, a matter of a week, no rain had fallen. So, instead of <u>casting about</u> among the trees for fallen twigs, I began leaping up and dragging down branches. Very soon I had a choking smoky fire of green wood and dry sticks, and could economize my camphor. Then I turned to where Weena lay beside my iron mace. I tried what I could to revive her, but she <u>lay like one dead</u>. I could not even satisfy myself whether or not <u>she breathed</u>.

'Now, the smoke of the fire <u>beat over</u> towards me, and it must have <u>made me heavy of a sudden</u>. Moreover, the vapour of camphor was in the air. My fire would not need replenishing for an hour or so. I felt very weary after my exertion, and sat down. The wood, too, was full of a slumbrous murmur that I did not understand. I seemed just to nod and open my eyes. But all was dark, and the Morlocks had their hands upon me. Flinging off their clinging fingers I hastily felt in my pocket for the matchbox, and — it had gone! Then they gripped and <u>closed with me</u> again. In a moment I knew what had happened. I had slept, and my fire had gone out, and the bitterness of death came over my soul. The forest seemed full of the smell of burning wood. I was caught by the neck, by the hair, by the arms, and pulled down. It was indescribably horrible in the darkness to feel all these soft creatures heaped upon me. I felt as if I was in a monstrous spider's web. I was overpowered, and went down. I felt little teeth nipping at my neck. I rolled over, and as I did so <u>my hand came against</u> my iron lever. It gave me strength. I struggled up, shaking the human rats from me, and, <u>holding the bar short</u>, I thrust where I judged their faces might be. I could feel the succulent giving of flesh and bone under my blows, and for a moment I was free.

Task 72

To help you to fully understand and become acquainted with the horrific scene, read it out loud to your partner or a group with expression, imagining you are experiencing it yourself. Then listen to your partner's public reading.

You will notice that I have underlined some parts of the original extract above where changes need to be made to update the text. Read the passage again carefully to ascertain how to adapt the original text into today's English. Write down your alterations.

Wells' novel called *The Invisible Man*, shows how the exploration of science has power to corrupt. In the story, Griffin has developed a process that enables him to become invisible, but he desperately wants to find the antidote. The English in the extract below has some old fashioned features, but the biggest challenge to understanding the passage is visualising the complicated series of events due to the invisible man getting angry.

Extract 73

They saw someone whisk round the corner towards the down road, and Mr

Huxter executing a complicated leap in the air that ended on his face and shoulder. Down the street people were standing astonished or running towards them.

Mr Huxter was stunned. Henfrey stopped to discover this, but Hall and the two labourers from the Tap rushed at once to the corner, shouting incoherent things, and saw Mr Marvel vanishing by the corner of the church wall. They appear to have jumped to the impossible conclusion that this was the Invisible Man suddenly become visible, and set off at once along the lane in pursuit. But Hall had hardly run a dozen yards before he gave a loud shout of astonishment and went flying headlong sideways, clutching one of the labourers and bringing him to the ground. He had been charged just as one charges a man at football. The second labourer came round in a circle, stared, and conceiving that Hall had tumbled over of his own accord, turned to resume the pursuit, only to be tripped by the ankle just as Huxter had been. Then, as the first labourer struggled to his feet, he was kicked sideways by a blow that might have felled an ox.

As he went down, the rush from the direction of the village green came round the corner. The first to appear was the proprietor of the coconut shy, a burly man in a blue jersey. He was astonished to see the lane empty save for three men sprawling absurdly on the ground. And then something happened to his rearmost foot, and he went headlong and rolled sideways just in time to graze the feet of his brother and partner, following headlong. The two were then kicked, knelt on, fallen over, and cursed by quite a number of over-hasty people.

Task 73

In your opinion, does the exploration of science corrupt humanity? Why? Why not? To what extent? Discuss this in a group.

Bram Stoker

Bram Stoker (1847–1912) was an Irish author, who wrote *Dracula* (1897), a Gothic Horror novel that introduces us to a <u>vampire</u> called Count Dracula. This book is the pre-runner to all the countless books, films and TV series about vampires.

In the story, Jonathan Harker, a solicitor from England, visits Count Dracula at his castle in Transylvania (in Romania) to provide legal support for a real estate transaction. Count Dracula is hospitable, but then Harker begins to realise he has become a prisoner in the castle.

Dracula sets off for England, leaving Harker at the mercy of three female vampires, but Harker manages to escape. Dracula's intention is to find new blood and spread the curse of the undead. Dracula's ship eventually runs aground on the shores of Whitby in England. The story also introduces us to Professor Abraham Van Helsing, the Dutch doctor who fights against Count Dracula and his horrible plans.

The book is written in epistolary format, meaning in the form of letters, diary entries, newspaper articles, ships' log entries and so on.

The following extract is part of Jonathan Harker's journal.

Extract 74

When I found that I was a prisoner a sort of wild feeling came over me. I rushed up and down the stairs, trying every door and peering out of every window I could find, but after a little the conviction of my helplessness overpowered all other feelings. When I look back after a few hours I think I must have been mad for the time, for I behaved much as a rat does in a trap. When, however, the conviction had come to me that I was helpless I sat down quietly, as quietly as I have ever done anything in my life, and began to think over what was best to be done. I am thinking still, and as yet have come to no definite conclusion. Of one thing only am I certain. That it is no use making my ideas known to the Count. He knows well that I am imprisoned, and as he has done it himself, and has doubtless his own motives for it, he would only deceive me if I trusted him fully with the facts. So far as I can see, my only plan will be to keep my knowledge and my fears to myself, and my eyes open.

Glossary

for the time	at the time
for I behaved much as a rat	because I behaved just like a rat
what was best	what the best thing was
I am thinking still	I am still thinking

Task 74

For this task, I would like you to read the introduction to the book again, and reread the extract several times, to fully grasp the predicament Jonathan Harker has found himself in.

The next extract from *Dracula* describes something very peculiar about Count Dracula. From high up in the castle, Harker is looking outside into the dark with his head out of a window. He can see Count Dracula's head sticking out of another window.

Extract 75a

What I saw was the Count's head coming out from the window. I did not see the face, but I knew the man by the neck and the movement of his back and arms. In any case I could not mistake the hands with which I had had some many opportunities of studying. I was at first interested and somewhat amused, for it is wonderful how small a matter will interest and amuse a man when he is a prisoner. But my very feelings changed to revulsion and terror when I saw the whole man slowly emerge from the window and begin to crawl down the castle wall over the dreadful abyss, face down with his cloak spreading out around him like great wings. At first I could not believe my eyes. I thought it was some trick of the moonlight, some weird effect of shadow, but I kept looking, and it could be no delusion. I saw the fingers and toes grasp the corners of the stones, worn clear of the mortar by the stress of years, and by thus using every projection and inequality move downwards with considerable speed, just as a lizard moves along a wall.

Note: The phrase, 'with which I had had...,' has a double 'had.' This is normal, even in today's English.

Below is the same extract updated. I have underlined the areas where I have made changes.

Extract 75b

What I saw was the Count's head coming out from the window. I did not see the face, but I knew the man by the neck and the movement of his back and arms. <u>Anyway</u> I could not mistake the hands with which I had had <u>so many opportunities</u> of studying. I was at first interested and a <u>little</u> amused, <u>because</u> it is wonderful how small a matter will interest and amuse a man when he is a prisoner. But my very feelings changed to revulsion and terror when I saw the whole man slowly emerge from the window and begin to crawl down the castle wall over the dreadful abyss, face down with his cloak spreading out around him like great wings. At first I could not believe my eyes. I thought it was some trick of the moonlight, some weird effect of shadow, but I kept looking, <u>and I could not have been mistaken</u>. I saw the fingers and toes grasp the corners of the stones, worn clear of the mortar by the stress of years, <u>and by using every projection and rough surface in this way</u> move downwards with considerable speed, just as a lizard moves along a wall.

Task 75

I have listed all my changes here, starting with my alteration and the original underneath. Look carefully at each alteration and remember them so that you can apply this knowledge to other samples of English Literature.

<u>*Anyway*</u>
In any case
<u>*so many opportunities*</u>
some many opportunities
<u>*a little*</u>
somewhat
<u>*because*</u>
for
<u>*and I could not have been mistaken*</u>
and it could be no delusion
<u>*and by using every projection and rough surface in this way*</u>
and by thus using every projection and inequality
Now write a note for each one, explaining why the change is necessary.

The following extract describes Harker's encounter with the female vampires at the castle.

<u>Extract 76</u>

In the moonlight opposite me were three young women, ladies by their dress and manner. I thought at the time that I must be dreaming when I saw them, they threw no shadow on the floor. They came close to me, and looked at me for some time, and then whispered together. Two were dark, and had high aquiline noses, like the Count, and great dark, piercing eyes, that seemed to be almost red when contrasted with the pale yellow moon. The other was fair, as fair as can be, with great masses of golden hair and eyes like pale sapphires. I seemed somehow to know her face, and to know it in connection with some dreamy fear, but I could not recollect at the moment how or where. All three had brilliant white teeth that shone like pearls against the ruby of their voluptuous lips. There was something about them that made me uneasy, some longing and at the same time some deadly fear. I felt in my heart a wicked, burning desire that they would kiss me with those red lips.

Task 76

The language used in this extract is almost identical to today's English, with just a couple of exceptions: The word 'as' should be added to the beginning of *'they threw no shadow on the floor'* and the clause should probably use 'cast' instead of 'threw.' Another one is the phrase *'that they would'* in the last sentence, which should be 'for them to.'

Even after taking account of the above issues, the overall impression of the passage is still that it was written in an old fashioned style (even though the English is correct by today's expectations in regard to grammar and structure). A similar book would not be written like this today for many complex reasons.

Now rewrite this extract in your own modern style, staying faithful to the content and most of the original structure, but allowing some freedom of expression to make it into literature typical of today.

Picture Books

Beatrix Potter (1866–1943) was an English author, illustrator, natural scientist and conservationist. She is well-known for her children's books featuring animals. At the latter end of the nineteenth century, modern picture books began to emerge—illustrated poems, short stories, novels and children's books; and Beatrix Potter's *The Tale of Peter Rabbit* (1901) is a prime example, as Potter not only wrote the book, but illustrated it herself.

Additional Notes for Unit 6
第6单元附加注释

Nationalistic pride amongst the British (English speaking) colonies, and a desire for independence, started to take hold after North America proclaimed their independence in 1776, which was achieved through armed force, leading to the establishment of the United States of America. Britain wanted to avoid a repeat of this in their other territories, so they tried to pre-empt it with Canada (which was next door to the United States), by giving them a form of self-governance in 1867. This was followed by giving Dominion Status to Australia in 1901, New Zealand in 1907 and South Africa in 1910. In 1931, these dominions were officially linked to Britain under the monarchy, creating what is called the 'Commonwealth.' This is now called the 'Commonwealth of Nations' which today covers a third of the world's population. The last country to join the Commonwealth was Rwanda, Central Africa, in 2009. This demonstrates just how international a language English has become; it has been an international language for a very long time. David Crystal estimates that from the end of the reign of Queen Elizabeth I (1603) to the beginning of Queen Elizabeth Ⅱ's reign (1952), four-fifths of English-speakers lived outside of the British Isles.

Glossary for Unit 6

Dante's *Inferno* 但丁的《地狱》
　　'Inferno' is the Italian for Hell. It is the name of the first part of Dante Alighieri's fourteenth century epic poem called *Divine Comedy*.
fable 寓言

A fable is a literary genre. It is a fictional story in prose or verse (poetry) that has animals, mythical creatures, plants, objects or forces of nature displaying human characteristics, especially speech. This story always has a moral lesson for the reader or hearer. This moral may be specified at the end of the story. The writer of a fable is called a fabulist.

A fable is different to a parable as parables are true-to-life stories, with realistic characters and events.

chimney sweep 烟囱清扫工

This is a person who cleans chimneys using special long brushes. In Victorian times, children were often used for these jobs which was very dangerous for them.

puns 双关语

A pun (also called 'paronomasia') is a 'play on words', a form of wordplay in which two or more meanings of words (or even similar-sounding words) are used for humorous effect.

Scottish Bar 苏格兰法庭

To join the Scottish Bar is to begin working in a courtroom as a representative of the laws of Scotland.

double standards 双重标准

To have 'double standards' is to be hypocritical; for example, to expect good behaviour from everyone but yourself.

pros and cons 有利有弊

advantages and disadvantages

vampire 吸血鬼

A vampire is a dead person who rises at night to drink the blood of the living.

Unit 7

Literature from the First Half of the 20th Century 20世纪上半叶文学

Chapter 18   The Second and Third Decade of the 20th Century
第18章   20世纪20与30年代

Chapter 19   Mysteries and Whodunnits
第19章   推理和侦探小说

Chapter 20   The 1930s and 1940s
第20章   20世纪30与40年代

Chapter 21   Tolkien and Lewis
第21章   托尔金与刘易斯

Additional Notes for Unit 7
第7单元附加注释

Chapter 18 The Second and Third Decade of the 20th Century
第18章 20世纪20与30年代

This Unit covers the literature of the last quarter of the Modern English Period (The Modern English Period lasts from 1750 to 1950).

Of course, not only has punctuation, grammar and the use of vocabulary changed over the centuries, but also the way in which words are spoken, for example in regard to stress, which increasingly tended to fall on the first syllable of words. Each word has a given number of syllables (individual beats or sounds), and many of the weakly stressed syllables have been relegated to a schwa.

The following notes explaining the use of the schwa in pronunciation are taken from Andrew Harrison's *As Time Approaches* (《滴答滴答》 published in 2015 by NPUP):

'The Schwa only occurs in unstressed syllables. For example, the word 'protect' has the 2 syllables 'pro' and 'tect.' The second syllable is stressed and the first syllable has the neutral vowel sound (schwa). In the word 'doctor,' the first syllable is stressed and the second syllable has the schwa. The word 'atmosphere' has 3 syllables, only one of which has a schwa. Do you know which one? Some words that do not have a schwa when standing alone, do so when they are part of a spoken sentence. For example, the word 'of' does not have a schwa unless it is within a sentence.'

本单元涵盖现代英语时期（1750—1950）后50年的文学作品。

几个世纪以来，不仅标点符号、语法和词汇的使用发生了变化，单词的读法也有所改变，例如重音越来越倾向于落在单词的第一个音节上。每个单词都有一定数量的音节（指单个的节拍或声音），许多弱读的音节都被归为弱读央元音（或非重读央元音）。

下文解释了发音中"弱读央元音"的用法，摘自安德鲁·哈里森（Andrew Harrison）撰写的《滴答滴答》一书（2015年西北工业大学出版社出版）：

'弱读央元音仅出现在非重读音节中。例如：'protect' 一词中有两个音节，'pro' 和 'tect'。第二个音节是重读音节，而第一个音节含有央元音（schwa）。在 'doctor' 一词中，第一个音节是重读音节，第二个音节中含有央元音。'atmosphere' 有三个音节，但只有一个中含有央元音，你知道是哪个吗？有些词单独出现的时候不存在央元音，但在一句说出来的话中就可能存在。如 'of' 只有在一句话中才会出弱读央元音。'

Galsworthy and Forster

John Galsworthy (1867-1933), a prominent English writer of the time, studied Law at Oxford University and was called to the Bar in 1890. He also wrote prose fiction such as *The Country House* (1907), *The Patrician* (1911), *The Dark Flower* (1913), *The Freelands* (1915) and a collection of short stories called *Caravan* (1925), but he is particularly famous for *The Forsyte Chronicles* which includes *The Forsyte Saga*. *The Forsyte Saga* became an extremely popular TV series in the 1960s. The stories concern the Edwardian upper-middle classes.

The Man of Property (1906) was the first novel of *The Forsyte Saga*, a story about bourgeois morality and society.

E.M. Forster (1879-1970) was an English novelist, short story writer and essayist. His novels were ironic and well-plotted, emphasising class difference and hypocrisy in twentieth century British society.

He was born in London and studied at King's College, Cambridge in 1897. He wrote 6 novels, including *Where Angels Fear to Tread* (1905), *The Longest Journey* (1907), *A Room with a View* (1908), and *Howards End* (1910).

Howards End

Howards End is a story about two sisters and their opposite lives, in a tale of irony and humour. Here is an extract from the book.

Extract 77

Most people thought Paul handsomer than his brother. He was certainly a better shot, though not so good at golf. And when Paul appeared, flushed with the triumph of getting through an examination, and ready to flirt with any pretty girl, Helen met him halfway, or more than halfway, and turned towards him on the Sunday evening.

He had been talking of his approaching exile in Nigeria, and he should have continued to talk of it, and allowed their guest to recover. But the heave of her bosom flattered him. Passion was possible, and he became passionate. Deep down in him something whispered: 'This girl would let you kiss her; you might not have such a chance again.'

That was 'how it happened', or, rather, how Helen described it to her sister, using words more unsympathetic than my own. But the poetry of that kiss, the wonder of it, the magic that there was in life for hours after it — who can describe that?

Task 77

Taking note of the information on the use of stressed and unstressed syllables, and the schwa, at the beginning of this chapter, read the extract above out loud several times, and identify where the stressed syllables and the schwas are. Annotate the text clearly where the stressed syllables and schwas are. Remember that some words that have no schwa when spoken in

isolation, may have a schwa within a spoken sentence.

Then, ask a native English speaker to read the text to you, and listen carefully to check whether you have annotated the stressed syllables and schwas correctly, bearing in mind that speech is often imprecise and interrupted by mistakes and pauses.

Kenneth Grahame and J.M. Barrie

Kenneth Grahame (1859-1932) was a Scottish writer, most famous for his children's book called *The Wind in the Willows* (1908) about rural life and the adventures of animal characters such as Mole, Ratty and Toad.

J.M. Barrie (1860-1937) was also a Scottish author, and a dramatist. Also popular amongst children's writers, he wrote the popular novel *Peter and Wendy* (1911), about a magical boy called Peter Pan who could fly. He took his friends, Wendy and her brothers, on adventures to the island of Neverland. It was a magical world, but it had a downside in the form of pirates, especially Captain Hook. Peter Pan also had a mischievous companion in the form of Tinker Bell the fairy.

Extract 78

The children often spent long summer days on this lagoon, swimming or floating most of the time, playing the mermaid games in the water and so forth. You must not think from this that the mermaids were on friendly terms with them; on the contrary, it was among Wendy's lasting regrets that all the time she was on the island she never had a civil word from one of them. When she stole softly to the edge of the lagoon she might see them by the score, especially on the Marooners' Rock, where they loved to bask, combing out their hair in a lazy way that quite irritated her; or she might even swim, on tiptoe as it were, to within a yard of them, but then they saw her and dived, probably splashing her with their tails, not by accident, but intentionally.

They treated all the boys in the same way, except of course Peter, who chatted with them on Marooners' Rock by the hour, and sat on their tails when they got cheeky. He gave Wendy one of their combs.

The most haunting time at which to see them is at the turn of the moon, when they utter strange wailing cries; but the lagoon is dangerous for mortals then, and until the evening of which we have now to tell, Wendy had never seen the lagoon by moonlight, less from fear, for of course Peter would have accompanied her, than because she had strict rules about every one being in bed by seven. She was often at the lagoon, however, on sunny days after rain, when the mermaids come up in extraordinary numbers to play with their bubbles.

Task 78

From the information available in this extract:
a Describe the mermaids' appearance.
b Describe the things that the mermaids like to do.
c Describe their behaviour and attitude towards all the children.

D.H. Lawrence

D.H. Lawrence (1885–1930) was an English novelist, poet and playwright. He wrote works such as *The White Peacock* (1911), *Sons and Lovers* (1913), and *The Rainbow* (1915).

Sons and Lovers takes place in Nottinghamshire, England. Paul, Gertrude Morel's son, cannot cope with his mother's over-protective hold on him. Gertrude is determined not to let her sons turn out like their father and end up working down the coal mines, but her son Paul rebels by entering into relationships with other women.

Extract 79

Paul was raw and irritable. He also wearied his mother very often.

She saw the sunshine going out of him, and she resented it.

As they were finishing breakfast, came the postman with a letter from Derby. Mrs Morel screwed up her eyes to look at the address.

"Give it here, blind eye!" exclaimed her son, snatching it away from her. She started and almost boxed his ears.

"It's from your son Arthur," he said.

"What now — !" cried Mrs Morel.

"'My dearest Mother,'" Paul read. "'I don't know what made me such a fool. I want you to come and fetch me back from here. I came with Jack Bredon yesterday, instead of going to work, and enlisted. He said he was sick of wearing the seat of a stool out, and like the idiot you know I am, I came away with him.

I have taken the King's Shilling, but perhaps if you came for me they would let me go back with you. I was a fool when I did it. I don't want to be in the army. My dear mother, I am nothing but a trouble to you. But if you get me out of this, I promise I will have more sense and consideration.—'"

Mrs Morel sat down in her rocking-chair.

"Well now," she cried, "let him stop!"

"Yes," said Paul. "Let him stop."

There was silence. The mother sat with her hands folded in her apron, her face set, thinking.

"If I'm not sick!" she cried suddenly. "Sick!!"

"Now!" said Paul, beginning to frown, "you're not going to worry your soul out about this, do you hear."

"I suppose I'm to take it as a blessing," she flashed, turning on her son.

"You're not going to mount it up to a tragedy, so there," he retorted.

"The fool! —the young fool!" she cried.

"He'll look well in uniform," said Paul, irritatingly.

His mother turned on him in a fury.

"Oh will he!" she cried. "Not in my eyes — !"

"He should get in a cavalry regiment — he'll have the time of his life, and will look an awful swell."

"Swell! — swell!! — a mighty swell indeed! — a common soldier!"

"Well," said Paul, "what am I but a common clerk?"

"A good deal, my boy," cried his mother, stung.

"What?"

"At any rate, a man, and not a thing in a red coat."

"I shouldn't mind being in a red coat — or dark blue, that would suit me better — if they didn't boss me about too much."

But his mother had ceased to listen.

Glossary

raw	blunt (impolite)
came the postman	the postman came
She started and almost boxed his ears	She was shocked at his words and almost slapped him round the face
enlisted	This indicates that he enlisted in the army.
taken the King's Shilling	officially agreed to serve as a soldier
"let him stop!"	"let him stay!"
her face set	looking serious
worry your soul out	worry yourself to death
she flashed	she snapped
mount it up to a tragedy	think of it as the end of the world
He'll look well	He'll look good
look an awful swell	look really important
Swell!	Important!
A good deal	A great deal
stung	offended

Task 79

Write an essay analysing this extract in regard to length of sentences, use of descriptive words, the context in which it is placed — including historical background, and the use of speech.

The title of your essay is:

A Brief Analysis of Extract 79 taken from Sons and Lovers

Virginia Woolf

Virginia Woolf (1882–1941) from England was a novelist, an essayist and a feminist. She is famous for novels such as *Mrs Dalloway* (1925) and *To the Lighthouse* (1927).

Below, an extract has been selected from *To the Lighthouse*, a novel that moves away from typical Victorian and Edwardian literary values. A small section of the passage has been removed for ease of reading.

Extract 80

Had there been an axe handy, a poker, or any weapon that would have gashed a hole in his father's breast and killed him, there and then, James would have seized it. Such were the extremes of emotion that Mr. Ramsay excited in his children's breasts by his mere presence; standing, as now, lean as a knife, narrow as the blade of one, grinning sarcastically, not only with the pleasure of disillusioning his son and casting ridicule upon his wife, who was ten thousand times better in every way than he was (James thought), but also with some secret conceit at his own accuracy of judgement. What he said was true. It was always true. He was incapable of untruth; never tampered with a fact; never altered a disagreeable word to suit the pleasure or convenience of any mortal being, least of all his own children, who, sprung from his loins, should be aware from childhood that life is difficult ....

'But it may be fine — I expect it will be fine,' said Mrs. Ramsay, making some little twist of the reddish-brown stocking she was knitting, impatiently. If she finished it tonight, if they did go to the Lighthouse after all, it was to be given to the Lighthouse keeper for his little boy, who was threatened with a tuberculous hip; together with a pile of old magazines, and some tobacco, indeed whatever she could find lying about, not really wanted, but only littering the room, to give those poor fellows who must be bored to death ...

Glossary

in his children's breasts	in his children
casting ridicule upon	ridiculing
conceit at his own accuracy	conceit over his own accuracy
making some little twist of	slightly twisting
threatened with	suffering from
those poor fellows	those poor people

Task 80a

Write an essay analysing this extract in regard to length of sentences, use of descriptive words, the context in which it is placed — including historical background, and the use of speech.

The title of your essay is:

A Brief Analysis of Extract 80 taken from To the Lighthouse

Additional Task D

Before you begin your essay for Task 80b, read and study the Sample

Essay in the Appendices with the title: *A Comparison of Shelly's To a Sky-Lark* (Extract 44) *with Keats' Ode to a Nightingale* (Extract 45), and answer the questions on the Sample essay below.

   a The first paragraph serves as an introduction to the whole essay (although there are also some important introductory comments at the beginning of the second paragraph). How long is the first paragraph in relation to the final word count?

   b The first paragraph expands on the meaning of the title and states more specifically how the title's purpose will be addressed in the main part of the essay. Is the title repeated in the first paragraph in exactly the same way? Does the first paragraph make any actual comparisons?

   c The last paragraph is the conclusion of the essay. How big is the conclusion in comparison to the introduction?

   d In what way does the conclusion link to the title and the main body of the essay?

   e Approximately how old were the two authors when they died?

   f What is an 'ode'?

   g In the main body of the essay (not including the introduction and the conclusion), approximately how many lines of the essay are devoted to Extract 44? How many lines of the essay are devoted to Extract 45? Is the content for each extract roughly the same?

   h In this essay of comparison, how many paragraphs in the main body deal with only one of the two extracts?

   i In this essay of comparison, how many paragraphs in the main body refer to both extracts?

   j Underline, or make a list of all the phrases that are used to switch from details of one of the extracts to the other, while comparing them.

   k Does the essay mention plenty of similarities AND differences?

   l Read both extracts again (See Extract 44 and 45). Which poem do you prefer? Clearly explain why you prefer it to your partner.

Task 80b

Now you have become familiar with the Sample Essay and how to use language of comparison, write an essay comparing this extract by Woolf (Extract 80) with the one by Lawrence (Extract 79) just before it. Use the information you have already discovered for Task 79 and Task 80, and add information about each author too. Your essay should be between 700 and 750 words long.

The title of your essay is:

A Comparison of Sons and Lovers (Extract 79) *with To the Lighthouse* (Extract 80)

A.A. Milne

A.A. Milne (1882–1956) is the author of the children's stories, *Winnie-the-Pooh* (1926), and *The House at Pooh Corner* (1928). The stories created well-known characters such as Winnie-the-Pooh, Eeyore, Piglet, Owl, Tigger, Kanga and Roo.

The following extract is taken from the first book *Winnie-the-Pooh*, and Pooh is out walking.

Extract 81

One day when he was out walking, he came to an open place in the middle of the forest, and in the middle of this place was a large oak-tree, and, from the top of the tree, there came a loud buzzing-noise.

Winnie-the-Pooh sat down at the foot of the tree, put his head between his paws and began to think.

First of all he said to himself: "That buzzing-noise means something. You don't get a buzzing-noise like that, just buzzing and buzzing, without its meaning something. If there's a buzzing-noise, somebody's making a buzzing-noise, and the only reason for making a buzzing-noise that I know of is because you're a bee."

Then he thought another long time, and said: "And the only reason for being a bee that I know of is making honey."

And then he got up, and said: "And the only reason for making honey is so as I can eat it." So he began to climb the tree.

He climbed and he climbed and he climbed, and as he climbed he sang a little song to himself. It went like this:

'Isn't it funny
How a bear likes honey?
Buzz! Buzz! Buzz!
I wonder why he does?'

Then he climbed a little further ... and a little further ... and then just a little further. By that time he had thought of another song.

'It's a very funny thought that, if Bears were Bees,
They'd build their nests at the bottom of trees.
And that being so (if the Bees were Bears),
We shouldn't have to climb up all these stairs.'

He was getting rather tired by this time, so that is why he sang a Complaining Song. He was nearly there now, and if he just stood on that branch ...

Crack!

Task 81

In this extract, Pooh sings a couple of short songs. They both consist of four lines. The lines are shorter in the first one.

Here is the first song. Read it aloud several times to become acquainted with the rhythm. Notice that the last two words of the first two lines rhyme, and the last two words of the last two lines rhyme.

'Isn't it funny

How a bear likes honey?

Buzz! Buzz! Buzz!

I wonder why he does?'

Now write your own song on any subject you like, but in the same style. Read it aloud (or sing it) to your partner.

Here is the second song. Read it aloud several times to become acquainted with the rhythm. Notice that the last two words of the first two lines rhyme, and the last two words of the last two lines rhyme.

'It's a very funny thought that, if Bears were Bees,

They'd build their nests at the bottom of trees.

And that being so (if the Bees were Bears),

We shouldn't have to climb up all these stairs.'

Now write your own song on any subject you like, but in the same style. Read it aloud (or sing it) to your partner.

The following extract is from the second book, *The House at Pooh Corner*. Pooh invented a game called Poohsticks, which he and his friends played on the edge of the forest. They would throw sticks off a bridge into the river, and go to the other side to see whose stick came out first.

Extract 82

Now one day Pooh and Piglet and Rabbit and Roo were all playing Poohsticks together. They had dropped their sticks in when Rabbit said "Go!" and then they had hurried across to the other side of the bridge, and now they were all leaning over the edge, waiting to see whose stick would come out first. But it was a long time coming, because the river was very lazy that day, and hardly seemed to mind if it didn't even get there at all.

"I can see mine!" cried Roo. "No, I can't, it's something else. Can you see

yours, Piglet? I thought I could see mine, but I couldn't. There it is! No, it isn't. Can you see yours, Pooh?"

"No," said Pooh.

"I expect my stick's stuck," said Roo. "Rabbit, my stick's stuck. Is your stick stuck, Piglet?"

"They always take longer than you think," said Rabbit.

"How long do you think they'll take?" asked Roo.

"I can see yours, Piglet," said Pooh suddenly.

"Mine's a sort of greyish one," said Piglet, not daring to lean too far over in case he fell in.

"Yes, that's what I can see. It's coming over on to my side."

Rabbit leant over further than ever, looking for his, and Roo wriggled up and down, calling out "Come on, stick! Stick, stick, stick!" and Piglet got very excited because his was the only one which had been seen, and that meant that he was winning.

"It's coming!" said Pooh.

"Are you sure it's mine?" squeaked Piglet excitedly.

"Yes, because it's grey. A big grey one. Here it comes! A very — big — grey — Oh, no, it isn't, it's Eeyore."

And out floated Eeyore.

"Eeyore!" cried everybody.

Looking very calm, very dignified, with his legs in the air, came Eeyore from beneath the bridge.

Task 82

Answer the following comprehension questions on the extract.

a What are the names of the characters that are playing this game of Poohsticks?

b Why did they initially think the sticks were taking so long to come out at the other side?

    c Who thought they could see their stick first?

    d Who asked Pooh if he could see his?

    e Who said he could see Piglet's stick?

    f What did Piglet's stick end up being?

Chapter 19 Mysteries and Whodunnits

第19章 推理和侦探小说

Denis Wheatley (1897-1977) was a writer from England who wrote thrillers and occult novels. He was one of the world's best-selling authors from the 1930s to 1960s. His writings inspired Ian Fleming, the author of the world renowned James Bond series of novels. One of Denis Wheatley's novels that was extremely popular was *The Devil Rides Out* (1934) which was made into a film by Hammer Film Productions (a British film and television production company) in 1968. The story is set in London and elsewhere in the south of England. The Duc de Richleau and Rex Van Ryan find out that Simon Aaron has become involved with a group of Devil worshippers, so they rescue him from a witches' ceremony on Salisbury Plain.

Agatha Christie

Agatha Christie (1890-1976) was a crime novelist from England. She is the world's best known mystery writer. After Shakespeare and the Holy Bible, Agatha Christie is the highest-selling author of all time, with up to 4 billion books having been published in 45 languages. More than one billion of these were in English, the original language of the novels.

She wrote 79 novels and short story collections, as well as 14 plays, of which 'The Mousetrap' is the longest-running theatre-play in history.

For most of her whodunnit Murder Mysteries, she created the famous Belgian private detective Hercule Poirot and the elderly English private detective

Miss Marple, the stories requiring their master private detective to identify the murderer. Her books have been widely used for TV productions and feature films.

Here is just a handful of her novels:

Mysteries
The Man in the Brown Suit
The Secret of Chimneys
The Hound of Death
Murder is Easy
And Then There Were None
Sparkling Cyanide
Crooked House

Poirot
The Murder of Roger Ackroyd
Murder on the Orient Express
The ABC Murders
Death on the Nile
Dead Man's Folly

Marple
The Murder at the Vicarage
They Do It With Mirrors
A Pocket Full of Rye
4.50 from Paddington

Tommy and Tuppence
Partners in Crime
By the Pricking of My Thumbs

Below are some famous quotations by Hercule Poirot in the stories published between 1920 and 1974:

Extract 83

'It is sometimes difficult for a dog to find a scent, but once he has found it, nothing on earth will make him leave it! That is if he is a good dog! And I, Hercule Poirot, am a very good dog.' (The Chocolate Box)

'Women observe subconsciously a thousand little details, without knowing that they are doing so. Their subconscious mind adds these little things together — and they call the result intuition.' (The Murder of Roger Ackroyd)

'Mothers are particularly ruthless when their children are in danger.' (Death on the Nile)

'I always make my plans well in advance. To succeed in life every detail should be arranged well beforehand.' (Death on the Nile)

'If the little grey cells are not exercised, they grow the rust.' (The ABC Murders)

'Instinct is a marvellous thing. It can neither be explained nor ignored.' (The Mysterious Affair at Styles)

Glossary

little grey cells Poirot often refers to his 'little grey cells' to mean the cells of his brain. He considers his own brain/mind and investigative skills to be second to none.

rust 'Rust' is the reddish-brown colour that envelopes metal objects over time.

Task 83

Read these quotations very carefully, and then one by one describe in your own words what each quotation means, and give an example of how

each quotation can be applied to life today.

The following is an extract from Christie's *Murder on the Orient Express* (1933) when Poirot seeks to solve a mysterious death on the train.

Extract 84

"The door was locked and chained on the inside," said Poirot thoughtfully. "It was not suicide — eh?"

The Greek doctor gave a sardonic laugh. "Does a man who commits suicide stab himself in ten — twelve — fifteen places?" he asked.

Poirot's eyes opened. "That is great ferocity," he said.

"It is a woman," said the chef de train, speaking for the first time. "Depend upon it, it was a woman. Only a woman would stab like that."

Dr. Constantine screwed up his face thoughtfully.

"She must have been a very strong woman," he said. "It is not my desire to speak technically — that is only confusing; but I can assure you that one or two of the blows were delivered with such force as to drive them through hard belts of bone and muscle."

"It was clearly not a scientific crime," said Poirot.

"It was most unscientific," returned Dr. Constantine. "The blows seem to have been delivered haphazard and at random. Some have glanced off, doing hardly any damage. It is as though somebody had shut his eyes and then in a frenzy struck blindly again and again."

"C'est une femme," said the chef de train again. "Women are like that. When they are enraged they have great strength." He nodded so sagely that everyone suspected a personal experience of his own.

"I have, perhaps, something to contribute to your store of knowledge," said Poirot. "M. Ratchett spoke to me yesterday. He told me, as far as I was able to understand him, that he was in danger of his life."

The Orient Express

Glossary

hard belts of bone and muscle   hard layers of bone and muscle
scientific crime   well-planned and organised crime
He nodded so sagely   He nodded with such wise certainty
he was in danger of his life   his life was in danger (Poirot is mixing Belgian French grammar with English)

Task 84

Read the extract carefully and make sure you fully understand the English. Can you see any French words? What are they? What do you think they mean?

Christie's *By the Pricking of My Thumbs* (1968) is not a Poirot or Marple mystery, but rather a 'Tommy and Tuppence' one, written much later than *Murder on the Orient Express*. In *By the Pricking of My Thumbs*, Tommy and Tuppence visit Ada, an elderly aunt, in her nursing home, and they initially find it hard to understand why she is so mistrusting of her doctors. That is until they hear of a poisoned mushroom stew and something strange behind the fireplace. The title of the book *By the Pricking of My Thumbs* is taken from a Shakespearean quote. In Shakespeare, it is uttered by a witch on the third appearance of the witches in the play called Macbeth. The quote is as follows:

'*By the pricking of my thumbs*
Something wicked this way comes.'
(Macbeth Act 4, Scene 1)

The extract below is taken from *By the Pricking of My Thumbs*. An elderly lady has disappeared from the nursing home.

Extract 85

'*It's a disappearance — no traceable address — no answer to letters — it's a planned disappearance. I'm more and more sure of it.*'

'*But —*'

Tuppence broke in upon his '*But*'.

'*Listen, Tommy — supposing that sometime or other a crime happened — It seemed all safe and covered up — But then suppose that someone in the family had seen something, or known something — someone elderly and garrulous —someone who chatted to people — someone whom you suddenly realized might be in danger to you — What would you do about it?*'

'*Arsenic in the soup?*' suggested Tommy cheerfully. '*Cosh them on the head — Push them down the staircase — ?*'

'*That's rather extreme — Sudden deaths attract attention. You'd look about for some simpler way — and you'd find one. A nice respectable Home for Elderly*

Ladies. You'd pay a visit to it, calling yourself Mrs Johnson or Mrs Robinson — or you would get yourself some unsuspecting third party to make arrangements — You'd fix the financial arrangements through a firm of reliable solicitors. You've already hinted, perhaps, that your elderly relative has fancies and mild delusions sometimes — so do a good many of the other old ladies — Nobody will think it odd — if she cackles on about poisoned milk, or dead children behind a fireplace, or a sinister kidnapping; nobody will really listen. They'll just think it's old Mrs So-and-So having her fancies again — nobody will take any notice at all.'

Glossary

about	around
has fancies	has a vivid imagination
having her fancies	with her vivid imagination

Apart from the few corrections in the glossary, the use of English in the extract is representative of today's modern English, which is not surprising as it is one of Christie's later novels.

Task 85

Tuppence explained what she thought was the best way to stop an elderly, chatty witness to a murder from effectively revealing information about a crime. What does Tuppence suggest is the best way? Why?

What methods does Tommy suggest are the best way?

Why does Tuppence not agree with him?

J.B. Priestly

J.B. Priestly (1894–1984) was an English novelist, playwright and broadcaster. He was born in Bradford in England and studied at Trinity Hall in Cambridge. He wrote a fiction novel called *The Good Companions* (1929) regarding the trials and tribulations of a concert party in England between World War I and World War II, which reflected his Yorkshire background. This novel got him noticed; however, he is best known for *An Inspector Calls* (1945), a popular play set in Edwardian England. It is in three Acts, and takes place on one night in April 1912 in the dining room of the Birlings' house in the North Midlands of England. The story focusses on the middle-class Birling family. The first theatre production of this work took place in October 1946.

Below is an extract taken from *An Inspector Calls*. It is the beginning of Act 1, just after a lengthy description of the opening scene.

Extract 86

BIRLING: *Giving us the port, Edna? That's right. [He pushes it towards ERIC.] You ought to like this port, Gerald. As a matter of fact, Finchley told me it's exactly the same port your father gets from him.*

GERALD: *Then it'll be all right. The governor prides himself on being a good judge of port. I don't pretend to know much about it.*

SHEILA: *[gaily, possessively]: I should jolly well think not, Gerald. I'd hate you to know all about port — like one of these purple-faced old men.*

BIRLING: *Here, I'm not a purple-faced old man.*

SHEILA: *No, not yet. But then you don't know all about port — do you?*

BIRLING: *[noticing that his wife has not taken any]: Now then, Sybil, you must take a little tonight. Special occasion, y'know, eh?*

SHEILA: *Yes, go on, Mummy. You must drink our health.*

MRS BIRLING *[smiling]: Very well, then. Just a little, thank you.*

[To EDNA, who is about to go, with tray] All right, Edna. I'll ring from the drawing-room when we want coffee. Probably in about half an hour.

EDNA *[going]: Yes, ma'am.*

[EDNA goes out. They now have all the glasses filled. BIRLING beams at

them and clearly relaxes.]

BIRLING: Well, well — this is very nice. Very nice. Good dinner too, Sybil. Tell cook from me.

GERALD *[politely]*: Absolutely first-class.

Later in the play, an Inspector calls and questions the Birling family in regard to the suicide of Eva Smith who had worked in one of Arthur's mills.

Task 86

The acting parts for the play are Arthur, Sybil, Sheila and Eric Birling, Gerald Croft, Edna, and Inspector Goole. Can you work out which parts 'Birling' and 'Mrs Birling' refer to?

Study and discuss this section of the play in a group of 6 people. There are 5 speaking parts (Birling, Gerald, Sheila, Mrs Birling and Edna) and 1 non-speaking part (Eric). Divide the parts between the 6 members of your group and practice the extract as a role play.

When you are confident, act out this part of the scene in front of others.

Chapter 20　The 1930s and 1940s
第20章　20世纪30与40年代

George Orwell (1903-1950) was a novelist, essayist, journalist and critic from England. He was famous for his allegorical novel and political satire *Animal Farm* (1945), which reflected events leading up to the Russian Revolution of 1917.

Daphne Du Maurier (1907-1989) was born in London, but lived most of her life in Cornwall, England. She was educated in both England and France. She became an author of melodramatic novels and a playwright. She is well-known for her novel *Jamaica Inn* (1936). Jamaica Inn is a real place in Cornwall, having been built in 1750. It became associated with smuggling, and as such, Daphne Du Maurier used it as the setting for her novel. But it was her novel *Rebecca* (1938) that made Daphne Du Maurier famous. After that, many of her works were adapted into film. *Jamaica Inn* was made into a film in 1939 (and produced a TV series in 1983). *Rebecca* was adapted for film in 1940. Her novel *The Birds* (1952) was made into a horror film by the British film producer Alfred Hitchcock in 1963.

Rebecca

Daphne Du Maurier's novel *Rebecca* is a Gothic crime mystery which includes romance. A woman marries a widower who was once married to Rebecca who died in a boating accident. The new couple live on the Cornish estate called Manderley. However, the sinister housekeeper, Mrs Danvers, is always trying to psychologically undermine the new Mrs de Winter, by comparing her to Rebecca. The housekeeper eventually tries to get Mrs de Winter to commit suicide.

Extract 87

Well, it is over now, finished and done with. I ride no more tormented, and both of us are free. Even my faithful Jasper has gone to the happy hunting grounds, and Manderley is no more. It lies like an empty shell amidst the tangle of the deep woods, even as I saw it in my dream. A multitude of weeds, a colony of birds. Sometimes perhaps a tramp will wander there, seeking shelter from a sudden shower of rain and, if he is stout-hearted, he may walk there with impunity. But your timid fellow, your nervous poacher — the woods of Manderley are not for him. He might stumble upon the little cottage in the cove and he would not be happy beneath its tumbled roof, the thin rain beating a tattoo. There might linger there still a certain atmosphere of stress ... That corner in the drive, too, where the trees encroach upon the gravel, is not a place in which to pause, not after the sun has set. When the leaves rustle, they sound very much like the stealthy movement of a woman in evening dress, and when they shiver suddenly, and fall, and scatter away along the ground, they might be the patter, patter, of a woman's hurrying footstep, and the mark in the gravel the imprint of a high-heeled satin shoe.

Glossary

But your timid fellow, your nervous poacher But as for a timid person or the nervous poacher

tattoo 'Tattoo' here refers to a drumbeat that summons soldiers.

Task 87

After you have carefully read and studied the extract from *Rebecca*, it is a good opportunity to write an essay comparing three extracts, all from different authors and time periods. I have rewritten the relevant extracts below. The first one is from *Emma* (1815) by Jane Austen (1775–1817), combining Extract 38 and 39, before reducing the final passage in size; the second one is from *Jane Eyre* (1847) by Charlotte Bronte (1816–1855), having reduced the size of Extract 49; the third passage is exactly the same as Extract 87 which is taken from *Rebecca* (1938) by Daphne Du Maurier (1907–1989). I have labelled the Extracts A, B and C respectively. Reread Extracts A, B and C, then do the task at the end.

<u>Jane Austen</u>
<u>(1775–1817)</u>

<u>Emma</u> (1815)

This extract is taken from the beginning of the novel. Then there is a break in the extract, jumping to a part showing something of what Mr Knightley, Emma's love interest, thinks about Emma's friendship with Harriet.

Extract A

Emma Woodhouse, handsome, clever, and rich, with a comfortable home and happy disposition, seemed to unite some of the best blessings of existence; and had lived nearly twenty-one years in the world with very little to distress or vex her.

She was the youngest of the two daughters of a most affectionate, indulgent father, and had, in consequence of her sister's marriage, been mistress of his house from a very early period. Her mother had died too long ago for her to have more than an indistinct remembrance of her caresses, and her place had been supplied by an excellent woman as governess, who had fallen little short of a mother in affection.

Sixteen years had Miss Taylor been in Mr Woodhouse's family, less as a governess than a friend, very fond of both daughters, but particularly of Emma.

....

'I do not know what your opinion may be, Mrs Weston,' said Mr Knightley, 'of this great intimacy between Emma and Harriet Smith, but I think it a bad thing.'

'A bad thing! Do you really think it a bad thing? — why so?'

'I think they will neither of them do the other any good.'

'You surprise me! Emma must do Harriet good: and by supplying her with a new object of interest, Harriet may be said to do Emma good. I have been seeing their intimacy with the greatest pleasure.'

231 words

Charlotte Bronte
(1816–1855)

Jane Eyre (1847)

In the following extract, Jane is talking to St. John about their friendship. St. John wants Jane to go to India with him. I have omitted some parts.

Extract B

"Must we part this way, St. John? And when you go to India, will you leave me so, without a kinder word than you have yet spoken?"

He now turned quite from the moon, and faced me.

"When I go to India, Jane, will I leave you? What! Do you not go to India?"

"You said I could not, unless I married you."

"And you will not marry me? You adhere to that resolution?"

...

"No, St. John, I will not marry you. I adhere to my resolution."

"Once more, why this refusal?" he asked.

"Formerly," I answered, "because you did not love me now, I reply, because you almost hate me. If I were to marry you, you would kill me. You are killing me now."

His lips and cheeks turned white — quite white.

"I should kill — I am killing you? Your words are such that ought not to be used; violent, unfeminine, and untrue. They betray an unfortunate state of mind; they merit severe reproof. They would seem inexcusable, but that it is the duty of man to forgive his fellow, even until seventy-and-seven times."

...

"Now you will indeed hate me," I said. "It is useless to attempt to conciliate you; I see I have made an eternal enemy of you."

A fresh wrong did these words inflict; the worse, because they touched on the truth.

229 words

Daphne Du Maurier
(1907–1989)

Rebecca (1938)
Extract C

Well, it is over now, finished and done with. I ride no more tormented, and both of us are free. Even my faithful Jasper has gone to the happy hunting grounds, and Manderley is no more. It lies like an empty shell amidst the tangle of the deep woods, even as I saw it in my dream. A multitude of weeds, a colony of birds. Sometimes perhaps a tramp will wander there, seeking shelter from a sudden shower of rain and, if he is stout-hearted, he may walk there with impunity. But your timid fellow, your nervous poacher — the woods of Manderley are not for him. He might stumble upon the little cottage in the cove and he would not be happy beneath its tumbled roof, the thin rain beating a tattoo. There might linger there still a certain atmosphere of stress ... That corner in the drive, too, where the trees encroach upon the gravel, is not a place in which to pause, not after the sun has set. When the leaves rustle, they sound very much like the stealthy movement of a woman in evening dress, and when they shiver suddenly, and fall, and scatter away along the ground, they might be the patter, patter, of a woman's hurrying footstep, and the mark in the gravel the imprint of a high-heeled satin shoe.

225 words

Write a 1,000-word essay comparing Extracts A, B and C. For hints on how to write a good essay, refer back to the Sample Essay in the Appendices.

The title of your essay is:

A Comparison Between Jane Austen's Emma (Extract A), *Charlotte Bronte's Jane Eyre* (Extract B), *and Daphne Du Maurier's Rebecca* (Extract C)

In your essay, refer to the context of each extract; the use of language and how much each extract represents today's English; the length of sentences, and the reasons for the similarities and differences; the use of vocabulary; the use of emotion; and as the authors are all female, how much feminine values are expressed or represented in each extract. Bear in mind the different historical backgrounds that the authors come from. You can use any information you choose from the relevant chapters in this book where the extracts and authors have already been discussed.

Enid Blyton

Enid Blyton (1897–1968) was a much loved author of children's books, for example, her Famous Five series, her Naughtiest Girl series (including *The Naughtiest Girl in the School, The Naughtiest Girl Again, The Naughtiest Girl is a Monitor,* and *Here's the Naughtiest Girl!*) and Noddy.

Here is an extract from *The Famous Five: Five on a Treasure Island* (1942). There is a shipwreck off Kirrin Island and the four children, with George's dog, want to know where the treasure is, but as they search for clues, someone else is doing the same.

Extract 88

'I'm going to land at the little cove I told you about the other day,' said George. 'There's only one way to it, but I know it very well. It's hidden away on the east side of the island.'

The girl cleverly worked her boat in and out of the rocks, and suddenly, as it rounded a low wall of sharp rocks, the children saw the cove she had spoken of. It was like a natural little harbour, and was a smooth inlet of water running up to a stretch of sand, sheltered between high rocks. The boat slid into the inlet, and at once stopped rocking, for here the water was like glass, and had hardly a wrinkle.

'I say — this is fine!' said Julian, his eyes shining with delight. George looked at him and her eyes shone too, as bright as the sea itself. It was the first time she had ever taken anyone to her precious island, and she was enjoying it.

They landed on the smooth yellow sand. 'We're really on the island!' said Anne, and she capered about, Tim joining her and looking as mad as she did. The others laughed. George pulled the boat high up on the sand.

'Why so far up?' said Julian, helping her. 'The tide's almost in, isn't it? Surely it won't come as high as this.'

'I told you I thought a storm was coming,' said George. 'If one does, the waves simply tear up this inlet and we don't want to lose our boat, do we?'

'Let's explore the island, let's explore the island!' yelled Anne, who was now at the top of the little natural harbour, climbing up the rocks there. 'Oh do come on!'

They all followed her. It really was a most exciting place. Rabbits were everywhere! They scuttled about as the children appeared, but did not go into their holes.

'Aren't they awfully tame?' said Julian, in surprise.

'Well, nobody ever comes here but me,' said George, 'and I don't frighten them. Tim! Tim, if you go after the rabbits, I'll be furious.'

Tim turned big sorrowful eyes on to George. He and George agreed about every single thing except rabbits. To him rabbits were made for one thing — to chase! He never could understand why George wouldn't let him do this. But he held himself in and walked solemnly by the children, his eyes watching the lolloping rabbits longingly.

'I believe they would almost eat out of my hand,' said Julian.

But George shook her head.

'No, I've tried that with them,' she said. 'They won't. Look at those baby ones. Aren't they lovely?'

'Woof!' said Tim, agreeing, and he took a few steps towards them. George made a warning noise in her throat, and Tim walked back, his tail down.

'There's the castle!' said Julian. 'Shall we explore that now? I do want to.'

'Yes, we will,' said George. 'Look — that is where the entrance used to be — through that big broken archway.'

The children gazed at the enormous old archway, now half-broken down. Behind it were ruined stone steps leading towards the centre of the castle.

'It had strong walls all round it, with two towers,' said George. 'One tower is almost gone, as you can see, but the other is not so bad. The jackdaws build in that every year. They've almost filled it up with their sticks!'

As they came near to the better tower of the two the jackdaws circled round them with loud cries of 'Chack, chack, chack!' Tim leapt into the air as if he thought he could get them, but they only called mockingly to him.

'This is the centre of the castle,' said George, as they entered through a ruined doorway into what looked like a great yard, whose stone floor was now overgrown with grass and other weeds. 'Here is where the people used to live. You can see where the rooms were — look, there's one almost whole there. Go through that little door and you'll see it.'

They trooped through a doorway and found themselves in a dark, stone-walled, stone-roofed room, with a space at one end where a fireplace must have been. Two slit-like windows lit the room. It felt very strange and mysterious.

'What a pity it's all broken down,' said Julian, wandering out again. 'That room seems to be the only one quite whole. There are some others here — but all of them seem to have either no roof, or one or other of the walls gone. That room is the only livable one. Was there an upstairs to the castle, George?'

'Of course,' said George. 'But the steps that led up are gone. Look! You can see part of an upstairs room there, by the jackdaw tower. You can't get up to

it, though, because I've tried. I nearly broke my neck trying to get up. The stones crumble away so.'

'Were there any dungeons?' asked Dick.

'I don't know,' said George. 'I expect so. But nobody could find them now—everywhere is so overgrown.'

It was indeed overgrown. Big blackberry bushes grew here and there, and a few gorse bushes forced their way into gaps and corners. The coarse green grass sprang everywhere, and pink thrift grew its cushions in holes and crannies.

'Well, I think it's a perfectly lovely place,' said Anne. 'Perfectly and absolutely lovely!'

'Do you really?' said George, pleased. 'I'm so glad. Look! We're right on the other side of the island now, facing the sea. Do you see those rocks, with those peculiar big birds sitting there?'

The children looked. They saw some rocks sticking up, with great black shining birds sitting on them in strange positions.

'They are cormorants,' said George. 'They've caught plenty of fish for their dinner, and they're sitting there digesting it. Hallo — they're all flying away. I wonder why?'

She soon knew — for, from the south-west there suddenly came an ominous rumble.

'Thunder!' said George. 'That's the storm. It's coming sooner than I thought!'

Glossary

'I say — this is fine!'	'Hey, this is great!'
capered about	jumped around
'Oh do come on!'	'Hurry up!'
'Aren't they awfully tame?'	'They're really tame!'
'Aren't they lovely?'	'Aren't they cute?'
'I do want to.'	'I really want to.'
'… look, there's one almost whole there.'	'… look, there's an almost complete one there.'

'… one quite whole.'	' … complete one.'
'… livable one.'	' … one that you could live in.'
'The stones crumble away so.'	'The stones crumble away too easily.'
'… a perfectly lovely place'	' … a really beautiful place'
'Perfectly and absolutely lovely!'	'An absolutely perfect place!'
'Hallo'	'Hello'

Notice that every glossary entry is a required update of speech (apart from 'capered about'). The narrative, however, is typical of today's English. The speech of the children represents a correct spoken form of British English from that period (i.e. 1942, which is 78 years ago).

Task 88

Write a 700–750 word essay comparing this *Five on a Treasure Island* extract (Extract 88) for children, with the *Treasure Island* extract (Extract 61) by Robert Louis Stevenson for young adults, writing about the following aspects:

a The type of characters (age, background, purpose for being on the island etc.).

b Type of island (e.g. climate, foliage, buildings and animals).

c The main events in the extract.

d The use of dialogue (e.g. historical period and cultural background).

e The use of English (e.g. vocabulary, grammar).

f The suitability of the extract for the targeted age group.

Remember to have a suitable introduction and conclusion according to the requirements indicated in the Sample Essay in the Appendices.

The title of your essay is:

A Comparison of Blyton's Five on a Treasure Island (Extract 88) *with Stevenson's Treasure Island* (Extract 61)

The following extract by Enid Blyton is from *The Naughtiest Girl is a Monitor* (1945). Elizabeth ('the Naughtiest Girl') is chosen to be a school monitor, and she is delighted, but she soon discovers that it brings responsibilities with it. However hard she tries, she does not seem to be able to improve her behaviour. In the extract it is still the school holidays, and Elizabeth's mother gives her a surprise.

Extract 89

It was in the middle of the Christmas holidays that Mother sprang a surprise on Elizabeth. Christmas was over, and Elizabeth had been to the pantomime and the circus, and to three parties.

Now she was beginning to look forward to going back to boarding-school again. It was dull being an only child, now that she had got used to living with so many girls and boys at Whyteleafe School. She missed their laughter and their chatter, the fun and games they had together.

'Mother, I love being at home — but I do miss Kathleen and Belinda and Nora and Harry and John and Richard,' she said, 'Joan has been over here to see me once or twice, but she's got a cousin staying with her now, and I don't expect I'll see her any more these hols.'

Then Mother gave Elizabeth a surprise.

'Well,' she said. 'I knew you would be lonely — so I have arranged for someone to come and keep you company for the last two weeks of these holidays, Elizabeth.'

'Mother! Who?' cried Elizabeth. 'Somebody I know?'

'No,' said Mother. 'It is a girl who is to go to Whyteleafe School next term — a girl called Arabella Buckley. I am sure you will like her.'

Glossary

Mother	Today, it is too formal to address your own mother as 'mother.' Almost everyone will use the word 'Mum.'

'It is a girl who is to go to Whyteleafe School next term — a girl called Arabella Buckley. I am sure you will like her.'

'It's a girl who's going to go to Whyteleafe School next term — a girl called Arabella Buckley. I'm sure you'll like her.'

This book was published in 1945, and it is difficult to know how much of the dialogue in the extract avoids some contractions such as 'It's' 'I'm' and 'you'll' simply due to the author's desire to promote correct, formal English, and how much of it is a genuine reflection of how children spoke in her days. The spoken language is very precise, but it is not commonly spoken like this today. The contractions I have written in the glossary are the norm in speech now.

In the glossary, I have also changed *'who is to go to'* into *'who's going to go to.'* The former phrase is not as common today, the latter being the most likely.

Task 89

We are told in the extract that, *'Elizabeth had been to the pantomime and the circus, and to three parties.'* Going to the circus is not so popular these days, but going to three parties at Christmas-time is quite normal. Pantomimes have a long history in England, and attending them and taking part in them at Christmas-time is very common today too.

Do some personal research to fulfil the following task:

Find out the names of ten pantomimes that are very popular these days in the UK. What can you discover about the origins of these specific pantomimes?

Chapter 21   Tolkien and Lewis
第21章 托尔金与刘易斯

J.R.R. Tolkien CBE (1892–1973) was a writer, poet, philologist and academic. He created a 'new mythology', putting traditional mythical beings into his own chronology using detailed research. The works he is most famous for are *The Hobbit*, and the three volumes of *The Lord of the Rings* series. *The Hobbit* (1937) is a prequel to *The Lord of the Rings*. It concerns thirteen dwarves who are in search of the ferocious dragon called Smaug the Magnificent which is guarding a hoard of gold. The dwarves plot to raid that hoard of treasure. There is a similar scene in the famous ancient story of *Beowulf*.

In *The Hobbit*, the dwarves have a reluctant companion in the form of Bilbo Baggins, who is one of a community of hobbits. There are trolls, elves and goblins in the novel too.

The Hobbit

The extract below has been taken from *The Hobbit*, when Smaug goes on the rampage. A section has been removed for ease of reading.

Extract 90

There was once more a tremendous excitement and enthusiasm. But the grim-voiced fellow ran hotfoot to the Master. "The dragon is coming or I am a fool!" he cried. "Cut the bridges! To arms! To arms!"

Then warning trumpets were suddenly sounded, and echoed along the rocky shores. The cheering stopped and the joy was turned to dread.

....

Fire leaped from the dragon's jaws. He circled for a while high in the air above them lighting all the lake; the trees by the shores shone like copper and like blood with leaping shadows of dense black at their feet. Then down he swooped straight through the arrow-storm, reckless in his rage, taking no heed to turn his scaly sides towards his foes, seeking only to set their town ablaze.

Task 90

The following quotations are from Extract 7 which can be found earlier in this text book. They are from Seamus Heaney's 1999 translation of the Old English text of *Beowulf*, renamed Extract D.

Extract D
'The dragon began to belch out flames
and burn bright homesteads ...
Then Beowulf was given bad news,
a hard truth: his own home,
the best of buildings, had been burnt to a cinder,
the throne-room of the Geats.
... the fire-dragon
had rased the coastal region and reduced
forts and earthworks to dust and ashes,
so the war-king planned and plotted his revenge.

Here is a section of Extract 90, from Tolkien's novel *The Hobbit* of 1937. I have renamed it Extract E.

Extract E
'Then warning trumpets were suddenly sounded, and echoed along the rocky shores. The cheering stopped and the joy was turned to dread.

....

Fire leaped from the dragon's jaws. He circled for a while high in the air above them lighting all the lake; the trees by the shores shone like copper and like blood with leaping shadows of dense black at their feet. Then down he swooped straight through the arrow-storm, reckless in his rage, taking no heed to turn his scaly sides towards his foes, seeking only to set their town ablaze.'

Reread these two extracts several times before making a detailed list of all the similarities between them.

Ferocious dragon guarding its treasure

Tolkien's *Lord of the Rings* series is found in the following three volumes:

Volume 1: *The Fellowship of the Ring* (1954)

Volume 2: *The Two Towers* (1954)

Volume 3: *The Return of the King* (1955)

All of these related stories by Tolkien have been made into a series of 6 major films, *The Hobbit* taking three films of its own.

The Fellowship of the Ring

The following extract is from *The Fellowship of the Ring*, in which the young hobbit Frodo Baggins of the Shire is given the huge task of crossing Middle-Earth to destroy a powerful ring. This is the only way to prevent the evil Dark Lord from having dominion over Middle-Earth.

Extract 91

Frodo drew the Ring out of his pocket again and looked at it ... It was an admirable thing and altogether precious. When he took it out he had intended to fling it from him into the very hottest part of the fire. But he found now that he could not do so, not without a great struggle. He weighed the Ring in his hand, hesitating, and forcing himself to remember all that Gandalf had told him ... but he found that he had to put it back in his pocket.

Gandalf laughed grimly. 'You see? Already you too, Frodo, cannot easily let it go, nor will to change it ... It has been said that dragon-fire could melt and consume the Rings of Power, but there is not now any dragon left on earth in which the old fire is hot enough ... There is only one way: to find the Cracks of Doom in the depths of Orodruin, the Fire-mountain, and cast the Ring in there, if you really wish to destroy it, to put it beyond the grasp of the Enemy for ever.'

Task 91

Read the extract carefully and then rewrite it in today's modern English.

The Two Towers

The following extract is from *The Two Towers*. Gandalf the Grey discovers that the ring in Frodo's possession is none other than the ruler of all the Rings of Power. Frodo and his companions travel through peril after peril towards the Fire-mountain, but they are followed by a mysterious creature called Gollum. In the extract, Gollum has grabbed hold of Sam, Frodo's travelling companion, and is biting into his shoulder. Frodo comes to the rescue.

Extract 92

Frodo sprang up, and drew Sting from its sheath. With his left hand he drew back Gollum's head by his thin lank hair, stretching his long neck, and forcing his pale venomous eyes to stare up at the sky.

'Let go! Gollum,' he said. 'This is Sting. You have seen it before once upon a time. Let go, or you'll feel it this time! I'll cut your throat.'

Gollum collapsed and went as loose as wet string. Sam got up, fingering his shoulder. His eyes smouldered with anger, but he could not avenge himself: his miserable enemy lay grovelling on the stones whimpering.

'Don't hurt us! Don't let them hurt us, precious! They won't hurt us will they, nice little hobbitses? We didn't mean no harm, but they jumps on us like cats on poor mices, they did, precious. And we're so lonely, "gollum." We'll be nice to them, very nice, if they'll be nice to us, won't we, yes, yess.'

'Well, what's to be done with it?' said Sam. 'Tie it up, so as it can't come sneaking after us no more, I say.'

'But that would kill us, kill us,' whimpered Gollum. 'Cruel little hobbitses. Tie us up in the cold hard lands and leave us "gollum" "gollum."' Sobs welled up in his gobbling throat.

Glossary

Sting	This is the name of a special sword.
"gollum"	This is a sound that Gollum makes intermittently, hence his name.
precious	The word 'precious' is full of meaning in the story. The ring

that Frodo now has once belonged to Gollum. The ring is literally a 'precious' object, but the ring must be destroyed. However, when Gollum calls the ring 'precious,' he uses it as a term of endearment, as though it is a 'being,' such as a human being or something even more powerful. In addition to this, the ring has supernatural power over Gollum, so this has made him mentally ill, giving him a split personality. From this extract, it sounds like the ring is directly associated with one of Gollum's personalities which he also calls 'precious,' or he could even be speaking directly to the ring as it is near him.

'Tie it up, so as it can't come sneaking after us no more, I say.'

When Sam speaks, he does not speak in Standard English, but in a manner typical of some spoken forms of English even today. In (Spoken) Standard English it should be something like, 'I say tie it up, so it can't come sneaking after us again.'

The narrative in the extract is typical of today's Standard English.

Task 92

Gollum's speech is very unusual, as it uses plural forms in the wrong places. This is to convey the schizophrenic nature of Gollum, as though he has at least two personalities in one body. Not only does he use plural forms, and therefore increase the use of the letter 's' to indicate plurality, but he also increases the use of the 'sss' sound, resulting in a hissing reminiscent of a snake. In western thought, a snake is often associated with something sneaky, untrustworthy, dangerous and even evil. So the connotations we get from this passage are somewhat subliminal, yet very strong.

Correct the grammar in the following statements by Gollum, assuming he is talking to a human companion called Precious.

'Don't hurt us! Don't let them hurt us, precious!'

'They won't hurt us will they, nice little hobbitses?'

'We didn't mean no harm, but they jumps on use like cats on poor mices, they did, precious.'

'And we're so lonely …'

'We'll be nice to them, very nice, if they'll be nice to us, won't we, yes, yess.'

'But that would kill us, kill us …'

'Cruel little hobbitses. Tie us up in the cold hard lands and leave us …'

The Return of the King

The following extract is from *The Return of the King*. The armies of the Dark Lord are gathering. Men, Dwarves, Ents (walking, moving trees) and Elves come together to fight against him. Meanwhile, Frodo continues his journey to Mordor to destroy the evil Ring of Power, until he finally reaches Mount Doom.

Extract 93a

Then Frodo stirred and spoke with a clear voice, indeed with a voice clearer and more powerful than Sam had ever heard him use, and it rose above the throb and turmoil of Mount Doom, ringing in the roof and walls.

'I have come,' he said. 'But I do not choose now to do what I came to do. I will not do this deed. The Ring is mine!' And suddenly, as he set it on his finger, he vanished from Sam's sight. Sam gasped, but he had no chance to cry out, for at that moment many things happened.

Something struck Sam violently in the back, his legs were knocked from under him and he was flung aside …

… Sam got up. He was dazed, and blood streaming from his head dripped in his eyes. He groped forward, and then he saw a strange and terrible thing. Gollum on the edge of the abyss was fighting like a mad thing with an unseen

foe. To and fro he swayed, now so near the brink that almost he tumbled in, now dragging back, falling to the ground, rising, and falling again ...

Eventually, Gollum gets the ring back off Frodo and then accidentally stumbles into the burning abyss, destroying Gollum together with the ring.

This passage represents the Standard English of 1955 (65 years ago), so I have rewritten it below in today's English. I have underlined all the areas where changes have been necessary.

Extract 93b

Then Frodo stirred and spoke with a clear voice, indeed with a voice clearer and more powerful than Sam had ever heard him use, and it rose above the throb and turmoil of Mount Doom, ringing in the roof and walls.

'I have <u>arrived</u>,' he said. 'But I <u>have now decided not</u> to do what I came to do. I will not do <u>this</u>. The Ring is mine!' And suddenly, as he <u>put</u> it on his finger, he vanished from Sam's sight. Sam gasped, but he had no chance to cry out, for at that moment many things happened.

Something struck Sam violently in the back, his legs were knocked from under him and he was flung aside ...

... Sam got up. He was dazed, and blood streaming from his head dripped in his eyes. He groped forward, and then he saw a strange and terrible thing. Gollum on the edge of the abyss was fighting like a mad thing with an unseen foe. To and fro he swayed, now so near the brink that <u>he almost</u> tumbled in, now dragging back, falling to the ground, rising, and falling again ...

Task 93

To help you to remember the differences between 1955 English and today's English, write out a list of all the original words or phrases (from

Extract 93a) twinned with their corrections in Extract 93b (I have underlined the words and phrases to help you).

C.S. Lewis

C.S. Lewis (1898–1963) was born in Ireland; he studied at Oxford University, receiving a triple First Degree. He eventually became Professor of Mediaeval and Renaissance Literature at Cambridge University in 1954. He was an atheist until he became a Christian in 1929.

In regard to Jesus Christ he is remembered for the following quotation. C.S. Lewis said:

'A man who was merely a man and said the sort of things Jesus said wouldn't be a great moral teacher. He'd be either a lunatic — on a level with a man who says he's a poached egg — or else he'd be the Devil of Hell. You must make your choice. Either this man was, and is, the Son of God, or else a madman or something worse. You can shut him up for a fool, you can spit at him and kill him as a demon; or you can fall at his feet and call him Lord and God. But let us not come with any patronizing nonsense about his being a great human teacher. He has not left that open to us.'

C.S. Lewis is very famous for *The Chronicles of Narnia* series, which has spawned films and TV series. But he is also known for his other books such as *Surprised by Joy*, *The Problem of Pain*, and *The Screwtape Letters*.

The Screwtape Letters (1942) is a selection of fictional letters sent between demonic beings. Demonic beings are evil angels who hate God, the Creator of all things, and they will do everything in their power to stop people worshipping God. In the following extract (a series of highlighted parts of a chapter from the book), a senior demon (Screwtape) is writing a letter to his subordinate (Wormwood), giving instructions on how to stop humans (mortals) from praying, or if he cannot stop them from praying, make sure that their prayers are misdirected, because if the prayers of a mortal ('the patient') to their Creator ('the Enemy') are strong, that will cause the demons extreme problems.

Extract 94

My Dear Wormwood,

The amateurish suggestions in your last letter warn me that it is high time for me to write to you fully on the painful subject of prayer....

One of their poets, Coleridge, has recorded that he did not pray "with moving lips and bended knees" but merely "composed his spirit to love" and indulged "a sense of supplication". That is exactly the sort of prayer we want ...

It is funny how mortals always picture us as putting things into their minds: in reality our best work is done by keeping things out.

If this fails, you must fall back on subtler misdirection of his intention. Whenever they are attending to the Enemy Himself we are defeated, but there are ways of preventing them from doing so ...

I have known cases where what the patient called his "God" was actually located — up and to the left at the corner of the bedroom ceiling, or inside his own head, or in a crucifix on the wall. But whatever the nature of the composite object, you must keep him praying to it — to the thing that he has made, not to the Person who has made him ... or, if ... the man trusts himself to the completely real, external, invisible Presence, there with him in the room and never knowable by him as he is known by it — why, then it is that the incalculable may occur....

Your affectionate uncle
Screwtape.

Task 94

The senior demon Screwtape tells his subordinate Wormwood how to stop humans from getting close to God. Make a list of the advice he gives. Some of his suggestions may surprise you.

Unlike *Screwtape Letters*, C.S. Lewis' *Chronicles of Narnia* series was written for children. In the series' chronical order (not necessarily the order of publication), the first book to be read is, *The Magician's Nephew* (1955), in which two friends, Polly and Digory, explore the attic of an old house, where they meet someone who leads them to another world, one in which an evil sorceress tries to enslave them.

Next is *The Lion, the Witch and the Wardrobe* (1950), in which four children, Peter, Susan, Edmund and Lucy explore an old house. Lucy hides inside a wardrobe, but then she discovers that through the back of it is an entrance to the magical world of Narnia which is enslaved by the power of the White Witch. Aslan the lion sacrifices his life to save them.

The Horse and His Boy (1954) comes next. Bree, the talking horse, whisks Shasta away into dangerous adventures on their search for Narnia.

This book is followed by *Prince Caspian* (1951). In *Prince Caspian*, Peter, Susan, Lucy and Edmund are in Narnia when a Dwarf tells them that civil war is destroying Narnia. Spurned Prince Caspian gathers an army to remove the reign of a false king, but he needs the help of Aslan the lion.

Following this is *The Voyage of the Dawn Treader* (1952). Lucy and Edmund find themselves on a ship with Prince Caspian in his search for the seven friends of his father. They embark on a voyage to the very ends of the world, but they find that the world's end is only the beginning.

The Silver Chair (1953) comes next, in which the noble group of friends, through great dangers and deep, dark caverns, are sent to rescue the son of King Caspian who is held captive.

The series ends with *The Last Battle* (1956), in which the greatest battle of all will determine the future of the Kingdom of Narnia. Peter, Edmund and Lucy join Jill and Eustace to help defeat the enemy.

The following extract is taken from *The Magician's Nephew*.

Extract 95

First came the hansom, There was no one in the driver's seat. On the roof — not sitting, but standing on the roof — swaying with superb balance as it came at full speed round the corner with one wheel in the air — was Jadis the Queen of Queens and the Terror of Charn. Her teeth were bared, her eyes shone like fire, and her long hair streamed out behind her like a comet's tail. She was flogging the horse without mercy. Its nostrils were wide and red and its sides were spotted with foam. It galloped madly up to the front door, missing the lamp-post by an inch, and then reared up on its hind legs. The hansom crashed into the lamp-post and shattered into several pieces. The Witch, with a magnificent jump, had sprung clear just in time and landed on the horse's back. She settled herself astride and leaned forward, whispering things in its ear. They must have been things meant not to quieten it but to madden it. It was on its hind legs again in a moment, and its neigh was like a scream; it was all hoofs and teeth and eyes and tossing mane. Only a splendid rider could have stayed on its back.

Glossary

hansom — This is a two-wheeled horse-drawn carriage.
a splendid rider — an excellent rider

The English in this extract is representative of today's English, except in the use of the word 'splendid.'

Task 95

This extract describes the arrival and character of Jadis, the Queen of Queens, superbly. Read it several times and allow your imagination to picture the event in detail.

The most well-known book in the series is *The Lion, the Witch and the Wardrobe*, which has inspired so many people, from young to old.

Read the following extract from the book.

Extract 96

"This must be a simply enormous wardrobe!" thought Lucy, going still further in and pushing the soft folds of the coats aside to make room for her. Then she noticed that there was something crunching under her feet. "I wonder is that more mothballs?" she thought, stooping down to feel it with her hand. But instead of feeling the hard, smooth wood of the floor of the wardrobe, she felt something soft and powdery and extremely cold. "This is very queer," she said, and went on a step or two further.

Next moment she found that what was rubbing against her face and hands was no longer soft fur but something hard and rough and even prickly. "Why, it is just like branches of trees!" exclaimed Lucy. And then she saw that there was a light ahead of her; not a few inches away where the back of the wardrobe ought

Aslan, the great lion

to have been, but a long way off. Something cold and soft was falling on her. A moment later she found that she was standing in the middle of a wood at night-time with snow under her feet and snowflakes falling through the air.

The narrative is representative of today's English, but the speech is not typical of today's speech.

Task 96

Lucy's words are different to today's English. Study the examples of her speech below, and rewrite them in today's English.

"This must be a simply enormous wardrobe!"
"I wonder is that more mothballs?"
"This is very queer"
"Why, it is just like branches of trees!"

The following extract is taken from *The Silver Chair*, when the Witch changes into a great serpent.

Extract 97

The Prince caught the creature's neck in his left hand, trying to squeeze it till it choked. This held its face (if you could call it a face) about five inches from his own. The forked tongue flickered horribly in and out, but could not reach him. With his right hand he drew back his sword for the strongest blow he could give. Meanwhile Scrubb and Puddleglum had drawn their weapons and rushed to his aid. All three blows fell at once: Scrubb's (which did not even pierce the scales and did no good) on the body of the snake below the Prince's hand, but the Prince's own blow and Puddleglum's both on its neck. Even that did not quite kill it, though it began to loosen its hold on Rilian's legs and chest. With repeated blows they hacked off its head. The horrible thing went on coiling and moving like a bit of wire long *after it had died; and the floor, as you may imagine, was a nasty mess.*

Glossary

till   until

The extract represents 1953 Standard English. It is easily understood by today's native speakers of English, but the style of writing does feel old fashioned (i.e. not typical of novels today). I will pick out just a couple of examples:

One example is in the use of the word 'horrible;' the snake's *'forked tongue flickered horribly in and out.'* 'Horror' is an ideal word to use when describing evil, hideous events, but the adverb ('horribly') is not used very often — it was, however, common in the days of C.S. Lewis and Enid Blyton.

Another example is the following construction:

'All three blows fell at once: Scrubb's (which did not even pierce the scales and did no good) on the body of the snake below the Prince's hand, but the Prince's own blow and Puddleglum's both on its neck.

Today's readers (apart from experts in the study of English Literature) may struggle to retain all the information on the first reading due to the unfamiliar sentence structure. Their minds may be more adjusted to something like the following:

'All three blows struck at the same time: Scrubb's blow hit the body of the snake below the Prince's hand, although it was useless because it did not even pierce the scales, but both the Prince's own blow and Puddleglum's struck its neck.'

Can you see the difference? Does it feel more comfortable to read? This latter adaption is more typical of today's literature.

Task 97

Here are the two versions of the selected sentence from the extract again. The first is the original from 1953, the second is my adaption for today's readers. Study the two versions, compare them carefully, and write comments on what changes have been made, and why?

C.S. Lewis

'All three blows fell at once: Scrubb's (which did not even pierce the scales and did no good) on the body of the snake below the Prince's hand, but the Prince's own blow and Puddleglum's both on its neck.'

Adapted Version

'All three blows struck at the same time: Scrubb's blow hit the body of the snake below the Prince's hand, although it was useless because it did not even pierce the scales, but both the Prince's own blow and Puddleglum's struck its neck.'

The following extract is taken from *The Last Battle*, with the following characters: King Tirian, the last King of Narnia; Jewel the Unicorn; Puzzle the Donkey; and Farsight the Eagle.

Extract 98

"Kiss me, Jewel," he said. "For certainly this is our last night on earth. And if ever I offended against you in any matter great or small, forgive me now."

"Dear King," said the Unicorn, "I could almost wish you had, so that I might forgive it. If Aslan gave me my choice I would choose no other life than the life I have had and no other death than the one we go to."

Then they woke up Farsight, who was asleep with his head under his wing (it made him look as if he had no head at all), and crept forward to the stable. They left Puzzle (not without a kind word, for no one was angry with him now) *just behind it, telling him not to move till someone came to fetch him, and took up their position at one end of the stable.*

Glossary

For certainly this is offended against	Because this is definitely offended
"I could almost wish you had, so that I might forgive it."	"I almost wish you had, so that I could forgive you."
till	until
fetch	get

Task 98

There is an interesting sentiment in this extract: The King asks Jewel the Unicorn to forgive him if he has ever offended her. She said she almost wishes he had offended her so she could forgive him. They clearly loved and trusted one another, even if they were not perfect.

How easy do you find it to forgive a person who has offended you? Discuss this with your partner. You will need to consider things such as:

What is forgiveness?

What is the difference between forgiveness and trust?

What are the connections between forgiveness and trust?

How does forgiveness help you personally, whether you are the guilty or innocent party?

How does forgiveness help the other person in the dispute?

Is there anyone you need to forgive today?

Additional Notes for Unit 7
第7单元附加注释

Spoken English

There are differences between the various 'Standard Englishes' of the world. These standard varieties include Standard English English (The Standard English of England), Standard Scottish English and Standard US English, among others. But the differences between Standard Englishes are not as great as one would imagine. There are far more differences between the regional nonstandard varieties, but even they have more similarities to Standard English than divergencies from it.

Another important observation to make is the fact that standardisation of any variety of English is primarily based on written rather than spoken English, as spoken English often mixes standard and nonstandard elements, for example, in the use of colloquialisms.

Having said that, there are many studies examining the differences in pronunciation between the world's standard varieties. 'Received Pronunciation' (RP), the standard pronunciation of England, is often used to help with this comparison, but we must bear in mind the fact that even RP has variants of its own, and as far as linguists are concerned, all accents undergo change and are never absolute.

Amongst the member states of the Commonwealth of Nations, there are significant variants in pronunciation between their respective standard varieties. Variation in intonation is also significant. For example, Australian English has a distinctive intonation feature in the use of a High Rising Tone at the end of declarative sentences. If we were to hear a sentence like, 'I didn't think it was her fault,' the last word would be pronounced with a high intonation in Australian English, even though the speaker is not asking a question.

Singaporean English has what could be described as a 'staccato' effect. Words in a sentence are individually pronounced and cut off from each other. This is partly due to the use of the <u>glottal stop</u> when Singaporeans omit the verbalisation of consonants (especially consonants at the end of words). When this type of speech is written down, an apostrophe replaces the consonant, for example, *what* is written as *wha'*.

Additional Task E

Throughout this text book, I have added glossaries to the various extracts. Sometimes I have described the meanings of words and phrases, but most of the time, I have given an alternative word or phrase. It might be useful to write a list of all the alternative phrases I have provided in the glossaries under the extracts. The resulting list will give you a stock of phrases to use in your own writing and speaking, at the same time helping you to avoid common mistakes that learners of English (as a second language) make by relying on old literary sources.

Work through the text book now and write your list of phrases typical of today's modern English.

Glossary for Unit 7

schwa 非重读央元音、弱读央元音

The schwa is represented as an upside-down 'e' in the IPA (International Phonetic Alphabet). An example of the sound can be found in the pronunciation of the word 'about;' the 'a' in 'about' is an unstressed syllable, and it has a schwa-sound.

Salisbury Plain 索尔兹伯里平原

This is a plain in the southern county of Wiltshire in England. The world-famous Stonehenge (a megalithic stone circle monument whose origins began 5,000 years ago) is situated on Salisbury Plain.

Alfred Hitchcock 阿尔弗雷德·希区柯克

Alfred Hitchcock (1899−1980) was an English film director and producer as well as a screenwriter. He was born in Essex, England. He was referred to as 'The Master of Suspense,' and directed over 50 films such as *The 39 Steps* in 1935 and *The Lady Vanishes* in 1938. He was eventually persuaded to move to the US, after which he produced *Vertigo* in 1954, *North by Northwest* in 1959, and his iconic *Psycho* in 1960. Hitchcockian style includes using the camera to mimic the movement of a person's gaze.

glottal stop 喉塞音

This is a type of consonantal sound produced by obstructing airflow in the vocal tract.

Unit 8

Literature from Late 20th to Early 21st Century　20世纪下半叶到21世纪初的文学

Chapter 22　The 1950s
第22章　20世纪50年代

Chapter 23　The 1960s to 1990s
第23章　20世纪60—90年代

Chapter 24　Translations and a Resurgence of Murder Mysteries
第24章　谋杀推理小说的翻译与复兴

Chapter 25　The 21st Century
第25章　21世纪

Additional Notes for Unit 8
第8单元附加注释

Chapter 22　The 1950s
第22章　20世纪50年代

This final Unit looks at English Literature from 1950 until today, officially named the Late Modern English Period. In this Unit you will see lots of extracts that use English very familiar to today's native speakers. However, the first few extracts we meet here still display what could be considered to be old fashioned English language.

本书最后一个单元介绍的是从1950年到今天的英国文学,该时期被称为现代英语晚期。在本单元中,你将看到许多英文节选。这些节选对如今英语为母语的读者来说耳熟能详。但所列的前几篇仍可能被认为是过时的英语。

John Wyndham

John Wyndham (1903-1969), a science fiction writer from England, wrote the well-known novel called *The Day of the Triffids* (1951). In the story, Bill Masen wakes up in hospital blindfolded, but after removing his bandages he realises—ironically—that he is the only person who can see; everyone else, including the other patients and even the doctors, are blind due to having watched a meteor shower in the sky. In fact this blindness has affected the entire world. This makes it easier for alien plants called Triffids to get away with walking around the earth and eating human beings. The novel was made into a feature film in 1962, and 2 TV series in 1981 and 2009. It was also adapted for radio.

Wyndham also wrote *The Kraken Wakes* (1953) about the world being drowned by rising sea levels, *The Chrysalids* (1955) which is about genetic mutation, and *The Midwich Cuckoos* (1957) which was adapted for film twice under the title *Village of the Damned*.

The following extract is from *The Day of the Triffids*.

Extract 99

When it 'walked' it moved rather like a man on crutches. Two of the blunt 'legs' slid forward, then the whole thing lurched as the rear one drew almost level with them, then the two in front slid forward again. At each 'step' the long stem whipped violently back and forth: it gave one a kind of seasick feeling to watch it. As a method of progress it looked both strenuous and clumsy — faintly reminiscent of young elephants at play. One felt that if it were to go on lurching for long in that fashion it would be bound to strip all its leaves if it did not actually break its stem. Nevertheless, ungainly though it looked, it was contriving to cover the ground at something like an average walking pace.

....

About ten minutes after I got home I was digging round our triffid, carefully loosening the earth near it to encourage it to 'walk.'

Unfortunately there was an aspect of this self-propelled plant discovery which the news-reel people had either not experienced, or chosen for some reason of their own not to reveal. There was no warning, either. I was bending down intent on clearing the earth without harming the plant, when something from nowhere hit me one terrific slam, and knocked me out ...

I woke up to find myself in bed, with my mother, my father, and the doctor watching me anxiously. My head felt as if it were split open, I was aching all over, and, as I later discovered, one side of my face was decorated with a blotchy-red raised weal.

Task 99

The following quotations are taken from the above *The Day of the*

Triffids extract. The English is not typical of today. Spend some time working out how to rewrite them in today's English before recording your adaptions on paper.

'... it gave one a kind of seasick feeling to watch it.'

'As a method of progress it looked both strenuous and clumsy'

'One felt that if it were to go on lurching for long in that fashion it would be bound to strip all its leaves'

'... it was contriving to cover the ground at something like an average walking pace.'

'... hit me one terrific slam'

Dylan Thomas

Dylan Thomas (1914-1953) was a famous Welsh writer and poet, who wrote exclusively in English. He was born in Swansea, Wales, and is well-known for his poem *Do Not Go Gentle into that Good Night* (1952). His radio recordings for the BBC during the late 1940s brought him to the attention of the public.

His poem *Do Not Go Gentle into that Good Night* was part of a collection of his works entitled *In Country Sleep, And Other Poems* (1952). The poem is believed to have been written for his dying father, encouraging him not to give up without a fight. The title of the six-stanza poem is also a refrain throughout. The first two lines of the poem are:

'Do not go gentle into that good night,
Old age should burn and rave at close of day.'

Ian Fleming

Ian Fleming (1908-1964), was a British author born in London, who later worked in British Intelligence. He is famous for his James Bond series which has inspired over thirty feature films throughout the last 6 decades. *Casino Royale*, published in 1953, was Fleming's first Bond novel, and several feature films were based on this book alone. Fleming also wrote the children's story *Chitty Chitty Bang Bang: The Magical Car* (1964), which was made into a musical film in 1968. The script of the film was actually written by Roald Dahl of *Charlie and the Chocolate Factory* fame.

His James Bond books are as follows:

Casino Royale (1953)

Live and Let Die (1954)

Moonraker (1955)

Diamonds are Forever (1956)

From Russia with Love (1957)

Doctor No (1958)

Goldfinger (1959)

For your Eyes Only (1960)

Thunderball (1961)

The Spy Who Loved Me (1962)

On Her Majesty's Secret Service (1963)

You Only Live Twice (1964)

The Man with the Golden Gun (1965)

Octopussy and The Living Daylights (1966)

All of these books have been made into film and more titles have been added into the Bond franchise.

In *Casino Royale*, James Bond (Secret Agent 007—pronounced "double 'o' seven") is on a mission to thwart Le Chiffre, a banker who supports terrorists, by winning against him at the baccarat table (in a poker game) at the casino of the same name. This would remove a fortune from him, money that he would otherwise use for evil purposes. Below is an extract from *Casino Royale*, in which Bond gets ready in his hotel room before going downstairs to the restaurant to have dinner with a beautiful young lady called Vesper.

Extract 100

Bond walked up to his room, which again showed no sign of trespass, threw off his clothes, took a long hot bath followed by an ice-cold shower and lay down on his bed. There remained an hour in which to rest and compose his thoughts before he met the girl in the Splendide bar, an hour to examine minutely the details of his plans for the game, and for after the game, in all the various circumstances of victory or defeat ...

As he tied his thin, double-ended, black satin tie, he paused for a moment and examined himself levelly in the mirror. His grey-blue eyes looked calmly back with a hint of ironical inquiry ....

....

'And now have you decided what you would like to have for dinner? Please be expensive,' he added as he sensed her hesitation, 'or you'll let down that beautiful frock.'

'I'd made two choices, she laughed, 'and either would have been delicious, but behaving like a millionaire occasionally is a wonderful treat and if you're sure ... well, I'd like to start with caviar and then have a plain grilled rognon de veau with pommes souffles. And then I'd like to have fraises des bois with a lot of cream. Is it very shameless to be so certain and so expensive?' She smiled at him inquiringly.

'It's a virtue, and anyway it's only a good plain wholesome meal.' He turned to the maitre d' hotel, 'and bring plenty of toast.'

'The trouble always is,' he explained to Vesper, 'not how to get enough caviar, but how to get enough toast with it.'

Glossary

Splendide bar 'splendide' is the French for 'splendid' or 'magnificent.' The French word has a capital letter here, so it must be the name of the bar, meaning 'Splendid Bar.' But this sounds peculiar in English, so if a bar in England were to have a name conveying the same sentiment, it could be called, 'The Bar of Magnificence,' although it would sound a little <u>tongue-in-cheek</u>. Something like, 'Paradise Lounge,' would be more likely.

or you'll let down that beautiful frock To 'let down' here means to 'disappoint.' 'Frock' is an old fashioned word for 'dress.' So, an updated version of this clause would be: '... or you'll let down that beautiful dress.'

maitre d' hotel This is the French for a restaurant attendant.

There is good British humour in the James Bond books, this also being an essential ingredient in most film adaptions. Combining this humour with what are very serious spy stories creates a winning formula.

This passage uses a lot of French names for dishes in the restaurant. Actually, French cuisine is also very important in restaurants in Bond's own home country of England, French terminology always being part of an expensive British restaurant's menu.

Task 100

Update this extract into today's English. Note that the French does not need to be translated, as the author intends the French names to be present to carefully construct an accurate context.

William Golding

Sir William Golding (1911-1993) was a novelist, playwright and poet who was born in Cornwall in England. He studied English Literature at Oxford University, and was a Nobel Prize winner for Literature in 1983. Among his various novels, Golding is best known for his *Lord of the Flies* (1954), an <u>allegorical</u>, <u>dystopian</u> novel, in which a group of British boys are stuck on an uninhabited island. They try to govern themselves, with disastrous results; they forget all the typical civilised behaviour they have been taught and start to kill each other. By using the community of children symbolically, Golding is trying to convey the message that human nature is flawed, and that that is why 'normal' society has terrible problems.

The term 'Lord of the Flies' comes from the word 'Beelzebub,' which also means '(Evil) Prince of Demons.'

Philippa Pearce

Philippa Pearce (1920–2006), from England, was a writer of children's books. She is very well-known for her story, *Tom's Midnight Garden* (1958). In this story, the grandfather clock strikes thirteen while everyone is asleep. Tom, who is staying at his aunt and uncle's house for the summer, hears the clock, and goes out of the house to find a Midnight Garden. He keeps revisiting this garden every time the clock strikes thirteen, and befriends a girl called Hatty who is from a different time. She grows much older every time he sees her, until eventually she does not see him. Is she a ghost? Or is Tom the ghost?

The following extract is taken from *Tom's Midnight Garden*.

Extract 101

Every night now Tom slipped downstairs to the garden. At first he used to be afraid that it might not be there. Once, with his hand already upon the garden door to open it, he turned back ...

...but, later the same night, he had forced himself to go again and open the door: there the garden was. It had not failed him.

He saw the garden at many times of its day, and at different seasons — its favourite season was summer, with perfect weather. In earliest summer hyacinths were still out in the crescent beds on the lawn, and wallflowers in the round ones. Then the hyacinths bowed and died; and the wallflowers were uprooted, and stocks and asters bloomed in their stead. There was a clipped box bush by the greenhouse, with a cavity like a great mouth cut into the side of it; this was stacked full of pots of geraniums in flower. Along the sundial path, heavy red poppies came out, and roses; and, in summer dusk, the evening primroses glimmered like little moons. In the latest summer the pears on the wall were muffled in muslin bags for safe ripening.

Glossary

and at different seasons	and in different seasons
in their stead	in their place
In the latest summer	Last summer

Task 101

Imagine that when you were a child, you found a Midnight Garden and met a child of the same age with whom you became very friendly. But he/she became older each night by 2 or 3 years. What do you think would happen eventually? Discuss all the possible outcomes you can think of with your study-partner.

Chapter 23　The 1960s to 1990s
第23章　20世纪60—90年代

From this point, we meet many examples of literature that are completely representative of today's written and spoken English.

The British children's writer called Roald Dahl (1916–1990) spent his childhood in Wales. He is very famous for books such as *Charlie and the Chocolate Factory* (1964), *Matilda* (1988) and countless more, many of which have been made into films.

Charlie and the Chocolate Factory

Charlie and the Chocolate Factory has been made into several films. It has characters such as the child called Charlie Bucket, the hero of the story, and of course Mr Willy Wonka who owns the chocolate factory, and his workers called 'Oompa-Loopas.' Other significant child-characters are Augustus Gloop, the greedy boy; Mike Teavee, who does nothing but watch television; Veruca Salt, who is spoiled by her parents; and Violet Beauregarde who chews chewing-gum all day long.

Extract 102

Charlie saw a long table, and on the table there were rows and rows of small white square-shaped sweets. The sweets looked very much like square sugar lumps — except that each of them had a funny little pink face painted on one side. At the end of the table, a number of Oompa-Loompas were busily painting more *faces on more sweets.*

'There you are!' cried Mr Wonka. 'Square sweets that look round!'

'They don't look round to me,' said Mike Teavee.

'They look square,' said Veruca Salt. 'They look completely square.'

'But they are square,' said Mr Wonka. 'I never said they weren't.'

'You said they were round!' said Veruca Salt.

'I never said anything of the sort,' said Mr Wonka. 'I said they looked round.'

'But they don't look round!' said Veruca Salt. 'They look square!'

'They look round,' insisted Mr Wonka.

'They most certainly do not look round!' cried Veruca Salt.

'Veruca, darling,' said Mrs Salt, 'pay no attention to Mr Wonka! He's lying to you!'

'My dear old fish,' said Mr Wonka, 'go and boil your head!'

'How dare you speak to me like that!' shouted Mrs Salt.

'Oh, do shut up,' said Mr Wonka. 'Now watch this!'

He took a key from his pocket, and unlocked the door, and flung it open ... and suddenly ... at the sound of the door opening, all the rows of little square sweets looked quickly round to see who was coming in.

The English in this extract is representative of today's English even though it was published in 1964.

Task 102

Do you understand the 'play on words' regarding the 'square sweets that look round'? Explain it to your partner in your own words.

At the end of the story, Mr Wonka gives his entire chocolate factory to Charlie, who is from a poor family, because he was the most honest, best behaved child who visited his factory, and because Mr Wonka had no children of his own to give the factory to.

Matilda

The following extract is from Roald Dahl's *Matilda*. Matilda is a school pupil of the evil headmistress Miss Trunchbull, but she has special powers to save herself and her classmates from Trunchbull's bullying.

Extract 103

'Eight threes,' the Trunchbull shouted, swinging Wilfred from side to side by his ankle, 'eight threes is the same as three eights and three eights are twenty-four! Repeat that!'

At that moment Nigel, at the other end of the room, jumped to his feet and started pointing excitedly at the blackboard and screaming, 'The chalk! The chalk! Look at the chalk! It's moving all on its own!'

So hysterical and shrill was Nigel's scream that everyone in the place, including the Trunchbull, looked up at the blackboard. And there, sure enough, a brand-new piece of chalk was hovering near the grey-black writing surface of the blackboard.

'It's writing something!' screamed Nigel. 'The chalk is writing something!'

And indeed it was.

'What the blazes is this?' yelled the Trunchbull. It had shaken her to see her own name being written like that by an invisible hand. She dropped Wilfred on to the floor. Then she yelled at nobody in particular, 'Who's doing this? Who's writing it?'

The chalk continued to write.

Everyone in the place heard the gasp that came from the Trunchbull's throat. 'No!' she cried.

Glossary

Eight threes	'Eight threes' and 'three eights' is a normal way to express multiplication in Mathematics. It means '8×3' and '3×8,' respectively. Other ways to say this are 'eight times three' 'three times eight' 'eight multiplied by three,' and 'three multiplied by eight.' The mathematical way to say 'the same as,' is 'equals,' represented by the symbol '=' giving $8 \times 3 = 24$ and $3 \times 8 = 24$.
the Trunchbull	The use of the definite article 'the' and the surname of the headmistress without her title 'Miss' is very derogatory.

The English in this extract is representative of today's English. Roald Dahl's books are used extensively in Primary Schools in western education.

Task 103

After reading and carefully analysing the extract, use your imagination and try to guess what the chalk is going to write and why. Share your ideas with your study-partner.

Richard Adams

Richard Adams (1920–2016), born in Berkshire, England, was famous for his survival and adventure novel *Watership Down* (1972), a story that he originally told his children on a long car journey. It is set around Hampshire in southern England. The story features a group of rabbits who live in their natural environment, but they have human-like characteristics: they have their own culture, language, proverbs and poetry. The rabbits attempt to escape their warren, which is going to be destroyed, to find a new home on the hill of Watership Down.

The following extract is from *Watership Down*.

Extract 104

In the first moments after they had recognized the poor creature under the hemlock, Hazel and Dandelion felt completely stupefied, as though they had come upon a squirrel underground or a stream that flowed uphill. They could not trust their senses. The voice in the dark had proved not to be supernatural, but the reality was frightening enough. How could Captain Holly be here, at the foot of the down? And what could have reduced him — of all rabbits — to this state?

Hazel pulled himself together. Whatever the explanation might be, the immediate need was to take first things first. They were in open country, at night, away from any refuge but an overgrown ditch, with a rabbit who smelt of blood, was crying uncontrollably and looked as though he could not move. There might very well be a stoat on his trail at this moment. If they were going to help him they had better be quick.

Glossary

down	The downlands in the south of England are an open area of chalk hills in the countryside.
pulled himself together	This is a common way to say that a person forced himself/herself to think rationally and not to be overcome with a particular problem.
take first things first	This is a common way to say, 'do things one step at a time.'

This extract is representative of today's English.

Task 104

The following grammatical structure may not be familiar to you. Can you explain—using your own words—exactly what this statement means?

'They were in open country, at night, away from any refuge but an overgrown ditch.'

Douglas Adams

Douglas Adams (1952–2001) was a writer and dramatist from England. He created the popular comedy science fiction series called *The Hitchhikers Guide to the Galaxy*. It began as a radio comedy broadcast on BBC Radio 4 in 1978, then it later developed into a series of 5 books, and also generated a TV series. The titles of the 5 books are:

The Hitchhiker's Guide to the Galaxy
The Restaurant at the End of the Universe
Life, the Universe, and Everything
So Long, and Thanks for all the Fish
Mostly Harmless

The humour in this series of books can be immediately seen in the book titles themselves. For example, book 1 suggests that someone could hitchhike to places anywhere in our galaxy, just like a person who is <u>thumbing a lift</u> to merely travel from one city to another. The size of the galaxy makes this concept ridiculous and therefore funny.

Task 105a

Can you identify the humour in the other four book titles? Explain the humour for each one in the same way that I have done for book 1.

In the first book of the series, *The Hitchhiker's Guide to the Galaxy* (1979), the earth gets demolished to make way for a hyperspace bypass. After his house is demolished, Arthur Dent begins to find out more about our strange galaxy. In the extract below, from the first book in the series, the readers are introduced to the Babel Fish as a helpful ear parasite. A couple of brief sections have been removed for ease of reading.

Extract 105

[Ford said,] 'You'd better be prepared for the jump into hyperspace. It's unpleasantly like being drunk.'

'What's so unpleasant about being drunk?'

'You ask a glass of water.'

Arthur thought about this.

'Ford,' he said.

'Yeah?'

'What's this fish doing in my ear?'

'It's translating for you. It's a Babel fish. Look it up in the book if you like.'

He tossed over 'The Hitchhiker's Guide to the Galaxy' and then curled up into a foetal ball to prepare himself for the jump.

At that moment the bottom fell out of Arthur's mind.

His eyes turned inside out. His feet began to leak out of the top of his head.

The room folded flat around him, spun around, shifted out of existence, and left him sliding into his own navel.

They were passing through hyperspace.

'The Babel fish,' said 'The Hitchhiker's Guide to the Galaxy,' quietly, '... feeds on brainwave energy received not from its carrier but from those around it. It absorbs all unconscious mental frequencies from this brainwave energy to nourish itself with. ... The practical upshot of all this is that if you stick a Babel fish in your ear you can instantly understand anything said to you in any form of language. ...

'Meanwhile, the poor Babel fish, by effectively removing all barriers to communication between different races and cultures, has caused more and bloodier wars than anything else in the history of creation.'

Glossary

You ask a glass of water This imperative form is the same as saying 'Ask a glass of water, and see what it says to you.'

Babel This name comes from a story in the Old Testament section of the Holy Bible. In its original language, Hebrew, 'Babel' (later called 'Babylon') is the name given to a city that was being built by humankind to construct a tower to reach Heaven. This tower is referred to as the Tower of Babel. God confounded this attempt by confusing their languages so that people could no longer understand each other. The word 'Babel' was later used to create the English verb 'to babble,' meaning to talk senselessly.

This extract is representative of today's English.

Task 105b

Do you understand the play on words joke about 'being drunk'? Discuss it with your partner.

Task 105c

Do you agree with the passage that if all communication barriers were removed between countries, there would be MORE wars? Why? Why not? Discuss this with your group.

Chapter 24　Translations and a Resurgence of Murder Mysteries
第24章　谋杀推理小说的翻译与复兴

Ruth Rendell CBE (1930-2015), was born in Essex, England, and was a famous author of psychological thrillers and murder mysteries, especially her Chief Inspector Wexford novels which produced a popular TV series. The first novel in her Wexford series was called *From Doon with Death* (1964). One of her novels not connected with the Wexford series was *Tigerlily's Orchids* (2010), her 60th published novel, from which we will see an extract in the last chapter of this book.

Caroline Graham, the English playwright, screenwriter and novelist, was born in Nuneaton, England in 1931. She studied at the University of Birmingham, and with the Open University (like me). *The Killings of Badger's Drift* (1987) was the first in a series of novels about Chief Inspector Barnaby, a series that was dramatised for TV under the name *Midsomer Murders*. The stories are typical Whodunnit Murder Mysteries, a genre which is always very popular in the western world.

Titles from her published Chief Inspector Barnaby series of novels:

The Killings of Badger's Drift (1987)

Death of a Hollow Man (1989)

Death in Disguise (1992)

Written in Blood (1994)

Faithful unto Death (1996)

A Place of Safety (1999)

A Ghost in the Machine (2004)

Colin Dexter

The British author Colin Dexter OBE (1930–2017). He graduated from Cambridge University in 1953. His first published book was *Last Bus to Woodstock* (1975). This marked the beginning of his Inspector Morse series, from which the hugely popular TV series called *Inspector Morse* arose (from 1987–2000), in which John Thaw played Morse. This in turn inspired two spin-off TV series, one called *Lewis*, featuring Morse's former sergeant, and a prequal called *Endeavour*, featuring Inspector Morse in his younger days.

Here is a list of Colin Dexter's Inspector Morse mystery novels (from 1975–1999):

Last Bus to Woodstock
Last Seen Wearing
The Silent World of Nicholas Quinn
Service of All the Dead
The Dead of Jericho
The Riddle of the Third Mile
The Secret of Annex 3
The Wench Is Dead
The Jewel that Was Ours
The Way Through the Woods
The Daughters of Cain
Death Is Now My Neighbour
The Remorseful Day

The following extract is taken from *The Daughters of Cain* (1994). As was often the case, Chief Superintendent Strange believed not enough progress had been made on the case; in his opinion, nothing had been achieved since the discovery of a dead body in a flat in Oxford, killed by a single stab wound to the stomach. But Chief Inspector Morse and his sergeant, Lewis, discovered new information about the death of Dr Felix McClure.

In this extract, the teacher Julia Stevens is looking through her pupils' exam results. The style of English used in the passage fits snugly with how people view Oxford, the home of Oxford University, around which the 'Morse' novels are based. Therefore, the narrative sounds very academic, more academic than would be expected in everyday life. It gives the impression that an elderly academic gentleman with old fashioned values is describing the events in a providential manner. This is also how 'Morse' himself is portrayed in the novels and TV series.

Extract 106

Like every self-respecting teacher, she wanted to discover the relative success of the pupils she herself had taught.

In former days it had often been difficult enough for some pupils to sit examinations, let alone pass them. And even in the comparatively recent years of Julia's girlhood several of her own classmates had been deemed not to possess the requisite acumen even to attempt the 11 Plus. It was a question of the sheep and the goats — just like the division between those who were lost and those who were saved in the New Testament — a work with which the young Julia had become increasingly familiar, through the crusading fervour of a local curate with whom (aged ten and a half) she had fallen passionately in love.

How things had changed.

Now, in 1994, it was an occasion for considerable surprise if anyone somehow managed to fail an examination. Indeed, to be recorded in the Unclassified ranks of the GCSE was, in Julia's view, a feat of quite astonishing incompetence, which carried with it a sort of bravura badge of monumental under-achievement....

She looked through 5C's English results. Very much as she'd expected. Then looked a little more closely at the results of the only pupil in the class whose name had begun with 'C'. Costyn, K: Religious Education, 'Unclassified': English, 'D'; Maths, 'Unclassified'; Geography, 'Unclassified'; Metalwork, 'Unclassified'. Well, at least he'd got something — after twelve years of schooling ... thirty-six terms. But it was difficult to imagine him getting much further than the Job Centre. Nowhere else for him to go, was there — except to jail, perhaps?

Glossary

11 Plus	This is an examination (exam) taken by some 11 year old school pupils to see if they are strong enough academically to go to a Grammar School instead of a local Secondary School.
GCSE	This stands for 'General Certificate of Secondary Education.'
bravura	This is the Italian for 'skill'.

In this extract, some aspects of the educational system of England are mentioned. In Julia's childhood (prior to 1994), it was difficult for some of her classmates to be even considered academically strong enough to have been permitted to take the 11 Plus exam. The writer likens this distinction between school pupils (students) to the New Testament section of the Bible's prophesy of the separation between the saved and the lost people at the Last Judgement (the sheep and the goats, respectively). But this strict distinction in regard to education was no longer in place in 1994, according to the writer, as it had become more difficult to fail an exam.

In 1994 (and now), at 16 years of age, students took exams called GCSEs ('General Certificate of Secondary Education' examinations). An extremely low score would grant the label 'unclassified,' in other words utterly useless. In the extract, Julia the Secondary School teacher, is checking the results of her pupils. One class was called '5C.' From among the pupils in that class, she looked at K. Costyn's GCSE results. He had not taken many exams and they were all fails (unclassified) except for a pass (albeit a low grade) in English. The author refers to twelve years of schooling, which is the same as thirty-six terms. This is because each school year in England consists of three terms (not two semesters). Julia, the teacher, considered that K. Costyn's chances of getting a good job were very low, so he would need to go to the 'Job Centre' (a place to go for assistance in finding a lower paid job). Julia would not be surprised if he ended up in prison because of his behaviour.

Task 106

The educational system in England is frequently changing. For example, in the extract above K. Costyn acquired grade D in English, but the grading system for GCSEs is different now.

Read Rebekah Benson's article about England's Educational System for 11–18 year olds today at the end of this Unit under 'Additional Notes for Unit 8.' The name of her article is 'Secondary Education in England.'

English Translations of Ancient Greek and Latin Classics

There have been many great translations of western literature throughout the history of the English language, and these translations have had a huge influence throughout the west in the areas of language and culture. Translators of ancient Latin and Greek works are among those worth mentioning here.

One example is David West (1926–2013) who was born in Aberdeen and then educated in Scotland as well as Cambridge University in England. He became Professor of Latin at Newcastle University. He has translated many classics, one of which was *The Aeneid* (1990).

The Aeneid was originally written by Virgil (born in 70 BC) in Latin, for the purpose of honouring the Roman Emperor Augustus by praising Aeneas, the emperor's ancestor. Augustus is credited with the beginning of the Roman Empire in 27 BC, which at its peak included lands in Europe, Africa and Asia, until it was divided in 395 AD.

The original Latin work was completed a couple of decades before the birth of Jesus Christ, and a thousand years after Homer's two ancient Greek epics, *The Iliad*, and *The Odyssey*, in whose style *The Aeneid* was written.

The story concerns Aeneas who lived over 3,000 years ago in the city of Troy, also called Ilium, which was located where today's Turkey lies. But Troy was finally defeated after ten years of fighting by the Greeks, the cunning Greek soldier Ulixes (Ulysses/Odysseus) having devised the plan to construct the Trojan Horse. The Trojans took the giant wooden horse into their city in spite of the warnings given by Laocoon the priest of Neptune (Neptune is the Roman name for the Greek god Poseidon), who said they should never trust the Greeks.

Aeneas survived the defeat of Troy (Ilium) and fled with his father and son, eventually meeting and falling in love with Queen Dido of Carthage, located in northern Africa.

After many years of wandering, Aeneas arrived in Italy and fought against the peoples of Latium (the Latin people) before making an alliance with them, thereby founding his city of Lavinium. Over three hundred years later, in 753 BC, the city of Rome was founded by Aeneas' descendant Romulus, the twin brother of Remus. Romulus and Remus are said to have been weaned by a she-wolf after they were abandoned. The name 'Rome' comes from the name 'Romulus.'

The Aeneid

Here is a group of extracts from West's translation of *The Aeneid*, in which he stays faithful to the original Latin. The extracts concern the story of the Trojan Horse.

Extract 107

Year after year the leaders of the Greeks had been broken in war and denied by the Fates, until, with the aid of the divine skill of Pallas Athene, they built a horse the size of a mountain, cutting pine trees to weave into it for ribs. They pretended it was a votive offering for their safe return to Greece ... Then they chose some men by lot from their best warriors and shut them up in the darkness of its belly, filling the vast cavern of its womb with armed soldiers.

Laocoon came running down in a blaze of fury from the heights of the citadel, shouting ... 'O you poor fools! Are you out of your minds, you Trojans? Do you seriously believe that your enemies have sailed away? Do you imagine Greeks ever give gifts without some devious purpose? Is this all you know about Ulixes? I tell you there are Greeks hiding in her, shut up in all this wood ... or else there is some other trick we cannot see. Do not trust the horse, Trojans. Whatever it is, I am afraid of Greeks, even when they bear gifts.'

We breached the walls and laid open the buildings of our city. ... setting wheels to roll beneath the horse's feet and stretching ropes of flax to its neck. The engine of Fate mounted our walls, teeming with armed men.

Sinon ... stealthily undid the pine bolts of the horse and freed the Greeks from its womb. The wooden horse was open, and the Greeks were pouring gratefully out of its hollow chambers into the fresh air ... fierce Ulixes sliding down the rope they had lowered, and ... Menelaus and Epeos himself, the maker of the horse that tricked the Trojans.

Glossary

Ulixes This is one of several versions of the name of Odysseus, the form 'Ulixes' reflecting the Latin original. Another form of the name that we have met in this book is Ulysses. It was Ulixes that thought up the successful battle plan for the construction of the Trojan Horse.

Sinon Sinon had been left behind by the Greeks to persuade the Trojans to take the huge wooden horse, secretly containing Greek soldiers, into the city of Troy.

The Trojan horse

Task 107

The Trojan Horse story is clearly expressed in the selection of extracts. Summarise the content of the extracts and put them together into one complete, continuous narrative. There are approximately 300 words in Extract 107; a summary of 200 words is adequate.

The Iliad and The Odyssey

Homer (c.700 BC) is considered to be the poet of these two ancient, epic Greek poems, *The Iliad* and *The Odyssey*. *The Iliad* is the story of Achilles, the Greeks' greatest warrior 3,000 years ago, at the beginning of the ten year Trojan War. This war was fought between the Greeks and the Trojans (the same war as that from which Aeneas escaped in *The Aeneid*). Helen, the beautiful wife of Menelaus, had been abducted by Paris of Troy, so, the Greeks sailed to Troy to recover Helen, this being the sole reason for the ten year war. The Trojan War ended with the plot using the Trojan Horse, causing Troy to be burnt to the ground. Helen is said to have been 'the face that launched a thousand ships,' by one of William Shakespeare's contemporaries called Christopher Marlowe (1564–1593), also a poet and playwright from England. He wrote:

'Was this the face that launched a thousand ships
And burnt the topless towers of Illiam?
Sweet Helen, make me immortal with a kiss ...'

Glossary

Illiam   Ilium/Troy

E.V. Rieu (1887–1972), a classicist, publisher and poet, was born in London. He was also a scholar at St. Paul's School and Balliol College at Oxford University. He translated *Homer: The Iliad* in 1950 from the ancient Greek, and it was revised in 2003 by Peter Jones. Peter Jones M.B.E. was born in 1942. He is a Cambridge graduate with a Doctorate on Homer; he became senior lecturer in Classics at the University of Newcastle upon Tyne (Newcastle University).

E.V. Rieu also translated *Homer: The Odyssey* in 1946 from ancient Greek, and this was revised by his son D.C.H. Rieu in 1991. D.C.H. Rieu read Classics and English at Queen's College, Oxford University.

The Odyssey concerns the wanderings of Odysseus (Ulixes/Ulysses) immediately after the defeat of Troy (just as Virgil's Aeneid concerns the wanderings of Aeneas immediately after the defeat of Troy). The wanderings of Odysseus took ten years, and his destination was his home, his native Ithaca, a Greek island in the Ionian Sea. During his journey he encountered both natural and supernatural threats such as shipwrecks, battles and mythical gods and creatures.

The Odyssey

In the following extract, clever Odysseus (Ulysses/Ulixes) comes across a man-eating giant with one eye. In English, we refer to him as the Cyclops (one member of a community of giants called the Cyclopes).

Extract 108

And we came to the land of the Cyclopes, a fierce, lawless people who never lift a hand to plant or plough but just leave everything to the immortal gods. All the crops they require spring up unsown and untilled, wheat and barley and vines with generous clusters that swell with the rain from heaven to yield wine. The Cyclopes have no assemblies for the making of laws, nor any established legal codes, but live in hollow caverns in the mountain heights, where each man is lawgiver to his own children and women, and nobody has the slightest interest in what his neighbours decide.

The use of English language in this extract, taken from the 1991 edition, is typical of today's English.

This 104-word paragraph is made up of only 3 sentences. The last sentence is 46 words long. Long sentences like this are common in today's English, especially in descriptions of scenes and locations. This is all thanks to a well-developed, yet extremely complex, grammatical system. The position of words within a sentence are stricter in some ways in Modern English than in Old and Middle English because English is no longer an inflectional language. But we must realise that this does not make things simpler, because today's reliance on word order, sentence structure and other grammatical patterns, has produced numerous nuances of meaning depending upon the slightest of adjustments to any given sentence.

These factors in the present reality of today's English allow precision in legal agreements and contracts, and enable a clear expression of hopes and intentions in the international arena.

Task 108

In spite of the fact that these giants had everything they needed and they

had no need to work, they were described as lawless and did not care what their neighbours were doing, good or bad.

This is an example to us. Do you think we should work hard to be better people? Do you think having a very easy life makes you a more moral (kinder, more responsible) person, or a more fierce, uncaring person? Discuss these things with your partner and tell your group what your conclusions are. Then as a group, discuss what we can learn from this extract.

Odysseus pleaded with the giant Cyclops for some simple hospitality, but the giant treated him and his companions cruelly, eating two sailors, and keeping the other sailors, including Odysseus, in his cave; they were prisoners because the stone covering the exit from the cave was too heavy for humans to move.

Clever Odysseus secretly made a stake with a sharp end out of an olive-wood pole in the cave. Meanwhile, Odysseus also tried to develop a rapport with the giant as part of his scheme for escape, including his plan to lie about his name. Odysseus told the giant his name was 'Nobody.' The giant responded with, 'Of all his company I will eat Nobody last, and the rest before him.' Then the giant fell asleep, and while he slept, Odysseus and his men drove the sharpened olive-wood pole into the giant's single eye to blind him.

The Cyclops woke up screaming and pulled the stake out of his eye.

Extract 109

Then he hurled it away from him with frenzied hands and raised a great shout to the other Cyclopes who lived in neighbouring caves along the windy heights. Hearing his screams they came up from every quarter, and gathering outside the cave asked him what the matter was.

"What on earth is wrong with you, Polyphemus? Why must you disturb the peaceful night and spoil our sleep with all this shouting? Is a robber driving off your sheep, or is somebody trying by treachery or violence to kill you?"

Out of the cave came mighty Polyphemus' voice in reply: "O my friends, it's Nobody's treachery, not violence, that is doing me to death."

"Well then," came the immediate reply, "if you are alone and nobody is assaulting you, you must be sick and sickness comes from almighty Zeus and cannot be helped. All you can do is to pray to your father, the Lord Poseidon."

And off they went, while I laughed to myself at the way in which my cunning notion of a false name had taken them in.

Glossary

raised a great shout	shouted out loud
Why must you disturb the peaceful night	Why do you have to disturb our peaceful night
is somebody trying by treachery or violence to kill you?	is somebody trying to kill you by treachery or violence?
O my friends, it's Nobody's treachery, not violence, that is doing me to death.	Friends, it's by Nobody's treachery and violence that I'm dying.
had taken them in	This phrase is normal in today's English, and means 'had fooled them.'

In the end, when the giant removed the stone from the cave exit, Odysseus and his men tied themselves to groups of sheep so that as the now blind Cyclops felt with his hand to make sure it was only sheep leaving his cave, the sailors were not noticed tied underneath. Then they finally sailed away in their ship.

Task 109

We can see from the extract that the uncaring attitude of the giants to their neighbours backfired in several ways for the Cyclops. If the Cyclops were ill, his neighbours would not help anyway because they said sickness comes from Zeus. This was an excuse not to care. Regardless of whether or not the Cyclops was ill, he was in distress, but the only thing his neighbours were concerned about was their sleep. They left him in distress. And because of the Cyclops' arrogance, he was too conceited to consider how clever Odysseus was, which led to his defeat.

With your partner, discuss what things we do or do not do in our daily lives that displays the same uncaring attitude as the Cyclopes. What can we do to change our poor behaviour?

Chapter 25　The 21st Century

第25章　21世纪

The following extracts are all representative of today's English.

The British author J.K. Rowling was born in Gloucestershire, England in 1965. Her father worked as a Rolls-Royce aircraft engineer. Her Harry Potter series for young adults is the best-selling book series in world history. The seven books were published between 1997 and 2007, and they were adapted into 8 films between 2001 and 2011. The story explores the wizarding world of Harry Potter and his friends Hermione Granger and Ron Weasley, all students at Hogwarts School of Witchcraft and Wizardry in Scotland (incidentally, to many people's surprise, this school does not really exist).

The books have been widely used in educational institutions in the western world, but not without some controversy as there are people who consider witchcraft to be dangerous, and many children have become interested in witchcraft due to reading the books. The books also contain spells, which some parents and teachers believe will literally conjure up evil demonic powers, causing children to become involved in spiritually dangerous <u>occult practices</u>. The same issue is not applied to the works of C.S. Lewis and J.R.R. Tolkien as unlike Harry Potter's world, which exists alongside the real world, C.S. Lewis' magical world is in another dimension, and Tolkien's Middle-Earth is from a mythical past; this distances the magic and witchcraft from real life.

Harry Potter

Each of the seven Harry Potter books, listed below, represent one year in

Harry's life from 1991 to 1998.

In *Harry Potter and the Philosopher's Stone* (1997), Harry is orphaned, but on his eleventh birthday he receives a letter telling him he is invited to Hogwarts School, where he will ride a broomstick, play Quidditch and get clothes of invisibility. But then a magic stone appears which will affect the present and future of the whole world.

In *Harry Potter and the Chamber of Secrets* (1998), Harry receives predictions from a House-elf called Dobby, which appear to come true when Harry's friends are turned to 'stone.'

In this extract, Harry finds the Chamber of Secrets.

Extract 110

The tunnel turned again and again. Every nerve in Harry's body was tingling unpleasantly. He wanted the tunnel to end, yet dreaded what he'd find when it did. And then, at last, as he crept around yet another bend, he saw a solid wall ahead on which two entwined serpents were carved, their eyes set with great, glinting emeralds.

Harry approached, his throat very dry. There was no need to pretend these stone snakes were real, their eyes looked strangely alive.

He could guess what he had to do. He cleared his throat, and the emerald eyes seemed to flicker.

'Open,' said Harry, in a low, faint hiss.

The serpents parted as the wall cracked open, the halves slid smoothly out of sight, and Harry, shaking from head to foot, walked inside.

Task 110

The last sentence comprises of a simple list with a slight interlude in the middle of the last item. Remember this simple and common structure for

your own writing in the future, whether it is an academic essay or a story.

'The serpents parted as the wall cracked open, the halves slid smoothly out of sight, and Harry, shaking from head to foot, walked inside.'

The first item is 'The serpents parted as the wall cracked open'; the second item is 'the halves slid smoothly out of sight'; and the third item (according to normal convention) begins with 'and,' giving 'and Harry, shaking from head to foot, walked inside.'

The simplest form of the third item would be 'and Harry walked inside,' but the author wanted to add some extra information, so she put 'shaking from head to foot' in the middle, separating it with commas.

In *Harry Potter and Prisoner of Azkaban* (1999), Harry hears that Sirius Black, a follower of Lord Voldemort, is coming after him.

Harry Potter and the Goblet of Fire (2000) comes next in which Hogwarts School holds the Triwizard Tournament on Halloween, and Harry faces three tasks involving dragons and dark wizards.

Harry Potter and the Order of the Phoenix (2003) introduces us to Harry's fifth year at Hogwarts, and Professor Snape teaches Harry how to protect himself from Voldemort's attacks. In this extract, the Sorting Hat sings as follows (it has been shortened for this extract):

Extract 111

The whole school waited with bated breath. Then the rip near the hat's brim opened wide like a mouth and the Sorting Hat burst into song:
In times of old when I was new
And Hogwarts barely started
The founders of our noble school

Thought never to be parted:
United by a common goal,
They had the selfsame yearning,
To make the world's best magic school
And pass along their learning;
'Together we will build and teach!'
The four good friends decided
And never did they dream that they
Might some day be divided,
For were there such friends anywhere
As Slytherin and Gryffindor?
Unless it was the second pair
Of Hufflepuff and Ravenclaw?
....
Oh, know the perils, read the signs,
The warning history shows,
For our Hogwarts is in danger
From external, deadly foes
And we must unite inside her
Or we'll crumble from within.
I have told you, I have warned you ...
Let the Sorting now begin.

The Hat became motionless once more; applause broke out, though it was punctured, for the first time in Harry's memory, with muttering and whispers.

Task 111

The song in the extract has many rhyming words. Read it to yourself several times until you identify each rhyming pair.

In *Harry Potter and the Half-Blood Prince* (2005), hanging in the sky is a blazing green skull with a serpent tongue. This is the mark of the Death Eaters, and Harry believes there is a Death Eater amongst them.

The final instalment is *Harry Potter and the Deathly Hallows* (2007), in which Voldemort promises that Hogwarts School will not be harmed if they give him Harry Potter. Harry has no choice but to face his enemy.

Extract 112

... Voldemort had frozen where he stood, but his red eyes had found Harry, and he stared as Harry moved towards him, with nothing but the fire between them.

Then a voice yelled —

'HARRY! NO!'

He turned: Hagrid was bound and trussed, tied to a tree nearby. His massive body shook the branches overhead as he struggled, desperate.

'NO! NO! HARRY, WHAT' RE YEH — ?'

'QUIET!' shouted Rowle, and with a flick of his wand Hagrid was silenced.

Bellatrix, who had leapt to her feet, was looking eagerly from Voldemort to Harry, her breast heaving. The only things that moved were the flames and the snake, coiling and uncoiling in the glittering cage behind Voldemort's head.

... and a singularly mirthless smile curled the lipless mouth [of Voldemort].

Task 112

Why do you think some of the words are capitalised? The words in question from the extract are:

'HARRY! NO!'

'NO! NO! HARRY, WHAT' RE YEH — ?'

'QUIET!'

What do you think 'WHAT' RE YEH — ?' means?

Later in *Deathly Hallows*, Harry has a conversation with Dumbledore in an other-worldly place. Harry eventually comes to the conclusion that it must have been his imagination as he realised he was unconscious.

Extract 113

'Tell me one last thing,' said Harry. 'Is this real? Or has this been happening inside my head?'

Dumbledore beamed at him, and his voice sounded loud and strong in Harry's ears even though the night mist was descending again, obscuring his figure.

'Of course it is happening inside your head, Harry, but why on earth should that mean that it is not real?'

Task 113

Do you understand the words of Dumbledore? Do you think everything inside your head is unreal? Or are some things (or all things) that take place in your mind real? Discuss this with your partner.

The English in the Potter extracts above is typical of today's English, totally familiar to native English speakers, and the grammar is not too complex either, as the stories were written for young adults.

Tigerlily's Orchids

Ruth Rendell (1930–2015) was mentioned earlier in this book, an author whose published novels spanned more than 50 years. *Tigerlily's Orchids* (2010) was her 60th published book, a story which shows that crimes, whether big or small, have a great effect on a community. In the story, Stuart Font has a house-warming party in his new flat in Lichfield House. He invites everyone in the building, but he chooses not to invite Claudia as he would also have to invite her husband, which he does not want to do. Entering the mix is a very mysterious Asian resident whom Stuart nicknames Tigerlily.

Here is an extract from the novel, in which Stuart is determined not to rely on his mobile phone.

Extract 114

Nothing leads to the making of discoveries like an enforced change in one's lifestyle. Stuart, determined to escape from Claudia's phone calls, had begun going out a great deal. Long walks were taken, he twice went to the cinema, met his old friends Jack and Martin on Tuesday night, had a drink with an ex-girlfriend for old times' sake on Wednesday and next day even visited his parents. He had found that it was unnecessary to take his mobile with him. This was a revelation to him; it wasn't since his mid-teens that he had been anywhere without carrying it or one of its predecessors. But without it in his pocket the heavens didn't fall, retribution didn't descend on him, no vengeful illness struck him down. It was even quite peaceful not hearing 'Nessun dorma' every five minutes, restful not having to speak to Claudia.

When he got home the messages were piling up, two from Claudia, one from his mother from whom he had parted three hours before, one from Martin inviting him to Sunday lunch with himself and his girlfriend. Stuart deleted them all and still lightning didn't strike him or the earth open.

Glossary

for old times' sake   This has the same meaning as 'For auld lang syne,' from Robert Burns' poetry. 'For old times sake' is a

	common phrase in today's English. In this context it is expressing the fact that he had a significant relationship with his ex-girlfriend in the past and they both wanted to recapture something of their past relationship by meeting for a drink.
mobile	This means 'mobile phone,' the word 'mobile' being enough to express this.
'Nessun dorma'	This is Italian for, 'None shall sleep.' It is a very popular aria (An aria is an elaborate song for one voice) from Giacomo Puccini's opera Turandot. It is sung by a Prince who falls in love at first sight with the beautiful but cold-hearted Turandot. Anyone who wants to marry her must answer three riddles correctly, or they will be beheaded. This simple reference to Stuart's mobile phone ring tone may have significance in the story.

In this passage we have three good examples of the typical list structure that I mentioned earlier for Extract 110. Here are the three examples from Extract 114:

'Long walks were taken, he twice went to the cinema, met his old friends Jack and Martin on Tuesday night, had a drink with an ex-girlfriend for old times' sake on Wednesday and next day even visited his parents.

In this first example, the final item on the list, *'and next day even visited his parents,'* does not have a comma just before it (before 'and'), possibly because the phrase is so closely linked to the phrase just prior to it, as it was the next day after the Wednesday, not the Tuesday, that he visited his parents.

In the first part of the sentence we have, *'Long walks were taken, he twice went to the cinema...,'* the author has decided to use the word 'he' in the second item on the list, whereas you might expect 'he' in the first item ('He went on long walks, went to the cinema twice ...') This shows flexibility in sentence structure is still very normal in English. It does not always change the meaning.

'But without it in his pocket the heavens didn't fall, retribution didn't descend on him, no vengeful illness struck him down.'

In the second example above, the key phrase is 'But without it in his pocket...' The three phrases that follow are the consequences (in this case the negative consequences did not occur). The first one is connected comfortably to the key phrase with no comma. The final two 'consequences' are separated by commas. The final phrase, however, does not have the conventional 'and' at the beginning. This does not matter, and in fact its absence gives a feeling of continuation, as if you are expected to add several 'consequences' in your own imagination. This shows how just the removal of a simple conjunction such as 'and' can be powerful in English.

'When he got home the messages were piling up, two from Claudia, one from his mother from whom he had parted three hours before, one from Martin inviting him to Sunday lunch with himself and his girlfriend.'

For this third example, see the task below.

Task 114a

So far, I have made comments on three examples of sentences containing lists: one from **Extract 110** and two from **Extract 114**. Analyse the final example below from **Extract 114** in a similar manner.

'When he got home the messages were piling up, two from Claudia, one from his mother from whom he had parted three hours before, one from Martin inviting him to Sunday lunch with himself and his girlfriend.'

Task 114b

In this extract the author appears to be supporting the idea of reducing dependence on mobile phones. This is expressed in the following statements:

'But without it in his pocket the heavens didn't fall, retribution didn't descend on him, no vengeful illness struck him down. It was even quite peaceful not hearing 'Nessun dorma' every five minutes, restful not having to speak to Claudia.'

'When he got home the messages were piling up ... Stuart deleted them all and still lightning didn't strike him or the earth open.'

How are you and the people around you affected by the use of mobile phones? First discuss this with your partner, then with a group. You will need to address issues such as those described in the notes below:

How many hours you spend using your phone each day.

What you spend most of your time doing on your phone.

How your phone's presence affects your work, play, and face to face relationships.

The noise from yours and other people's phones affecting the people around you.

The temptation to respond to messages immediately.

The temptation to spend more money than you should because the phone enables you to do this wherever you are.

The temptation to play computer games every time you sit down.

The dangers of reading your phone while walking.

The dangers of using a phone while driving.

Andrew Harrison

Andrew Harrison was born in Yorkshire in 1962. He has lived in China for many years teaching in several universities. He wrote the novel *As Time Approaches* (《滴答滴答》published in 2015 by NPUP) specifically for Chinese university students to give them a resource for learning today's Standard English. This concept of a native English speaker writing a novel with the sole intention of teaching today's Standard English to Chinese university students, was a new idea.

The author wanted to ensure that the mistaken use of old fashioned English and the common mistakes typical of those who speak English as a second language were addressed. This is also supported by the questions contained throughout the novel. Many aspects of western culture are contained within the story to enable students of English to grasp deeper nuances of English Language in their original contexts.

In *As Time Approaches*, humankind does not realise that the end of the world as they know it is coming soon. Chris and Michelle, university graduates from England, try to live a normal life in a world plagued by earthquakes, famine, disease and disaster.

In the second novel of the series, *Time Will Tell* (2018), the story begins immediately after the end of the previous era. The earth is left in chaos, and Michelle is left alone to fend for herself and her daughter Tina. Who can she trust now that her family and so many other good people are gone?

Death and Hades (2018), the third book, is a whodunnit, a classic Murder Mystery written as a play. Venessa, one of Michelle's community at the Old Mill in Cornwall, is found dead and hanging from the mill's waterwheel. The team work together to discover the murderer(s).

In the fourth novel, *The Mark of the Beast* (2018), Christaff the Beast is controlling almost the whole of the troubled world, picking off his opponents one by one. Will he succeed? Or will the world be delivered from this impossible situation in the lead up to the Battle of all battles?

Below is an extract from *As Time Approaches*, in which George, a member of a reading club, is suddenly becoming controlled by another force!

Extract 115

George, a stereotypical 'nutty professor' lookalike, wasn't the slightest bit interested in Maths, Physics or Chemistry. He had however always been an avid reader. Now he was retired he was a loyal and very mature student at the weekly

Leeds Readers' Association meetings. It kept his brain ticking over and gave him a regular retirement pursuit to occupy himself with. He enjoyed going through the preparatory work before the next class, and actually seemed to put more effort into his homework than anyone else. His English Literature classes were really leaving a lasting impression on him; **twas brillig**, or so he thought.

After the class he packed his briefcase with 'Through The Looking Glass, And What Alice Found There' along with the accompanying class notes. He admired the style of Lewis Carroll's 'literary nonsense'.

The metal object's razor sharp edge twinkled.

"*Snicker-snack! Snicker-snack!*" it whispered.

Stepping out into the Autumn evening, sidestepping the muddy fallen leaves, he strode down the **tulgey** street. A misty haze shrouded his mind's eye above his forehead bringing with it a headache. Although he found it hard to focus his thoughts he could picture his fellow students sat in the classroom. He liked his class-mates... 'although some are **slithy toves**, especially the one in the striped T-shirt!' He couldn't shake off an image of a fellow student talking and talking and talking... 'and dominating the WHOLE CLASS! **The jaws that bite, the claws that catch! Beware the Jubjub bird!**' George's right hand twitched and tried to clench itself tight.

The stainless steel object of death spoke again,
 growing impatient, vibrating in expectation.

"*Snicker-snack! Snicker-snack!*" it called.

"*Beware the Jabberwock, my son!*"

'Then there's that sleazy young man, thinking he's the teacher's pet, trying to get ALL the attention, **THE FRUMIOUS BANDERSNATCH!**'

"*Snicker-snack! Snicker-snack!*" throbbed the lonesome
 object, the metal blade now feeling assured.

On the table it lay, reclining and waiting for its fun.

"*Snicker-snack! Snicker-snack!*" it whispered
 faster and more...

"Snicker-snack! Snicker-snack!"

'I like my literature class, I've learnt so much and become ... I hate those smug intellectuals who think they own the world!' Suddenly, all went calm as he inserted his key into the lock of his front door. The handle turned, the familiar voice of his wife rang out from the kitchen ... and a whisper met his ears:

"Take me, use me, I will release you. **Snicker-snack!**

Snicker-snack! Snicker-snack! Snicker-snack!*"*

He managed to ignore the whispers and hunched his shoulders. Something was on his back, invisible but heavy...

"Take me, use me, I will release you. **Snicker-snack!***"*

Entering the dining room **he took his vorpal sword in hand**. It spoke to him. That moment his wife **came whiffling** into the room. He **stood awhile in thought**. Having picked up the tool of release and **with eyes aflame: One, two! One, two! And through and through the vorpal blade went snicker-snack! Snicker-snack! Snicker-snack! Snicker-snack! Snicker-snack! Snicker-snack! Snicker-snack! He left it dead ... with its head** hanging back ......

"And hast thou slain the Jabberwock?
Come to my arms my beamish boy!
O frabjous day! Callooh! Callay!"
Twas brillig, and the slithy toves *ceased*
gyring ***and gimbling in the wabe.***
And now, at last, ***all mimsy were the borogoves****,*
And no longer feared he if ***the mome raths outgrabed****.*
In ***uffish thought*** *he trudged with short hunched steps*
into the living room,
so rested he by the Tumtum tree.
Meanwhile, lifeless around the floor she lay
in the dining room,
Raw flesh razored, sliced and diced for all to see.
O frabjous day!

O frabjous day!
Timeless and motionless rested he
in no man's land free
this was meant to be
he and only he
all else is history
'No more for me!'
"What's for tea?"
Can't they see?
"Sorry!"
'See.'

This extract frequently makes use of words and phrases from Lewis Carroll's nonsense verse poem called 'Jabberwocky' (see Extract 59). The original poem 'Jabberwocky' was published in Carroll's book called *Through the Looking Glass and What Alice Found There* in 1871. The words from the poem used in the chapter are emboldened.

Task 115

The words and phrases from Carroll's 'Jabberwocky' poem are used to indicate the process of George becoming mentally ill. Harrison has deliberately chosen to use Carroll's novel (*Through the Looking Glass and What Alice Found There*) because it contains the 'Jabberwocky' poem. This is the novel that George is studying in his reading club, from which he is in the process of returning home.

Explain in more detail why Harrison uses words and phrases from 'Jabberwocky' in this extract?

Now, by checking Extract 59 and Task 59 to help you, identify the 'nonsense' words used in Extract 115, and replace them with English words that make sense.

Share your results with your partner, and reread Extract 116, replacing the 'Jabberwocky' words and phrases with your own.

The following is an extract from Andrew Harrison's futuristic play *Death and Hades*, a murder mystery (2018).

Extract 116

Narrator: Pierre cannot believe his eyes! He is the first one to find Venessa tied to the old mill's water wheel, looking limp and lifeless, fastened in an undignified star shape. He had thought she was still travelling back late from Stonehenge, as she was not in bed, but now he knows otherwise.

Pierre: Venessa! VENESSA! (Climbing up the wheel to slap her face in an attempt to get a response. He sees a gash on the side of her head.) MURDER! MURDER!

Michelle: Pierre, what's wrong? OH NO! VENESSA!

Pierre: She's dead!

Michelle: Who would do something like this? Is she definitely dead? Venessa! Venessa!

Pierre: She's dead alright, and the one who killed her will be too!

Michelle: We have a murderer in our midst, I can't believe it.

Pierre: (Trying to untie Venessa's hands to get her down off the water wheel) Quick Michelle, get me some scissors or a knife.

Michelle: No wait! We need to preserve the evidence.

Pierre: I can't leave her up here!

Michelle: Not for long; we just need to take pictures.

Bridget: (Running towards them) Don't do anything. Pierre, you didn't touch the body did you?

Pierre: That body's got a name, it's Venessa!

Bridget: *Of course. I'm a nurse so I'll just check her pulse and temperature. (Bridget climbs steadily to check the body over). She's stone cold and there's no pulse. I'm afraid she is gone. She was killed by a blow to the head and then tied up by the murderer for us all to see.*

Pierre: *WHY! WHY! WHY! (Michelle comforts Pierre as he falls to his knees.)*

Gustav: *(Just arriving) What's happened? What's all the screaming about?*

Pierre: *Venessa's dead!*

Gustav: *What! (Looking at Pierre) What did you do to her?*

Pierre: *What do you mean? I did nothing to her!*

Gustav: *Who found the body?*

Pierre: *I did.*

Gustav: *Well, doesn't that seem a little suspicious?*

Michelle: *Why is that suspicious?*

Gustav: *Have you touched the body?*

Bridget: *Yes he did.*

Gustav: *Convenient.*

Pierre: *(Pushing Gustav to the ground) You don't know what you're talking about.*

Gustav: *Well there needs to be an investigation, and you are suspect number one.*

Michelle: *Don't jump to conclusions. I suggest you and I investigate together, Gustav. You've had experience as a policeman in the Middle East, and I'm responsible for the whole team, so we are the best for the job.*

First of all, we need to collect evidence from the crime scene and calmly break the news to the others; remember we have children.

Narrator: *No one has the opportunity to gently break the news to the rest of the team, because just then the whole household emerges, including the children, to see what all the shouting is about.*

After Gustav, Bridget and Michelle gather as many clues as they can from the scene, Pierre endeavours to take the body down off the water wheel.

Pierre: That's enough! I am taking her down now! I'm not leaving her up there like this for the murderer to gloat at her.

Michelle: Let me help.

Narrator: Pierre holds tightly onto Venessa's torso as he attempts to untie her arms from the wheel, but it is too difficult, so Michelle supports the body of Venessa while Pierre cuts the cords that are binding Venessa's hands and feet to the water wheel. As Venessa's body flops from the wheel, Michelle helps Pierre to take the weight.

Pierre takes Venessa off Michelle, carries her into the old mill and lays her body gently and respectfully on his bed.

Michelle: Her head is bruised but there's not much blood.

Jenny: Don't you think you're a bit out of your depth Michelle? Perhaps we should call the police.

Esther: What? The police are governed by the authorities at Stonehenge City! You must be joking!

Jenny: So who's gonna lead the investigation?

Michelle: We've already decided; Gustav because he used to be a policeman, and myself.

Jenny: Oh I might have guessed! Michelle Marple and Gustav Holmes.

Michelle: If you're going to be your obnoxious self, Jenny, then I think you can be excused completely from our group. I've had it up to here with your attitude. Someone ... no not someone ... one of our dear friends has been murdered and SOMEONE has to find out who did it. If you can think of anyone better to lead the investigation, then make a suggestion, otherwise shut up!

Jenny: No, you do it (walking off). I'm going to check on Pierre ... if that's okay with you (sarcastically).

Glossary

gash   A gash is a wound in the form of a cut or broken skin.

suspect number one	A suspect is someone whom the investigators consider to be guilty of a crime. By saying 'number one,' he is saying he is the most likely person to be guilty, and therefore evidence will be gathered to establish whether the investigators are right or not.
a blow to the head	This is the damage done to the head after being hit by something.

Don't jump to conclusions. Don't be too quick to conclude this.

Stonehenge City	In this novel, London is no longer the capital city of the UK, and instead a new city, having developed around the ancient monument called Stonehenge, has become the capital city of the whole of the British Isles. This new city is called Stonehenge City.
Michelle Marple	This is likening Michelle to Jane Marple, the fictional character created by British author Agatha Christie. Miss Marple was an old spinster who acted as an amateur consulting detective. She first appeared in a publication in 1927. Agatha Christie's first novel to involve Miss Marple was *The Murder at the Vicarage*, published in 1930.
Gustav Holmes	This is likening Gustav to Sherlock Holmes, the fictional private detective created by the British author Sir Arthur Conan Doyle. His character first appeared in Doyle's first novel *A Study in Scarlet* in 1887. Sherlock Holmes is well-known for his powers of deduction.

Task 116a

Answer the following comprehension questions on the text:
a Why does Gustav say 'Convenient'?

b Why does Michelle say 'Remember we have children'?

c Why does Jenny say 'Don't you think you're a bit out of your depth Michelle?'

Task 116b

Practice and perform a role play of this scene. There are 7 speaking parts (including the Narrator), and 8 non-speaking parts. And of course we also have Venessa, who is the 'dead body' tied to the water wheel.

The speaking parts are The Narrator, Michelle, Pierre, Gustav, Bridget, Jenny and Esther.

If you have enough people in your group, you can include the following non-speaking parts: Gloria, Victoria, Ben and Sheila, and the four children Tina, Suzy, Matthew and Rachel. Venessa can be a dummy, or Michelle and Pierre can mime carrying the body.

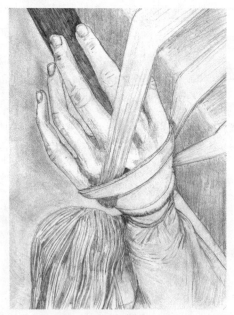

Venessa on the water wheel, by Andrew Harrison (2018)

Additional Notes for Unit 8

第8单元附加注释

Secondary Education in England

Article by Rebekah Benson

In England, children begin Secondary School in Year 7 at the age of 11 years old. Secondary Schools in England are funded or managed in different ways. A State School is attended by the majority of children. These schools are funded by the government and provide a free education for all children. Approximately 7% of children attend Independent Schools (also known as private or public schools), which are not funded by the government and require fees to be paid for attendance.

Most children move automatically from their local Primary School to their local Comprehensive School (a state funded Secondary School that accepts any child of the appropriate age). However, some state funded Secondary Schools are selective; these are called Grammar Schools. As they select on academic ability, children need to complete an entrance test (the 11 Plus) during Year 6, which tests their knowledge of non-verbal and verbal reasoning, English and Maths. Many Grammar Schools are oversubscribed, and as a result, passing the test is not a guarantee for a place. It is thought that parents may choose Grammar Schools for their child, rather than the local Comprehensive, as they focus on academic achievement and discipline, and in some cases, it can prevent a child from having to attend a local school that does not have a good reputation.

The most common state funded schools available in England consist of

Foundation Schools (where the governing body is the employer rather than the local council); Voluntary Schools (where a trust — usually of a religious faith — has some formal influence over the running of the school); Community Schools (controlled by the local council); Academies (run by the governing body and not the local council, and can follow their own curriculum called their Programme of Learning); and Grammar Schools (with the children's academic ability as the basis for selection). Other State Schools available include Faith Schools (associated with a particular religion); Special Schools (for children with learning difficulties or disabilities); Boarding Schools (free education but a fee is charged for the child to board); Free Schools (not run by the local council and so they have more control over how they do things, e.g. they do not have to follow the National Curriculum); and City Technology Colleges (independent schools but with free education, with a focus on teaching science and technology).

The large majority of state funded schools have to follow the National Curriculum and are inspected by OFSTED. OFSTED inspect schools to ensure they meet particular standards of education and welfare. They report their findings to the Government to hold schools responsible for their provision and to promote improvement.

England's examination and qualification system is organised by levels of learning. Children will study GCSEs from the age of 14 to 16, and A Levels (or other educational qualifications) from the age of 16 to 18.

The academic year begins on the 1st of September and finishes on the 31st of August. The year is divided into three sections (called 'terms'). Children have a two week holiday at 'Christmas' to mark the end of the first term, a two week holiday at 'Easter' to mark the end of the second term and the third term ends with a six week holiday over the summer. Each term is divided into two, marked by a one week holiday for the children (called 'half term'). This means children have 39 weeks of schooling per year.

Whilst at Secondary School students begin their education in Year 7 and study the Key Stage 3 curriculum until Year 9 (i.e. from age 11 to 14). During this time, children study a wide range of subjects as part of the National Curriculum, such as, Maths, English, Science, Music and Drama, Religious Studies, Geography, History, Physical Education, Citizenship, Modern Foreign Languages, Art and Design Technology, and IT (Information Technology).

Typically during Year 9 children choose their 'options' for GCSEs. They will begin to study these when they reach Year 10 (age 14) and continue their Key Stage 4 study until the end of Year 11 (age 16). This requires children to still study the 'core' compulsory subjects of Maths, English, Science, Physical Education and Religious Studies and Citizenship (approximately 60% of their timetable) and the subjects that they chose for their 'options' (approximately 40% of their timetable), which can consist of Geography, History, Religious Studies (including Philosophy and Ethics), Media, Design Technology (Food, Graphics, Electronics, Resistant Materials), Art, Photography, Triple Science, Physical Education, Music, Performing Arts and Dance. Children will usually study four option subjects, but in some cases it may be three or five, depending on the school's provision or the academic ability of the child.

During these two years of study, children will have to complete formal 'controlled assessments' in some subjects and complete examinations in all subjects at the end of Year 11. These combined assessments and examinations provide them with their GCSE results. The children will be awarded a grade for each of their subjects which provide evidence of their academic achievement from Secondary School education. The grading system is numbered from 9 to 1, with 9 being the highest grade and 1 being the lowest. A '4' is regarded a pass, with a '5' regarded a strong pass.

Once children have completed their GCSEs, they must remain in some form of education for the next two years, until the age of 18. This can be full time education, enrolling in an apprenticeship or part time education / training whilst in work.

The main pathway to University is for children to study A Levels, also known as GCEs. Many Secondary Schools provide the GCE programme of study, alternatively, some children choose to study them at a Sixth Form College. In both cases, this typically involves choosing three or four subjects to study, for which they have a wide range to choose from, including subjects such as English Language, English Literature, Mathematics, Further Maths, Physics, Chemistry, Biology, Performing Arts, History, Geography, Politics, and Psychology. At the end of their two years of study, the student completes their final examinations which will result in a grade from A* – E, with A* being the highest qualification.

However, other Post 16 (post 16 years old) options include Vocational qualifications. These are specific to a particular job or employment / industry sector, with a key focus on practical learning. There are many programmes available, covering a wide range of subjects. Some are studied in school, but they are mostly offered in colleges or alongside Apprenticeships. These qualifications help to provide skills, behaviours and knowledge needed for the world of work in a particular career. Work performance is assessed on observations on the job rather than examinations.

There are different types of vocational qualifications:

—**Vocational subjects** develop both practical skills and knowledge related to a broad area. They are offered in both schools and colleges and they include a significant amount of activities based in the classroom. Subjects include areas such as Leisure and Tourism, and Health and Social Care (These can include some BTEC subjects).

—**Vocational courses** provide training and qualifications for a specific job, e.g. plumber, hairdresser. They are usually offered in colleges and include learning in real life situations.

—**Apprenticeships** allow them to learn on the job, gaining skills and a qualification whilst earning money. Most of their time is spent in the workplace but they are also supported by a college to help build up their knowledge and qualifications. This training can take 1 to 4 years and there are different levels of apprenticeships.

Vocational qualifications include BTEC Diplomas, which are typically studied in college. This qualification is thought to give the skills needed and *'a route into employability much faster because it's giving you tools and techniques that can be very valuable to an employer'* (Albert Hitchcock — Chief Technology and Operations Office for Pearson's Examination Board). These are available at 7 levels and can be equivalent to other qualifications, e.g. Levels 1 and 2 (GCSE), Level 3 (A Level) and Levels 6 and 7 (Degree). This consists mostly of full time study, but can be offered as part time courses to provide career development opportunities for people within work. Students are assessed throughout the course through a variety of methods which regularly focus on practical exercises, as well as more traditional tests. At Levels 2–5, students can complete BTEC Apprenticeships which include on and off the job training.

Vocational qualifications also include NVQs (National Vocational Qualifications). These are work based qualifications which are usually delivered in the work place where work related practical skills are learned. This course is specifically focused on developing the knowledge and skills required to do a particular job effectively. They can be taken by college students with work placements / part time jobs or by full time employees. These qualifications are available within many employment sectors, such as catering, construction and engineering, with the courses ranging in difficulty from Levels 1 to 5.

These types of qualifications enable students to decide whether this job is the right one for them and it helps them to become effective employees. These qualifications can, therefore, lead to employment or further education, including University / Degree level.

This article is indebted to the information found on:
https://www.relocatemagazine.com/articles/education-system-in-england
Other sources used:
https://www.parentzone.careerpilot.org.uk/
https://www.uptonhigh.co.uk/page/?title=Curriculum&pid=35
https://www.gov.uk/national-curriculum
https://www.independenteducationconsultants.co.uk/what-is-ofsted-or-isi-

and-what-do-they-do/

Glossary

Secondary School	A Secondary School provides education for children from 11 to 16, or 11 to 18 years of age.
State School	This is a school funded by the government. The vast majority of Secondary Schools are state funded schools. Primary School This is a school that provides education from 5 to 11 years of age.
selective	Grammar Schools are 'selective' Secondary Schools in that they do not simply accept any 11 year old student; their academic level needs to be proven to be high enough before entry. This is unlike Comprehensive Secondary Schools which accept every student within a certain catchment area (the areas surrounding the school).
Grammar Schools	These are state funded schools that select their students according to their academic ability. They are not classed as Comprehensive Schools, which are state funded non-selective schools.
11 Plus	This is an examination taken by pupils who are 11 years old and want to be assessed to see if their academic ability is strong enough for entry to a Grammar School. Most pupils do not take this test as there are too few Grammar Schools.
oversubscribed	If something is oversubscribed, then there are too many people for admission.
National Curriculum	The National Curriculum is a set of standards and subjects used by schools to ensure children learn and achieve the same things.

OFSTED	OFSTED stands for 'Office for Standards in Education' which also assesses Children's Services and Skills.
GCSE	GCSE stands for 'General Certificate of Secondary Education.'
A Levels	These are subjects and examinations of an Advanced Level, taken by students aged 16–18 (See GCE below).
Key Stage 3	As indicated in the article, this is the provision of education for students between 11 and 14 years old (Years 7–9).
IT	This stands for Information Technology, the study of computer science.
Key Stage 4	As indicated in the article, this is the provision of education for students between 14 and 16 years old (Years 10–11).
controlled assessments	These are different to examinations in that a student's work projects during the academic year are carefully monitored and assessed. These results are then added to the final examination score.
GCE	GCE stands for 'General Certificate of Education.' This is the same as an A Level.
BTEC	BTEC stands for 'Business and Technology Education Council.'
BTEC Diplomas	These are BTEC qualifications.
Degree	In the article, 'Degree' refers to a Bachelor's Degree, taken at university. These are Undergraduate Degrees in Science or Arts, and usually take 3–4 years of study. 'Degree level' is therefore a higher academic level than A Level (GCE) subjects.

A brief example of how music can influence the use of spoken English

British rock and pop singers in the 1950s often tried to sound like singers from the US to appear more cool, but singers in the US ironically used a pronunciation closer to black singers, because many popular forms of music came from black music in the south of the US, such as 'Blues.'

An interesting example of this is in the way 'r' is pronounced. British singers pronounced their 'r's very clearly, unlike their own accent but more akin to US pronunciation; however, the US singers abandoned their 'r's to sound more like black singers.

The presence of the strong 'r' sound in the US stems from the 'Early Modern English' language of Britain in the sixteenth century. The early settlers took this English with them to America, but whereas London in England became 'r-less' later on, the US retained the pronunciation of their ancestors. This phenomenon in the US is an example of what is called 'colonial lag,' when distance from the original source causes a slower development of the language.

However, not all British musicians relied on 'American' pronunciation to sell <u>records</u>. The world famous Beatles, a group from England that was formed in 1960, had a distinctly Merseyside accent, as they were from the city of Liverpool, in England. Their singing style had a typical 'adenoidal' quality, not due to a blocked nose, but due to a certain positioning of the tongue, pharynx and larynx typical of Merseyside pronunciation.

Interestingly, at the time of writing (2019), it is 50 years since the Beatles first released their 1969 <u>album</u> *Abbey Road*. It has been released again this year and become top of the UK official album charts again—49 years and 252 days later. This makes it a <u>Guinness World Record</u>.

British English Literature in England's Rock Music

Article by Andrew Harrison (2019)

Music in England has promoted British English Literature with its various stories and plots, throughout the centuries. Among the countless examples are the seventeenth century works of Henry Purcell (1659-1695), the most important British composer of his day. Although his music had some elements of Italian and French styles, his compositions were prime examples of a uniquely British form of <u>Baroque</u> music, during what is called the Middle Baroque Period. He is famous for his songs, his <u>incidental music</u> to a version of Shakespeare's *Midsummer Night's Dream*, and especially his English tragic opera called *Dido and Aeneas*, which is part of the story of Virgil's Aeneid (written 2,000 years ago), already referred to in this book.

The more recent genre of Rock Music is no exception. It too has many examples of references to English Literature. For example, the composer and keyboardist Rick Wakeman, a vital member of the long-standing <u>Progressive Rock</u> band 'Yes,' created many solo works, including his third <u>Concept Album</u> called 'The Myths and Legends of King Arthur and the Knights of the Round Table,' the stories of which are the theme of many famous British authors' works. The titles of the <u>tracks</u> are *Arthur, Lady of the Lake, Guinevere, Sir Lancelot and the Black Knight, Merlin the Magician, Sir Galahad*, and *The Last Battle*. This Progressive Rock album, combining rock with classical music and other elements, is an outstanding piece of work, released by A and M Records in 1975. Rick Wakeman's other early concept albums were *The Six Wives of Henry VIII* (his first); *Journey to the Centre of the Earth*, which was recorded at The Royal Festival Hall, London in 1974 with the London Symphony Orchestra and The English Chamber Choir; and, after *King Arthur*, he created his fourth concept album called *No Earthly Connection*.

Although *The Six Wives of Henry VIII* is based on history rather than any specific work of literature (for example, Shakespeare's play *The Life of Henry VIII*), it perpetuates respect for British Literature and highly valued historical records, architecture and artefacts. It is no surprise that Rick Wakeman respects British Literature as he was trained in Classical Music, and as such his Rock Music has many classical elements, even in his work with the British Progressive Rock band 'Yes.'

British Literature is found in the work of other Rock musicians, too. Another extremely popular and influential Progressive Rock band was 'Emerson, Lake and Palmer,' who produced their studio version of William Blake's *Jerusalem*, according to the melody composed by Hubert Parry; this can be found on their fourth studio album called *Brain Salad Surgery*, released in 1973.

Kate Bush, a highly influential and unique singer-songwriter from England, topped the UK Singles Charts in 1978 at the age of 19 with her song *Wuthering Heights*, the topic of which was derived from Emily Bronte's novel of the same name. It also made Number 1 in Australia, Italy, New Zealand and Ireland. In the song, Kate Bush refers to Cathy (Catherine Earnshaw) in the First Person as she calls out to Heathcliff. The song appeared on her debut album *The Kick Inside*.

Pink Floyd, the British band responsible for the ground-breaking, extremely popular album *Dark Side of the Moon*, includes a track called *Money*. In the song, a well-known English saying is quoted:

'Money is the root of all evil.'

The song adds the word 'today,' making:

'Money is the root of all evil today.'

The common saying actually comes from the Bible, and because the saying uses the word 'the' instead of 'a,' it has obviously originated from a very old English translation of the Bible such as the KJV of 1611, which is an exquisite example of English Literature.

However, the original sentence in the KJV Bible states:

'The love of money is the root of all evil.' *(1 Timothy 6:10)*

Today, the same Greek authoritative manuscripts are translated in modern versions of the Bible as: 'The love of money is a root of all evil,' replacing 'the' with 'a,' which is quite different. To say that the love of money is the root of all evil is to say that ONLY the 'love of money' causes evil, whereas the original Greek (and the typical modern translation) suggests that not only does the love of money cause all kinds of evil, but other things can cause all kinds of evil too. There is some flexibility in regard to whether the English 'the' or 'a' should be used in the translation.

The order of the Greek words, more literally, suggests the following in today's English:

'A root of all evil is the love of money.'

Remaining with the theme of *Money*, we have another British Rock band to mention, and that is the world-famous Led Zeppelin. On their fourth studio album there was a track called *Stairway to Heaven*, released in 1971. This highly influential song was produced by guitarist Jimmy Page and vocalist Robert Plant. Among the lyrics is the interesting phrase:

'all that glitters is gold'

This is actually a misquote from Shakespeare, the original being:

'all that glisters is not gold'

This is usually (by replacing the unknown word 'glisters' with 'glitters') quoted as:

'all that glitters is not gold'

But in *Stairway to Heaven*, we are told that there is a lady who is sure 'all that glitters is gold' (omitting the word 'not'), because she thinks she can use her precious things to pay for a stairway that leads up to Heaven.

The theme is similar to Shakespeare, not only in regard to 'Money,' but also in its connection with 'Death.' In the western world, the concept of Heaven primarily refers to a perfect, eternally happy existence in Paradise after death, and the song *Stairway to Heaven* is about access to this blissful Heaven.

However, the song diverges from Shakespeare in that it implies money can bring happiness after death. Shakespeare, on the other hand, supports the Bible's teaching, for example, in the words of Jesus: 'It is easier for a camel to go through the eye of a needle than for a rich person to enter the kingdom of God

[Heaven]' (Matthew 19:24). Therefore, Shakespeare's words can be understood to mean, 'Expensive things do not guarantee happiness in life or in death.' Led Zeppelin cleverly twists this idea to say the opposite in regard to a particular, special lady.

In 1999, Cliff Richard produced a well-loved song to celebrate the world's passing from one millennium to another. It was called *Millennium Prayer*, being a combination of the music to Auld Lang Syne (the lyrics of which were penned by Robert Burns) and the words to the Lord's Prayer, using language from the King James Version of the Bible (KJV) from 1611.

It cannot be overestimated how much music contributes to the appreciation of English Literature. In addition to the examples above, we could go into the lyrics of many more popular, composed songs that are repeatedly played or sung over the decades, creating set phrases with their own connotations. And time and time again, the poetry of famous writers from throughout the centuries are adapted for song.

Additional Task F

In your group, discuss the following statement:
'A root of all evil is the love of money.'
While discussing this topic, you need to consider the following points:
What is 'the love of money'?
What is the 'root' of something?
What does 'all evil' mean?

Additional Task G

Throughout this book, there are 116 extracts. Among these extracts are many that are written in the first person; for example, in Jane Eyre, Jane herself is writing. This is quite an effective method for helping the reader to

identify closely with the events in the novel or poem.

Look through every extract and list all the extracts that have been written in the first person (i.e. the authors referring to themselves as I, we, my or our).

Glossary for Unit 8

tongue-in-cheek 随便说说的; 开玩笑的

If something is 'tongue-in-cheek,' it is not to be taken too seriously; it is meant humorously.

allegorical 寓言式的

An allegory is an extended metaphor (a metaphor being a description of something by referring to it as something else, suggesting there are common qualities between them). In this way, the allegorical novel describes events that illustrate complex ideas symbolically.

dystopian 反乌托邦的

Lord of the Flies is a dystopian novel, which means it presents a society or community that is not good, and one that leads to tragedy. The dystopian society is the opposite of a utopia.

play on words 双关语

This means the same as 'word play,' which is a literary technique using double meanings in words and phrases for effect or amusement.

thumbing a lift 搭便车

This means the same as 'hitchhiking,' that is, holding out your thumb to passing traffic with the hope of obtaining a lift to another location.

case （刑事）案件

Here the meaning is 'criminal case.' This is an investigation into a crime.

occult practices 作法

These are dangerous, mysterious practices that involve (supernatural) magic and spirits.

ring tone 铃声

The sound made by a telephone when you receive an incoming text or phone call is called a ring tone.

records 唱片

A 'record' means a disc (larger than a CD or a DVD) made out of vinyl containing music, to be played on a record player. These days, they are made only for collectors, as now music is either put onto CDs or downloaded from the internet.

album 专辑

An 'album' was a large vinyl record containing a selection of songs or pieces of music by an artist or music group (band). Each album was enclosed in an informative and decorative cover which was often just as important to people as the music itself. Today, the word 'album' is still used for a similar selection of music whether it is on CD or downloadable.

Guinness World Record 吉尼斯世界纪录

This is a reference document produced every year to record and celebrate the best achievements in a wide variety of fields and sporting activities. In this case, the Guinness World Record has recorded *Abbey Road* by the Beatles as representing the longest period of time before an album has returned to No. 1 in the UK. This record was also previously held by The Beatles with their *Sgt. Pepper's Lonely Hearts Club Band* album, which did the same in 2017, after 49 years and 125 days.

Baroque 巴洛克

This music genre of western music dates from 1600 to 1750. Typical musical instruments of this genre included the lute, violin, viola, cello and double bass, and brass instruments such as the trumpet and horn.

incidental music （电影、戏剧）配乐

In this context, the term means the music used in a play.

Progressive Rock 前卫摇滚

This is a genre of Rock Music that originated in the United Kingdom. It combined elements of a variety of genres, especially Rock and traditional

Classical. The tracks (see 'tracks' below) were usually much longer than Pop songs typically entered into the singles charts (see 'UK Singles Charts' below). Progressive Rock was not restricted to the theme of Romance, unlike most Pop songs.

Concept Album 概念专辑

A Concept Album is an album (see 'album' above) that is entirely united under one specific theme or story.

tracks 歌曲、乐曲

A song or piece of music on an album (see 'album' above) is called a track.

UK Singles Charts 英国单曲榜

This is the official list of contemporary songs in order according to popularity and sales.

the eye of a needle 针眼

A needle is used for sewing and repairing fabric, and its eye is the hole through which you can thread the needle (attach thread).

Appendices

附 录

Timeline
时间线

Task Answers
问题答案

Sample Essay
范文

Acknowledgements
致谢

Timeline

时间线

Pre-English Period (Before 450 AD)

The languages of the British Isles are Celtic.

After the Roman invasion, many communities become bilingual, speaking Celtic and Latin.

In 410 AD, the Romans leave Britain.

In 449 AD, the Anglo-Saxon invasion of Britain begins.

Early Old English (450–850 AD)

Anglo-Saxon settlers bring a variety of Germanic dialects from mainland Europe to the British Isles, which begin to form a new language (English).

In 700 AD, the first Old English written texts appear, borrowing many religious words from Latin.

In about 750 AD, the original Beowulf is composed.

In 787 AD, the Viking invasion of Britain begins.

King Egbert (Ecgherht) reigns as King of England 827–839.

Later Old English (850–1100 AD)

In the north of England, English dialects become strongly influenced by Scandinavian languages.

King Alfred (Alfred the Great) reigns as King of England 871–899.

Many Latin texts are translated into English.

The French Norman Conquest of England in 1066 AD.

Middle English (1100–1450 AD)

England is ruled by France.

English vocabulary and spelling is influenced by the French language.

French becomes the official language of England.

King Richard I reigns as King of England 1189–1199.

Educated English people become trilingual — French, Latin and English.

In 1300 AD, the population of the British Isles is about 5 million.

The 'Hundred Years War' begins in 1338 AD.

In 1348 AD, the Black Death (the bubonic plague) reaches England and eventually kills half of the population.

In 1362 AD, English becomes the official language of the British Parliament and Law Courts.

The New Testament is translated into English by Wycliff's followers in the 1380s.

Chaucer begins writing *The Canterbury Tales* in 1387.

Early Modern English (1450–1750 AD)

By 1453, all French lands are lost except for Calais, ending the 'Hundred Years War.'

In 1455, The 'Wars of the Roses' begin.

The roles of Latin and French start to decline, and English becomes the language of Science and Government.

In 1473, Caxton prints the first book in English.

King Henry VII reigns as King of England and Wales 1485–1509.

By 1487, the king has united the two warring houses of York and Lancaster, ending the 'Wars of the Roses.'

King Henry VIII reigns as King of England, Wales and Ireland 1509–1547.

Tyndale's English translation of *the Bible* (1526).

In 1534, King Henry VIII breaks with the Roman Catholic Church and the English Reformation begins. King Henry VIII declares himself 'Head of the Church of England'.

The English Renaissance Period begins.

The Universities of Oxford and Cambridge expand.

Queen Elizabeth I reigns as Queen of England, Wales and Ireland 1558–1603.

The Elizabethan Era is a time of peace.

In 1562, Hawkins starts the British Slave Trade.

In 1564, Shakespeare is born.

King James I reigns as King of Britain and Scotland (where he was known as James VI) 1603–1625.

In 1605, the Roman Catholic Guy Fawkes is stopped from blowing up King James and the Houses of Parliament, beginning the annual festival of Bonfire Night (Guy Fawkes Night).

In 1607, the first permanent English settlement in America in Jamestown.

The King James Bible is completed in 1611.

In 1618, the 'Thirty Years War' begins in England.

In 1620, the Pilgrim Fathers sail for America on board the Mayflower.

Colonisation of the Caribbean island country of Barbados (1627).

The English Civil War (1642–1645) between the forces of King Charles I and Oliver Cromwell, and Oliver Cromwell's success.

The Great Plague of 1665.

The Great Fire of London in 1666.

St. Paul's Cathedral is built by Sir Christopher Wren.

In 1707, the kingdoms of Scotland and England (including Wales) unite to become 'The United Kingdom of Great Britain.'

Modern English (1750–1950 AD)

1760 sees the beginning of the Industrial Revolution.

The American War of Independence (1775–1783).

In 1788, penal colonies are established in Australia.

In 1798, the Romantic Movement begins.

English becomes the medium of education in many parts of the world.

In 1800, the 'Act of Union' unites Great Britain and Ireland, producing the 'The United Kingdom of Great Britain and Ireland.'

The British Slave Trade ends in 1807.

Britain abolishes the Slave Trade in the colonies in 1833.

Telegraph comes into use in 1835.

Queen Victoria reigns as Queen of the United Kingdom, at the height of the British Empire 1837–1901.

Crimean War (1854); Florence Nightingale starts the nursing profession and ministers to the wounded in the Crimea.

In 1858, the Oxford English Dictionary is proposed.

The American Civil War (1861–1865).

Canada is given self-government (1867).

Boer War in South Africa (1899–1902).

King Edward VII reigns as King of the UK 1901–1910.

The Edwardian Age begins.

Australia is given self-government status (1901).

King George V reigns as King of the UK 1910–1936.

The First World War (The Great War) 1914–1918.

The Irish Free State (Irish Republic) is established in 1922, but Northern Ireland decides to remain in the UK.

In 1927, the official title of the UK becomes 'The United Kingdom of Great Britain and Northern Ireland.'

In 1928, the Oxford English Dictionary, the greatest dictionary of any language in the world, is completed.

The British Commonwealth is created in 1931.

1932 saw the beginning of royal broadcasts on Christmas Day.

King George VI reigns as King of the UK 1936–1952.

The Second World War 1939–1945.

The National Health Service (NHS) is started.

Late Modern English (1950 AD to today)

Queen Elizabeth II reigns as Queen of the UK 1952–present.

Queen Elizabeth's coronation is the first coronation to be televised.

English Language becomes the international language of communications technology.

English Language becomes the primary language for international communication and trade.

Task Answers
问题答案

Unit 1

Task 1

romwalusandreumwalustwoegen

Task 2

A typical modern English translation of the Old English carving would be:

I lifted up the great king, heaven's lord;
I did not dare to bend.
Men mocked us both together.
I was drenched with blood.

Task 3

A typical modern English translation of the extract would be:

On a certain occasion, he left the house of the feast and went out to the cattle shed, whose care was entrusted to him that night, and there, at the appointed time, he laid down his limbs in rest and fell asleep. Then a certain man stood before him in a dream and hailed and greeted him, and called him by his name, "Caedmon, sing me something!" Then he answered and said, "I don't know how to sing ..."

Task 4

He first made   on earth for men
Heaven as a roof   the Holy Creator

Here is an example of how to rewrite the extract in correct order:

He, the Holy Creator, first made Heaven as a roof for men on Earth.

Task 5

a There are so many names in such a short extract. They are as follows:
God the Creator, Guardian of Heaven's Kingdom, Father of Glory, Eternal Lord, Holy Creator, Guardian of Humankind, Everlasting Lord.

b He made Heaven as a roof for the people.

c He adorned the Earth for the people.

d 'adorned' here means he created the sea, birds, animals and plants.

e He asked Caedmon to sing about creation, because the Creator 'established the beginning of every wonder'. Therefore 'we must praise' God.

f Caedmon possessed the skill to compose and sing a song in the form he learnt in his dream.

Task 6

Here is an example of how it could be changed into modern English prose:

There was Shield Sheafson, who caused misery and death to many tribes while destroying the benches on which they sat to drink mead. With violence he assaulted his enemies in their famous halls and made a name for himself, from being nothing more than a deserted child to a powerful warrior of great renown through his conquests. Eventually, every clan overseas had no choice but to yield to him and speak of him with great honour. That was one good king.

Task 7

Here is an example of how these extracts can be rewritten in prose while considering the many connotations in the language of Seamus Heaney's translation:

In a certain mountain there was a dragon guarding a hoard, a trove of golden treasures, sparkling with jewels of many colours. The value of this stolen mound was beyond calculation, and it was within this glistening hoard that the dragon slept.

One day by chance, a wanderer stumbled across the secret passageway leading to the dragon's lair, and he could not comprehend his fortune as he clambered over the sparkling mound of neck-chains, ornate bowls and commemorative plates and rings, all made of gold and studded with precious stones. One such object was a goblet, which he caressed with delight. He did not hesitate to claim it as his own and steal it from the dragon, leaving swiftly by the same passageway along which he had come.

It was not long before the dragon noticed something was amiss, and this roused him from his sleep in a rage. He saw the indentations where a human had trodden upon the trove surrounding him, even up to the point where his head had been sleeping. The fire rose up inside the dragon's body and belched from his mouth as he charged through the tunnel and slithered down the mountain looking for the prowler.

Unable to find the thief, the dragon flew from the mountain, spewing out flames across every homestead he could find, communities once alive with merriment, now burnt to ashes. This continued until the whole coastal region was obliterated, even the forts and earthworks, such was the fury of the dragon.

Then Beowulf heard the news that his own home, the best of all buildings, had been burnt to a cinder, and it was beyond his ability to bear. This building was not only his home, but the throne-room of the Geats! But Beowulf was the King of War, and war was on his mind as he plotted and planned his revenge upon the fuming dragon.

Unit 2

Task 8

This is a modern version of the extract. Compare it with your own analysis.

The king reclined at Camelot at Christmastime
With many noble lords and honoured guests,
Including the rich brotherhood of the Round Table,
With great feasting in carefree mood.
Taking part in tournaments on many occasions,
The gentle knights joined in jousting competitions
Before coming to the court to join in with carols.
The feast was in full swing for fifteen days,

With all the meat and mirth humanly possible;
Such glee and gladness, glorious to hear,
Boisterous din by day and dancing by night,
All hearts were full throughout the halls and chambers
With lords and ladies that pleased him most.

Task 9

This exercise will help you to remember the content of the extract and develop your own descriptive skills.

Task 10

Here are some possible answers to the comprehension questions:

a The Green Knight has come to challenge the bravery of the knights in Arthur's kingdom, as they have the reputation of being the best in the World. This challenge is in the form of a deadly game involving an exchange of blows from the Green Knight's axe. But it is more than a simple deadly game, as it turns out that the Green Knight expects the willing knight to go on a quest to find him in a year's time to face an almost certain death. This will test the knight's faithfulness to his promise as well as his courage.

b The Green Knight looks around threateningly and he refuses to accept King Arthur's hospitality. He questions the bravery of the knights in the hall and laughs at them when nobody rises to his challenge.

c He compliments King Arthur's people when he says they are considered to be the best in the World, and his knights are always ready to fight. He comes in peace and hopes to part as friends.

Task 11

Your lists might look something like this:

a **that, with, his, the, of, March, to, and, bathed, every, in, which, is, inspired, holt, Ram, open, eye, so, Nature, folk, on, pilgrimages, palmers, for, specially, from, shires, they, were, flour** (but here it means 'flower'), **goon** (but here it means 'go on')

b **whan, Aprill, roote, engendred, sweete, breeth, heeth, tendre, yonge,** halfe, cours, smale, maken, melodye, slepen, al, nyght, straunge, sondry, ende, Engelond, Caunterbury, hooly, blissful, martir, seke, flour (meaning 'flower'). 'seeke' does not mean 'seek', but rather 'sick'.

c **shoures, soote, droghte, hath, perced, veyne, swich, licour, vertu, Zephirus, eek, croppes, sonne, yronne, foweles, priketh, corages, thane, strondes, ferne, halwes, kowthe, londes, wende, holpen**

Task 12

This exercise will help you to practice your skills of analysis.

Task 13a and Task 13b

I have arranged all of the descriptive words and qualities attributed to the knight into two contrasting lists below. The first list contains qualities that tend not to be associated with soldiers in today's thinking.

gentlemanly, chivalrous, truthful, courteous, wise, gentle, meek, man of good conduct and polite in speech

The second list below contains the typical qualities of a modern soldier:

fighter of battles, defeater of opponents, strong, skillful, brave

A third list could be made of words that may apply to either of the lists above. They are:

highly valued, worthy of honour, high ranking, famous, perfect, noble, lover of freedom

Task 13c

During your discussion you should become aware of just how important honourable behavior was to the knights of the Middle Ages (the Medieval Period). This description of just one knight is incredibly detailed for such a short extract. In western thought, a soldier is tough (emotionally detached and strong), willing to do terrible deeds for the sake of his or her country. Everything else is secondary. So the second list above would be perfectly suited to the modern western soldier. However, it is good to be reminded of the importance of the qualities in the first list for a soldier.

Task 13d

The knight was a good person at least from the time he started to travel throughout the World on his horse as a knight.

Task 13e

The knight looked plain as he was wearing simple clothes that were stained with rust from his coat of chain mail. But this plain appearance did not suggest he was poor, it was simply due to the fact that he had fought in so many battles in difficult conditions that the metal on his chain mail had rusted, and he did not have the opportunity to change his clothes; he arrived at the inn the moment he returned from his latest battle because he was so determined to go on the pilgrimage to Canterbury.

Task 14

Here is an example of how to convert the Middle English original passage into modern English.

This young wife was beautiful, although
her body was small and slender like a weasel.
She wore a striped girdle made of silk,
and an apron as white as morning milk
on her hips, made up of lots of material.
Her smock was white, embroidered at the front
and at the back, like her collar,
inside and outside, but black as coal.
The tapes holding her white cap
matched her collar;
her broad headband was made of silk, set high off her brow.

Unit 3

Task 15

Here is a modern English version of the text:

And it is certainly true that our language now has a usage varying to some extent from that which was used when I was born. For we English men have been born under the dominion of the moon, which is never still but ever wavering, waxing one season, and waning and decreasing another season. And the common English that is spoken in one shire varies from another, in so much that in my days it happened that some merchants were in a ship on the Thames with the intention of sailing over the sea to Zeeland, and for lack of wind, they waited at the foreland, and went inland to refresh themselves; and one of them called Sheffield, a mercer, went into a house and asked for meat; and he especially asked for eggs. And the good wife answered by saying that she could not speak any French. And the merchant was angry because he could not speak French either, but he wanted eggs, and she did not understand him. And then eventually another said that he wanted 'eyren' (eggs). Then the good wife said that she understood him well. So, what should a man write these days, 'eggs' or 'eyren'? Indeed, it is hard to please everyone because of the diversity and changes in language.

Task 16a

You should have the following words:

heauen, forme, uoyde, darknesse, deepe, mooued, saide, sawe, hee, euening, againe, bee, middes

Task 16b

The two main spelling differences are in the addition of the letter 'e' to many words, and the use of the letter 'u' where we would expect a 'v.'

Task 17a

It's all Greek to me means 'I do not understand any of it.'

It vanished into thin air means 'It could not be found anywhere.'

To refuse to budge an inch means 'To refuse to change your mind or change your actions, even a little bit.'

To be tongue-tied means 'To be unable to speak clearly due to embarrassment, anxiety or a similar reason.'

To be in a pickle means 'To be in a complicated and difficult situation.'

To not sleep a wink means 'To not be able to sleep even for a little while.'

<u>Task 17b</u>

The lady protests too much.

All the World's a stage, and all men and women merely actors.

To exist, or not to exist, that is the question.

'To be' means 'to exist,' so this is the correct way to update the English of this Shakespearean phrase. However, it is much better to leave it in its original form, as even though the English is not clear today, the form 'to be' allows the imagination to consider a multitude of connotations. For example, when we use the phrase 'to be,' we would expect something to be added to form a sentence ('To be …'). So, here are just a few possibilities:

'To be alive, or not to be alive'; 'To be dead, or not to be dead'; 'To be content with anything that comes my way, or not to be content with whatever comes my way'; 'To be living in a dream, or not to be living in a dream,' etc.

Oh Romeo, Romeo, why are you like this Romeo? (Also see Additional Notes for Unit 3)

Not everything that glitters is gold.

The course of true love never runs smoothly.

Friends, Romans, countrymen, listen carefully.

Here, I have changed 'lend me your ears' to 'listen carefully' even though 'lend me your ears' is grammatically correct in today's English. The vocabulary and spelling are also correct. The issue to deal with is the fact that nobody would use this phrase today unless they were quoting Shakespeare, as the phrase is humorous to today's English speakers.

<u>Task 18</u>

A couple of the sentences do not need to be changed.

Your words are blunt and so are you.

Vile pile of criminal dung.

There's no more faith in you than in a stewed prune.

A good apple rotten at the core.

Not worth a gooseberry.

You are not worth the dust which the raw wind blows in your face.

No more brain than a stone.

You have in your skull no more brain than I have in my elbows.

Your lips are rotting off.

If only you were clean enough to spit on.

If I were like you, I would throw myself away.

Task 19

See Extract 20 in the main text.

Task 20

It is common for people whose first language is English to memorise at least some Shakespeare.

Task 21a

<u>Blow, winds, and crack your cheeks! Rage! Blow!</u>

Here, Lear is commanding the wind to blow hard, to be strong and devastating ('Rage!'). He personifies the wind by suggesting that its cheeks (like the cheeks of a face) bulge as its mouth exhales powerfully.

<u>... oak-cleaving thunderbolts, Singe my white head! And thou all-shaking thunder, Strike flat the thick rotundity o' the world ...</u>

'Thunderbolts' are forks of lightning that strike the trees (oak trees), cleaving them (splitting them in two). Lear feels he deserves to be struck by such thunderbolts, and creates the image of his white hair being singed or burnt by the lightning. Likewise, he calls on the thunder to bring destruction on earth.

<u>Rumble thy bellyful! Spit, fire! Spout, rain!</u>

Thunder rumbles deeply, and anger rumbles inside a person, bringing out a growling roar. Again, Shakespeare uses personification, giving the thunder a stomach. And the storm's mouth spits the lightning that burns up everything it strikes. The wind's saliva is rain.

<u>Nor rain, wind, thunder, fire are my daughters.</u>
<u>I tax not you, you elements, with unkindness ...</u>

Lear is saying that the various elements of the storm (rain, wind, thunder and fire) are not his daughters, so he does not blame them for anything, even though they cause so much devastation. However, his daughters are guilty and have also caused personal devastation to King Lear's life.

Task 21b

Here's a night pities neither wise men nor fools.

The Fool speaks as though the 'night' has personal values and emotions, but the night is not kind enough to differentiate between wise people and fools, and so the storm recklessly destroys everything in its path. In normal English prose today, we would add the word 'that' as follows: 'Here's a night that pities neither wise men nor fools.'

Task 22

The sonnets can be said to have the following rhyming pattern:

ABAB CDCD EFEF GG.

Sonnet I:

Lines 1 and 3, lines 2 and 4, 5 and 7, 6 and 8, 9 and 11, 10 and 12, 13 and 14.

Sonnet II:

Lines 1 and 3, lines 2 and 4, 5 and 7, 6 and 8, 9 and 11, 10 and 12, 13 and 14.

Unit 4

Task 23a

The King James Version only has three examples:

forme, darkenesse and deepe

Whereas the older translation, *the Geneva Bible*, has eight examples:

forme, uoyde, darknesse, deepe, saide, sawe, hee, againe and bee

Task 23b

The first sentence in *the KJV* chooses to have a capital letter at the beginning of the word 'Heaven' and the word 'Earth,' unlike *the Geneva Bible*, but the converse is true for the words 'evening' and 'morning' which have lower case for the first letter in *the KJV* for *the Geneva Bible*'s capital letters.

Instead of 'upon the deep,' *the KJV* has 'upon the face of the deep'; and instead of 'upon the waters,' *the KJV* has 'upon the face of the waters.'

The Geneva Bible uses the word 'middes' whereas *the KJV* uses 'midst.'

The KJV uses the word 'divided' and 'divide' in place of 'separated' and 'separate.'

Here are some reasons for the above:

The seeming discrepancy in the use of upper case and lower case first letters is due to translators' preference. The original language that *the Book of Genesis* is translated from does not distinguish between upper and lower case letters.

Using or omitting 'face of the' has little or no effect upon the meaning, so there are two possibilities. Because both phrases mean the same thing, either can be used in translation. Alternatively, the extra words may be due to an alternative ancient manuscript.

The word 'middes' is not a word used in today's English. The word 'midst' is used today, although it sounds a little old fashioned. It is likely that fifty years after the publication of *the Geneva Bible*, the most commonly accepted form 'midst' was adopted for *the KJV*, and 'middes' was eventually abandoned.

Whether the translator used the verb 'to separate' or the verb 'to divide' is not very important as they both mean exactly the same thing in the context of the passage. The original Hebrew word from which the translation was made, can be translated either way. And both English synonyms are equally acceptable today.

Task 23c

There are no speech marks ('...', or "...") for 'Let there be light'.

A colon (:) is used when you would expect a semi-colon (;), a full stop (.) or a comma (,).

The KJV was published in 1611, and punctuation as we know it was not fully established until the 18th century. Most punctuation in English began with the arrival of the printing press, and the symbols used for Latin were often adopted. In earlier manuscripts, spaces and decoration were used. Speech marks were not used at this time.

In regard to the colon (:), if you were to see the original manuscript of the translation, you would notice that the first of the six verses has no colon, but the other 5 longer verses are each marked by a colon to mark a halfway point, or a pause between two important statements within the verse.

Task 24a

The words are *righteousnes* and *goodnes*. Today we would have double 's' at the end, making: *righteousness* and *goodness*.

Task 24b

'oyle' should be 'oil'; 'mercie' should be 'mercy'; 'daies' should be 'days'. In each case, the older form has been printed with an extra letter.

Task 24c and Task 24d

In the following answers, I have combined both tasks:

<u>The Third Person Singular Pronoun</u>

He maketh

He leadeth

He restoreth

My cup (It) runneth over

In all of these examples, the following verb ends with the suffix '-eth'.

<u>The Second Person Singular Pronoun</u>

Thou art (You are)

Thou preparest (You prepare)

Thou anointest (You anoint)

In two examples, the suffix '-est' is added to the verb, but in the use of 'art' in 'Thou art,' we have an irregular form. The verb 'to be' is irregular in today's English too.

<u>The Second Person Singular Possessive Pronoun</u>

Thy rod (Your rod)

Thy staff (Your staff)

In both cases, the possessive 'your' is written 'thy'.

The First Person Singular Possessive Pronoun

Mine enemies (My enemies)

The possessive pronoun 'my' is written as 'mine'.

Task 24e

Here is my translation of Psalm 23 in today's modern English. Your version should look something like this:

The LORD is my shepherd, I lack nothing.

He makes me lie down in green pastures;

he leads me beside still waters.

He restores my soul;

he guides me in paths of righteousness for his name's sake.

Even though I walk through the valley of the shadow of deep darkness, I will fear no evil;

for you are with me; your rod and your staff comfort me.

You prepare a table for me in the presence of my enemies;

you anoint my head with oil; my cup overflows.

Surely goodness and mercy will follow me all the days of my life;

and I will live in the house of the LORD forever.

Task 25

Here is an example of how the passage can be converted into today's English prose:

This is an account of humankind's first act of disobedience, and the fruit of that forbidden tree, whose mortal taste brought death into the world, and all our troubles. Eden was lost as a result, until a greater man could restore us.

Holy Spirit, Heaven hides nothing from you, neither does deep Hell, so tell us what caused our ancestral parents, who were in such a blissful state and so highly favoured in Heaven, to fall away from their Creator by disobeying him; if it were not for one single lack of restraint, they would have remained lords of the whole world. Who first seduced them to that foolish rebellion? It was the Serpent of Hell, whose scheming was stirred up by envy and a desire for revenge, that deceived the mother of humankind, because he had been cast out from Heaven with all his rebel angels. This was due to the fact that he considered himself to be of greater glory than those around him and even equal to the Most High, and he sought to obtain this position with the help of the rebel angels, by ambitiously opposing the throne and monarchy of God. In his pride, the Serpent of Hell started an unholy war in Heaven, but it was in vain, as he was hurled out in flames by the Almighty Power, falling down through the air until he reached the fires of the bottomless pit in disastrous defeat. There he must stay in unbreakable chains in the flames of punishment because he dared to defy the Omnipotent One in battle.

Task 26

Here are most of the phrases that you will have selected, all of them incorrect in today's English. I have given their equivalents in today's modern English for each one.

he had gone but a little way	he had only gone a little distance
he espied	he saw
Then did Christian begin to be afraid	Then Christian began to be afraid
and to cast in his mind	and to consider carefully
had I no more in my eye than the saving of my life	if I was only concerned about saving my life
his mouth was as the mouth of a lion	his mouth was like the mouth of a lion
Were it not that I hope that	If it wasn't for the fact that I am hoping that
your wages such as a man could not live on	and a person could not live on your wages
I might mend myself	I might improve my behaviour
what our country will afford	what our country can afford
I have let myself to another	I have given myself to another
return again unto me	return again to me
I am willing to pass by all	I am willing to forget it all
what I did as to my compliance with thee	what I did according to your

	expectations
leave off to persuade me further	don't try to persuade me anymore

<u>Task 27</u>

Here are most of them:

Thou hast	*You have*
Thy service	*Your service*
How dost thou	*How do you*
Thou didst faint	*You fainted*
Thou wast	*You were*
Thou didst attempt	*You attempted*
Thy burden	*Your burden*
Thou shouldest have	*You should have*
Thy Prince	*Your Prince*
Thou didst sinfully sleep	*You sinfully slept*
Thou talkest	*You talk*
Thou hast seen	*You have seen*
Thou art	*You are*
Thou sayest	*You say*
Thy country	*Your country*
To withstand thee	*To withstand you*
Prepare thyself	*Prepare yourself*
Thou shalt	*You shall*
Thy soul	*Your soul*

You will notice that in every case, the meaning of the Second Person Pronoun is singular as it is referring to one man. Without the context, it would be impossible to know from today's English, whether these phrases concern one person or more than one person (singular or plural).

<u>Task 28</u>

a Christian decided not to turn back because he had no armour on his back, and if he turned his back to the monster, it could easily kill him by firing arrows into him.

b He was very ugly, with scales that looked like the scales of a fish. He had wings like a dragon and feet like a bear. Fire and smoke came out of his stomach and his mouth was ferocious like a lion's mouth.

c i. The City was evil; ii. It belonged to the monster Apollyon who was its king; iii. Serving Apollyon was difficult and sinful; iv. Death was an inevitable consequence of living there; v. Christian wanted to improve his behaviour.

d i. He likes his wages; ii. His servants; iii. His governance; iv. His company; v. His country.

Task 29a

The phrases that are not typical of today's English writing and speech are as follows:

The perturbation of my mind

I slept unquiet

dreamed always frightful dreams

often started out of my sleep

In the day ... in the night

I dreamed often

justify the doing of it

for I marked all upon the post still

it blew a very great storm of wind all day

I know not what

my present condition

a noise of a gun

were quite of another kind

I started up

and in a trice clapped my ladder to

a flash of fire bade me listen

some ship in distress

Task 29b

Here are the updated phrases from Task 29b:

The tension in my mind

my sleep was restless

always had terrible dreams

often woke up with a start

During the day ... at night

I often dreamed

justify doing it

because I still marked everything on the post

there blew a great stormy wind all day

I do not know what

my present situation

the sound of a gun

were quite different

I quickly got up

and in the blink of an eye fastened my ladder to

a flash of fire caught my attention

a ship in distress

Task 30

This task is very good analysis practice.

Task 31

Here are the underlined sections with a possible equivalent in today's modern English.

<u>I looked about me</u>

I looked around me

<u>The country round appeared like a continued garden</u>

The countryside around me appeared like a continuous garden

<u>inclosed fields</u>

enclosed fields

woods of half a stang

woods half the height of a pole

and the tallest trees, as I could judge, appeared to be seven foot high

and the tallest trees, as far as I could tell, were seven foot high

For the better convenience of beholding him

So I could look at him better

but three yards off

only three yards away

I have had him since many times in my hand

Since then I have had him in my hand many times

cannot be deceived in the description

can describe him quite accurately

His dress was very plain

His form of dress was very plain

the fashion of it between the Asiatick and the European

a combination of Asian and European in style

if I should happen to break loose

in case I managed to break loose

most magnificently clad

dressed magnificently

to address themselves to me

to address me directly

to no purpose

to no avail

the impertinence, and probably the malice of the rabble, who were very impatient to croud about me as near as they durst

the impatient rabble, impertinently and probably maliciously, crowd around me as near as they dare

sate

sat

<u>whereof one</u>

of which one

<u>thought no punishment so proper as to deliver them bound</u>

thought there was no better punishment than to bind and deliver them

<u>accordingly did</u>

did accordingly

<u>and as to the sixth, I made a countenance as if I would</u>

and as for the sixth, I gave a look as though I was going to

<u>squalled terribly</u>

screamed in terror

<u>were in much pain</u>

were in great anguish

<u>put them out of fear; for, looking mildly</u>

allayed their fears by looking at them with a gentle expression

<u>highly obliged at this mark of my clemency</u>

very grateful for this act of clemency

Additional Task A

You will have found that some phrases make sense on their own, but as a whole sentence, none of the three latter combinations make sense. This is due to the fact that every word has its own unique nuance of meaning, so we must remember not to randomly pick synonyms from a dictionary to insert into any given sentence.

Additional Task B

*We decided not to get **divorced*** (original)

*We decided not to **separate***

It does not make sense here to say, 'We decided not to **get** separated', so the word 'get' had to be removed from the original clause. 'To get separated' is to suggest that some other person or action forced them to separate rather than it being a personal choice.

*We decided not to get **divorced*** (original)

*We decided not to **divide up** our possessions*

We simply should not use the word 'divide' here to express 'divorce,' and the clause, 'We decided not to get divided,' is incorrect English in this context. I had to use the synonym 'to divide' to express the possible consequences of a divorce, as an object is required after the verb.

*We decided not to get **divorced*** (original)

*We decided not to **split up***

Again, I have had to remove the word 'get', as 'We decided not to **get** split up' assumes the split was due to external forces rather than a personal decision, unlike divorce.

Additional Task C

This task will help you to appreciate the importance of choosing the right synonym for your written work, and of making sure you check the structure of your sentence is appropriate for the word you choose.

Here is one example of how you can design your synonym ladder for the subject of HAPPINESS:

```
           H A P P Y
        E C S T A T I C
          T H R I L L E D
       D E L I G H T E D
          P L E A S E D
         C O N T E N T
```

Unit 5

Task 32

Here are the words and phrases that are unique to Scots English in the poem *Auld Lang Syne*, listed with their accompanying meaning in today's modern Standard English.

auld	old
lang syne	long since
jo	dear
ye'll be your pint-stowp	you'll pay for your pint cup
tak a cup o'kindness yet	again offer a toast (take a cup of kindness still)
We twa hae run about the braes	We two have run around the slopes
pou'd the gowans fine	picked the beautiful daisies
mony a weary fit	many a weary foot
Sin	Since
paidl'd in the burn	paddled in the stream
Frae morning sun till dine	From morning sun till dinnertime
But seas between us braid hae roar'd	But the broad seas between us have roared
my trusty fiere	my good friend (my trusty friend)
gie's a hand o'thine	give me your hand (give us a hand of yours)
tak a right gude-willie-waught	wish good will by sharing a drink (a 'willie-waught' is a deep draft of ale)

Task 33

The only word in the poem that is unique to Scots is 'straths.' A strath is a large, wide river valley.

Task 34a

The first stanza suggests that the tiger must have been made by the most amazing immortal being (God the Creator). Only God *'Could frame thy fearful symmetry.'* This means that only God 'was able to create your awesome body.'

When this stanza is repeated at the end of the poem, the word 'could' is changed to 'dare.' This is because by the end of the poem you will understand not only how beautiful the tiger is but also how dangerous and powerful it is, so much so that only God would 'dare' to make such an animal.

Task 34b

Your lists should look something like this, but some parts are unclear as to the poet's original intentions. I have put a handful of phrases in brackets where it is open to individual interpretation.

<u>The words and phrases that directly refer to the Creator</u>

immortal hand or eye,

(what wings dare he aspire)

the hand

shoulder

(dread hand)

dread grasp

Dare

Did he smile his work to see?

Did he who made the lamb make thee?

<u>The words and phrases that directly refer to the tiger</u>

Tyger Tyger, burning bright

thy fearful symmetry

the fire of thine eyes

the sinews of thy heart

thy heart began to beat

(dread feet)

thy brain

its deadly terrors

<u>The words and phrases that describe the creative process</u>

Could frame

(Burnt the fire of thine eyes)

art

twist the sinews of thy heart

What the hammer? What the chain?

In what furnace was thy brain?

the anvil

dread grasp

Task 35a

This task will help you with your analytical skills.

Task 35b

10 lines end in a word that rhymes with another in the same quatrain. The rhyming words are listed with their partner below.

green, seen

hills, mills

gold, unfold

desire, fire

hand, land

Task 36

Here are the original sentences from *Pride and Prejudice,* with an alternative Standard English equivalent that would be used today.

A single man in possession of a good fortune must be in want of a wife.

A single person with a good fortune ('in possession of a good fortune' is also appropriate today) must be in need of a wife.

'Oh! single, my dear, to be sure!'

'Oh! Definitely single, darling!'

'What a fine thing for our girls!'

'That's promising for the girls!'

'How can you be so tiresome! You must know that I am thinking of his marrying one of them.'

'Why are you so awkward! You know I'm hoping he's going to marry one of them!'

'Is that his design in settling here?'

'Is that his reason for settling here?'

'How can you talk so!'

'How can you talk like that!'

'I see no occasion for that.'

'I can't see any reason to do that.'

'... for as you are as handsome as any of them, Mr Bingley might like you the best of the party.'

'... because you're just as beautiful as the girls, and Mr Bingley might like you the best of the bunch.'

Note that 'handsome' is not correct when referring to a woman now. We would say, 'beautiful' 'attractive' or 'good looking.' When referring to a man, the following are common: 'handsome' 'attractive' or 'good looking.'

Task 37

Here is my updated version of the extract:

'Miss Elizabeth, why aren't you dancing? — Mr Darcy, let me introduce you to this young lady who would make a wonderful dance partner for you. — You can't refuse to dance with her, surely; she is so beautiful. And taking her hand, he was going to give it to Mr Darcy, who, though extremely surprised, was happy to receive it, but she felt uncomfortable and instantly drew back, saying to Sir William,

'I'm afraid I have no desire to dance. — I hope you don't think I came over here to beg for a dancing partner.'

Mr Darcy respectfully requested to be allowed the honour of her hand; but in vain. Elizabeth was adamant, and Sir William could not shake her resolve however much he tried to persuade her.

'You are so good at dancing, Miss Eliza, that it is cruel to deny me the chance of watching you; and even though he doesn't particularly like dancing, he can't possibly object to sacrifice half an hour of his time.'

'Mr Darcy is very polite,' said Elizabeth, smiling.

'He is — but it's not surprising he's so willing, Eliza; who wouldn't dance with someone like you?'

Elizabeth gave a condescending look, and turned away.

In addition to the above changes, the names are not used correctly according to today's English. Today, it is not right to use Mr, Mrs or Miss followed by a

Christian name (Personal name). For example, the expression 'Miss Eliza' is very strange today. The correct options are: Miss Eliza Bennet, Miss Bennet, Miss Elizabeth Bennet, Elizabeth Bennet, Eliza Bennet, Elizabeth, or Eliza.

Task 38

Below are the phrases and sentences taken from *Emma*, with an alternative Standard English equivalent that would be used today.

Emma Woodhouse, handsome, clever, and rich.

Emma Woodhouse, attractive, clever, and rich.

She had, in consequence of her sister's marriage …

She had, as a consequence of her sister's marriage …

Her mother had died too long ago for her to have more than an indistinct remembrance of her caresses.

Her mother had died too long ago for her to have more than an indistinct memory of her caresses.

Task 39

Below are the phrases and sentences taken from *Emma*, with an alternative Standard English equivalent that would be used today.

'… but I think it a bad thing.'

'… but I think it's a bad thing.'

'Emma must do Harriet good.'

'How could Emma not do Harriet good!'

'I have been seeing their intimacy with the greatest pleasure.'

'I have really enjoyed watching just how well they get on.'

'How very differently we feel!'

'We feel so differently!'

'Perhaps you think I am come on purpose to quarrel with you, knowing Weston to be out.'

'Perhaps you think I've just come to quarrel with you, knowing Weston would be out.'

'… for he thinks exactly as I do on the subject.'

'... because he thinks exactly as I do on the subject.'

'We were speaking of it only yesterday.'

'We were talking about it only yesterday.'

Task 40

These are sample answers to the comprehension questions.

a What subjects did Victor Frankenstein study?

Natural philosophy and particularly chemistry.

b In your own words, according to Frankenstein, how does scientific pursuit differ from studying other subjects?

With other subjects, there is nothing new to discover, so you just have to learn all there is this to know. But with science, there is always something new to find out and marvel at.

c What did Frankenstein do to acquire the knowledge he needed?

He read the modern research with ardour, and attended lectures, and spent time with the scientists at the university. He tirelessly laboured day after day until he discovered something new.

d What was the result of his hard work?

He improved so rapidly that at the end of two years he made some new discoveries in the improvement of some chemical compounds, which procured him great esteem and admiration at the university.

He discovered the very cause of generation and life, and became capable of bestowing animation upon lifeless matter.

e The answers to this part will be varied. Discussing these questions will help you to identify with the scene that Mary Shelley is setting in her novel.

Task 41

These are sample answers to the comprehension questions.

a Why was Frankenstein so anxious to the point of agony?

He could have been fearful for several reasons: fear that all his efforts would be unsuccessful, fear that the monster might attack him, fear that life may never be the same and what that may entail, and a simple fear at the prospect of facing a human-creature made from the body parts of dead people come to life.

b Why did she call the human corpse a 'thing'?

It was difficult to think of the creature as a true single human being as it had been formed from the parts of dead bodies. Even if Frankenstein succeeded in bringing the creature to life, he did not know if it would have the typical characteristics of a human.

c Why do you think the author set this event on a late, dreary, rainy night, with his candle dim?

Horror stories often use this kind of background to increase the sense of horror or terror in the minds of the readers. The room was dimly lit, and many people are fearful of the dark as you cannot see clearly what is in the room.

d Why does he call his creation a 'wretch'?

In 'part b' we saw that the creature could not be fully considered to be a human being, and was therefore referred to as a 'thing.' The word 'wretch' implies the same, but with the added negativity of the creature being bad.

e What does the following quotation mean and why did he say it?:

'the beauty of the dream vanished, and breathless horror and disgust filled my heart'

Your answer to this question will be unique, so I have not answered it for you.

Task 42

This is a memorising task.

Task 43

This is a memorising task.

Task 44

I have not written the following in a paragraph because there are numerous ways to do so. However, I have written a possible list of descriptions that come directly from the poem in today's English, the content of which may be in your paragraph:

The skylark is amazing (worthy of praise).

More than just a bird, heavenly.

It naturally sings vibrantly, and its song is like art.

It springs up from the earth and flies higher and higher.

As it rises, it continues to sing and then hovers high in the sky.

In the evening, the sunlight reflects off the skylark, making it look like a star in the sky, but in the daylight, the bird is not so visible, although its shrill-sounding song can be easily heard.

Task 45

I have not written the following in a paragraph because there are numerous ways to do so. However, I have written a possible list of descriptions that come directly from the poem in today's English, the content of which may be in your paragraph:

Listening to the nightingale brings an ecstatic happiness.

The nightingale is like a heavenly being.

The nightingale has a happy life.

The delicate bird sings melodiously from the green trees and their many shadows.

It sings in the summer and its song reminds people of summertime.

The beautiful song helps you to relax and drift into pleasing imagination.

The bird's song helps you to forget your troubles and the onset of old age with its limitations.

Task 46

Here are the elements connected with the number 3 in the story.

Once upon a time there were three bears (all through the story)

One of them was a little, small, wee bear (three adjectives repeated each time the bear is referred to)

They each had a pot for their porridge (3 pots)

And they each had a chair to sit in (3 chairs)

And they each had a bed to sleep in (3 beds)

But she was an impudent, bad old woman (3 adjectives to describe the woman)

'... *in his great, rough, gruff voice*' (3 adjectives)

The woman tastes the 3 bowls of porridge, tries the 3 chairs and the 3 beds. Each 'try' is described with similar emphasis, giving 3 sets of 3 actions. Then the bears comment on each of the 3 bowls, the 3 chairs and then the 3 beds also with equal emphasis.

Unit 6

Task 47a

Here are a couple of phrases in which the author expresses sarcasm, with the real meaning underneath. You may have used different words to express the same thing.

<u>*the impious and profane offence of asking for more*</u>

the reasonable and understandable action of asking for more

<u>*by the wisdom and mercy of the board*</u>

by the stupidity and callousness of the board

Task 47b

This task will help you to empathise with Oliver Twist and orphans like him, and enable you to show greater responsibility towards those in need within your own society, just like Charles Dickens hoped to do in his days.

Task 48

This activity is time consuming but the rewards are great. Even if you do not at this stage understand the reason behind every change, this understanding will increase as you bear these things in mind when reading other works of English Literature.

Task 49

Here are some ideas for fulfilling the task.

Look at the two following quotations from the dialogue:

"Must we part this way, St. John? And when you go to India, will you leave

me so, without a kinder word than you have yet spoken?"

"When I go to India, Jane, will I leave you? What! Do you not go to India?"

Both examples are very indirect. Today, there would not be such an 'air of respectability.' There is a formal distance between Jane and St. John even though they are talking about something as intimate as marriage.

However, in this case, it is not only because such a culture of respect was common among the upper classes, but also because St. John was not actually in love with Jane. In those days, 'appropriate' marriages of convenience were more common, with factors such as position and financial security having a greater importance than today.

In regard to the first quote, today's Jane would be more direct with:

"I know you're upset that I'm not going to India with you, but can't we part with some nicer words?"

This is much shorter and to the point. Then St. John would say something like the following:

"What! So you're definitely not going, then?"

This is also shorter and more to the point.

It is also possible, of course, that Charlotte Bronte was making the dialogues and narration very formal in her novel to be accepted for publication, in the same way that the BBC would initially only televise productions where the actors spoke the Queen's English (It is quite the reverse now).

In regard to speech today, English speakers from all walks of society use contracted forms such as: I'm, he's, they'll, they've, he'd, I'd, etc., so I have altered the original text where necessary. It is far too long-winded, in speech, to say things like:

"And you will not marry me?"

"Your words are such that ought not to be used;"

Another example of excessive formality not often seen today, can be found in St. John's following long sentence. For narrative, such long sentences are appropriate, but in speech, we would not usually do this:

"*They betray an unfortunate state of mind; they merit severe reproof. They would seem inexcusable, but that it is the duty of man to forgive his fellow, even until seventy-and-seven times.*"

Another cultural feature of the upper classes during the Victorian Period, is the inability to express deep emotion. Jane is step by step ascertaining St. John's feelings, and at the same time, St. John is struggling to control his emotions, although his quivering lip is a little indicator of how hurt he is:

'*That bloodless lip quivered to a temporary spasm. I knew the steely ire I had whetted.*'

There is also the issue of inequality between men and women in Victorian times. The woman was expected to be dependent on her husband, and his career and aspirations were given priority. In this respect, Jane was not willing to be controlled. She was intelligent and more independent in her thinking than her society would expect. Even so, she was very tactful in the way she let St. John down. In her day, to offend a man like St. John too bluntly and insensitively, would attract disapproval from her peers, and give her a bad reputation. Today, it would be more appropriate to be open and honest about your feelings, to avoid misunderstandings.

Task 50

The skills of analysis used for this task are essential for anyone doing research into language development. They are also useful when learning how to use English correctly today.

Task 51

Keep this glossary for use with Extract 51a.

Task 52

This activity will help you to gain confidence in speaking English, work on your pronunciation, and become more familiar with English Literature.

Task 53

Here are some sample answers to the Task.

'Thy foot is on the skull which thou hast made'

The Son of God has power over each human being, the power of life and death.

'Thou wilt not leave us in the dust'

The Son of God will not leave us in terrible circumstances, and he demonstrated this by creating us from dust at the beginning.

'He thinks he was not made to die'

Human beings have an inner belief that they should stay alive and remain healthy, and that death is something to avoid.

'The highest, holiest manhood, Thou'

The Son of God is the best human to have ever existed, and as such has the highest position of all human beings. He is also the holiest person to have ever existed.

'Our wills are ours, we know not how'

We humans do not understand how we have an individual personality that makes private decisions, and has the freedom to choose how to think and act.

'Our wills are ours, to make them Thine'

We should use our individual freedom of choice by choosing to give our souls to the Son of God, as he is perfect Love.

Task 54a

Here are some sample explanatory paragraphs for each of the first 6 verses of Robert Browning's poem.

In the first verse of this monologue poem, the poet is describing the activities of the apothecary in the laboratory. It mentions the mask that the wife wears as she, through the smoke from the chemicals, watches him work on the devilish task; 'devilish' because of the intended use of the drug, which is to poison her husband's lover. There is alliteration in the last line with the repeated 'p.' This creates the rhythm of an excited heart-beat.

The next verse makes it clear that while this work is going on, her husband is at that same moment being unfaithful to her, and the lovers are aware that the wife knows about it. She believes that in spite of her tears, they are laughing about her together. They think she is taking solace in an empty church while she is actually revelling in her vengeful activity in the laboratory.

In the third verse, the poison-making process is described in the words 'grind' 'moisten' 'mash' and 'pound.' She uses the imperative mood as she urges the apothecary to continue at his work. The repeated alliterative 'p' sound (in 'paste' 'pound' and 'powder') and the assonance (repeated vowel sounds) in 'pound' and 'powder' verbally express the creative method taking place. She is not in a hurry, as she is having more fun sat there watching the devilish process than she would have dancing at the court of the king.

In the fourth verse, the wife is considering the wonder and beauty of the materials used for such an evil purpose, materials from nature itself, used for creating a poison. The blue chemical looks so beautiful that she imagines it must taste sweet, making her question whether it is possible for such a beautiful thing to have the result of a successful murder.

The following verse likens the poisons in the laboratory to typical feminine gifts and treasures such as earrings, caskets, fan-mounts and filigree baskets. She wishes she had all of these various poisons as a treasure, and she would delight in carrying them with her; in doing so, she would be carrying the delightful power to dole out death wherever and whenever she wanted as a gift, and nobody would know.

The sixth verse describes her generalised intentions. For example, at the court of the king, she could give a simple pill to Pauline and she would die in just half an hour; or she could light a simple tablet of incense creating poisonous fumes that would kill Elise, causing a quick and complete end to her life.

Task 54b

There is a clear pattern. Each verse is a quatrain with rhyming couplets in AABB format.

Task 55

This exercise will help with your analytical skills. You can also learn from your partner's conclusions.

Task 56

Here are some sample answers to the comprehension questions.

a Tom had been bullied and injured by Flashman.

b 'Flashey' is Flashman's nickname. He is the school bully, which means he enjoys frightening and hurting his fellow students.

c The phrase *'toadied himself back into favour again'* means he did good things for people to regain his position of influence.

d His good behaviour was not sincere, but a necessary step to increase in power again with the intention of returning to his bullying behaviour.

e Two or three boys helped Flashman to restrain Tom in front of an open fire.

Task 57

This exercise will help you to understand the importance of carefully analysing extracts of English Literature before you feel certain of the author's meaning, especially in view of the fact that grammatical structures are always changing, along with the choice and definition of words.

Task 58

Here are some sample answers:

a Obviously, the first statement means that the eater is able to see what he or she eats. The latter statement can mean a similar thing, for example, if the eater chooses only to eat things that he or she is able to see. However, the meanings diverge if you understand the latter statement to mean what immediately comes to mind: everything the eater sees, he or she will eat (from food to trees to people!). It is quite possible for the Hatter to be implying this meaning, as he is mad anyway; he is also trying to say these two statements are different.

b The meaning of 'I like what I get,' depends on the meaning of 'get,' which depends on the context of the conversation. Here, there is no context, so it depends on what you perceive the context might be. For example, if 'get' refers to everything that you 'buy' when you go shopping, the sentence is implying that you are always successful in buying something you like; you never regret having bought it.

However, if 'get,' is referring to everything you 'receive' (as a gift for example), then it means you fortunately always like those gifts.

In the former case (buy), personal decision making is key; in the latter case (receive), the gift you receive is based on the decision making of another person.

If ALL of the meanings mentioned above are understood to be meant by the word 'get,' then both statements ('I like what I get' and 'I get what I like') are identical. However, if the first statement applies only to 'buying' and the second statement applies only to 'receiving a gift,' — or vice versa — then the two statements do not mean the same thing; hence the ambiguity. It is difficult for Alice to challenge the trio over this, as there would need to be a lengthy discussion about context.

In addition to this, in a certain context, *'I get what I like,'* can mean 'I get whatever I like' (I am free to obtain or buy anything I want with no restrictions [however, that does not mean I will always like it when I get it]). In this case, the two statements are very different.

So, in this example, the evidence used by the trio to support their argument is more ambiguous, and therefore not as strong as the first one about 'seeing' and 'eating.'.

c Everybody breathes when they sleep, otherwise they would die. The second statement 'I sleep when I breathe,' can only sensibly mean, 'Every time I breathe, I sleep.' Even though this makes sense, it is actually 'senseless' as nobody would have a need to make this statement, and to sleep every time you breathe is ridiculous, unless you are in a coma of course. So the Dormouse is right to suggest these two statements are different, and just because the statements sound similar, does not mean they are one and the same thing. However, as it happens — ironically — in the case of the Dormouse, the two statements do mean the same thing.

So the three examples given to annoy Alice serve to confuse and frustrate her, because of all the mental twists and turns she has to endure.

d Alice is suggesting that the Hatter is wasting time. This is a reasonable statement. But the Hatter understands (or pretends to understand) Alice to be speaking of a person or humanlike animal, Time being the name of that being. The Hatter says he knows this 'person' well, and talking about 'wasting' that 'person' is rude. In Alice's case, 'time' is an abstract reality, which requires a small 't' within her sentences. The Hatter believes 'Time' is a 'person,' so that would require the first letter to be a capital 'T.' But this is a dialogue, so what we can understand by reading (and noticing the capital 'T'), is not as immediately obvious to Alice, as she is simply listening. So, she continues to be confused.

e Alice is not yet aware of the Hatter's understanding of 'time,' and adds *'I have to beat time when I learn music,'* meaning to innocently clap her hands to the beat. The Hatter says that 'Time' (the 'person') will not 'stand beating' ('stand beating' means 'accept or endure being punched'), as it will hurt.

f The Hatter goes on to give an example of why treating Time badly is inadvisable. Once, when the Hatter was singing to the Queen, she was not happy so she shouted *'He's murdering time!'* meaning he is 'wasting time badly,' which ironically takes us back to Alice's words at the beginning of this discussion, and defends what she said.

g The Hatter misunderstood the Queen's words to mean he was murdering a 'person' called Time.

Task 59

Here are a couple of sample versions. You must do your own of course. **'Twas** is a poetic form of **It was**, changing two syllables into one.

'Twas midnight, and the slimy toads

Did croak and leap in the logs;

All spooky were the haunted groves,

And the rat-infested bogs.

'Twas wonderful, and the singing larks
Did hover and glide in the sky;
All enchanting were the natural parks,
And the multi-various birds did fly.

Task 60

Some of the poetic language may be a little confusing at the beginning, but as you read it and study it properly, the meanings of the phrases should be quite clear.

Task 61

The purpose of changing the vernacular here into today's speech is simply to aid your understanding of the conversation. Obviously, it is more authentic to leave the speech as it is in the original account.

Here are some sample answers.

Long John Silver:

'Mate (My friend), it's because you are like gold dust to me – gold dust, and I mean it! If I hadn't taken to you so much, do you think I'd have been here warning you? It's done — you can't change the situation; I'm saying this to save your neck, and if one of those wild ones knew about it, where would I be, Tom, tell me, where would I be?'

Crew Member:

'Silver, you're old, and you're honest, or at least you have that reputation; and you've got money, too, which lots of poor sailors don't have; and you're brave, unless I'm wrong. And you're telling me you're going to let yourself be led astray by that kind of thing? Not you, surely! As God is my witness, I'd rather lose my hand ...'

Task 62

This discussion will help you to understand your responsibilities in regard to living as a good citizen. But this does not only relate to avoiding bad behaviour; it also relates to good behaviour that we should have. Sometimes simply avoiding situations where we could help others honestly is just as bad as doing bad things – an absence of action can be bad in itself.

Task 63

Here is my updated version.

'Mr. Utterson had already shuddered at the mention of Hyde's name; but when the stick was laid before him, he could not doubt it any longer; in spite of the fact that it was so broken and battered, he recognised it as the one he had given to Henry Jekyll himself, many years before.

"Is this Mr. Hyde a short person?" he inquired.

"Very short and particularly wicked-looking, according to the maid," said the officer.'

Task 64

This task will help you to appreciate the kind of atmosphere typical of many Gothic Horror stories.

Task 65

a:

Flossy catkins of the later kinds

Fern-fronds

The square headed moschatelle

Cuckoo-pint

Lady's-smocks

The toothwort

Nightshade

Black-petaled doleful-bells

b:

Mr Jan Coggan

Second shearer

Third shearer

Henry Fray

Susan Tall's husband

Joseph Poorglass

Cain Ball

Gabriel Oak as general supervisor

c:

The Shearing Barn

d:

'... the large side doors were thrown open towards the sun to admit a beautiful light ...'

'... the sun slanting in upon their bleached shirts, tanned arms, and the polished shears ...'

'... causing these to bristle with a thousand rays, strong enough to blind a weak-eyed man.'

Task 66

Tess and her mother Joan's speech can be updated as follows:

Joan:

"I want to go and get your father; but more than that, I want to tell you what's happened. You'll be really proud, poppet, when you know!"

Note: I have kept the word 'poppet' as there are countless words of endearment used throughout the world when speaking English. These words of endearment are usually specific to a particular locality. 'Poppet' is still used in many places.

Tess:

"Had it anything to do with Dad making such a fool of himself in that carriage this afternoon? — Unbelievable! I was so embarrassed, I wanted the ground to open up and swallow me!"

Joan:

"That was all to do with the excitement! We've been found to be from the best breeding in the whole county — reaching all the way back to long before Oliver Cromwell's time — to the days of the Pagan Turks — with monuments and vaults and crests and scutcheons ..."

"In Saint Charles' days we were made Knights of the Royal Oak, our real name being d'Urberville ... Doesn't that make you feel proud?"

Task 67a

There are 78 words in the first sentence.

Here is a sample sentence using Sir Arthur Conan Doyle's basic grammatical structure and punctuation from the first sentence. This exercise may be a little difficult, but you should try to write your own sample sentence too.

'*After looking over the student's essays from his three years of study from which I have throughout his time here assessed his English ability, I notice many excellent, some average, a large number very original, but none poor; because, working as he did rather for the pleasure of learning foreign languages than for simply passing exams, he did not neglect getting involved in extra-curricular activities which helped to improve his acquisition of foreign languages, especially English.*'

Task 67b

Here are my updated versions of Sherlock Holmes' speech:

'*but it seems to be the norm this morning. Mrs Hudson was knocked up, then she did the same to me, and I to you.*'

'*Apparently a young lady has arrived in a considerable state of distress, and she insists on seeing me. She's waiting in the sitting-room now.*'

Task 68

Here is one way to update the text, keeping the formality of the extract. Your updated example will not be identical to mine. I have underlined the areas that have required adaption.

'... *You have <u>come by</u> train this morning, I see.*'

'*You <u>already know about</u> me, then?*'

'*No, but I <u>can see</u> the second half of a return ticket in the palm of your left glove. You must have <u>set off early, but you also had a long drive</u> in a dog-cart, along <u>bumpy</u> roads, before you reached the station.*'

The lady <u>jerked violently</u>, and stared in bewilderment at my companion.

'*There is no mystery, my dear madam,*' <u>he said</u>, smiling. '*The left arm of your jacket is spattered with mud in no less than seven places. The marks are* *perfectly fresh. There is no vehicle <u>except for a</u> dog-cart which throws up mud in that way, and then only when you sit on the left-hand side of the driver.'*

'*Whatever your reasons may be, you are perfectly correct,*' <u>she said</u>.

Task 69

A good discussion should help you to identify with Mowgli in the story, and your conclusions should help to highlight issues concerning class distinction and intercultural communication.

Task 70a

This discussion will promote a greater understanding of social responsibility.

Task 70b

This task is not too difficult, so it does not need an example here.

Task 71

The word 'till' is still used today, but it is less formal now. In line with the relative formality of the passage, 'until' is necessary. 'Upon' is not as common today, and the simple 'on' is normal in these cases. 'Woke' is acceptable here, but 'woke up' is more likely today. These changes have very little significance.

Several words in the passage would be considered old fashioned today, such as 'visage,' so I have replaced the word with the verb 'to look' which is more typical of today's English; this also requires the sentence structure to change. The word 'splendid' is used today, and can be used in the same way as it is in the extract, but there are other words that are more likely to have been chosen if the novel were written today.

There is very little difference between the two versions of the extract because only 130 years have elapsed between the production of the novel and today. The English Language has existed for 1,500 years, so it is reasonable to assume the works of just over a hundred years ago are easily understood by the modern reader, especially narrative.

Task 72

When you have completed this task, you can share your results with your partner and compare your conclusions, assessing whether one is better than the other, or whether both are equally acceptable, and why.

Task 73

This discussion not only helps students to understand the passage better, but also understand society's corporate responsibility for ensuring ethical issues are taken seriously in everything we do.

Task 74

This exercise will prepare the student well for the following extracts.

Task 75

Anyway

In any case

Today, we use the phrase 'In any case,' but 'Anyway' is more likely in this situation.

so many opportunities

some many opportunities

Using the word 'some' in a phrase like this was very common in Victorian times, but it is not usual today.

a little

somewhat

The word 'somewhat' is much less commonly used today, and its use here sounds old fashioned.

because

for

Obviously, the word 'for' is extremely commonly used today, as a preposition for example, but it is not used to mean 'because' any more.

and I could not have been mistaken

and it could be no delusion

If Harker had stated: 'I was not deluding myself,' then it would not need to be updated. Although this ('I was not deluding myself') is probably what he meant, I wanted to keep the element of uncertainty indicated by the word 'could.' So, to retain 'could,' I needed to alter the word 'delusion.' I could have changed the phrase into: 'and it could be no mistake,' but that would sound too casual in comparison to the professional formality of the rest of the solicitor's journal.

and by using every projection and rough surface in this way

and by thus using every projection and inequality

The problem with this clause is the presence of the words 'thus' and 'inequality.' Both words make sense to us today, so there is no reason to misunderstand the meaning of the clause, but 'thus' sounds old fashioned, and 'inequality' is mostly used today when referring to a lack of equality between people or groups of people. I have therefore updated 'thus' to 'in this way' and used a more likely expression from today's English to replace the word 'inequality.'

Task 76

Here is my first version of the extract, making it more typical of today's literature, but staying as faithful as possible to the original text. The version you have created for this task will not be the same as mine — everyone's will be unique.

'In the moonlight opposite me there were three young women, who were dressed and acted as though they were dignified ladies. I thought at first that I must be dreaming because their bodies did not cast a shadow on the floor. They came close up to me, and studied me carefully with their eyes for quite a while, and then whispered to each other. Two of them were quite dark-skinned, with high aquiline noses, like the Count, and big dark, piercing eyes, that appeared dark-red when contrasted with the pale yellow moon. The other woman was pale, extremely pale, with great masses of golden hair and eyes like sparkling sapphires. I seemed to recognise her face somehow, but I could not work out where or how, except that it had some connection to a dreamy fear. All three had brilliant white teeth that shone like pearls against their voluptuous, ruby-coloured lips. There was something about them that made me feel uneasy, conjuring up some sort of longing inside me, and at the same time an inexplicable deadly fear. In my heart I felt a wicked, uncontrollable desire for them to kiss me with those

ruby-red lips.'

I have written another version below, being more flexible with the content, but remembering it is a diary entry. Again, the version you have created for this task will not be the same as mine — everyone's will be unique.

'In the moonlight opposite me, I could see three women coming closer and closer towards me. At first I thought they were ladies of noble birth by their behaviour and by the way they were dressed, but the strange thing was, I noticed they had no shadow in spite of the intense moonlight. At that point, I thought I must be dreaming. They came right up to me, studying me inquisitively with their eyes; this lasted for quite a while before they began whispering to each other. Two of them were quite dark-skinned, with high aquiline noses, like the Count, and they had big dark, piercing eyes, that looked red in the pale yellow moonlight. The other woman had a very pale face, eerily pale, and long, thick golden hair, her eyes sparkling like sapphires. I seemed to recognise her face somehow, but I couldn't work out how or from where, except that she gave me a strange dreamy recollection of having seen her in a horrific nightmare. All three of them had brilliant white teeth that shone like pearls against their voluptuous, ruby-coloured lips. There was something about them that made me feel a sense of dread along with a deep personal longing for something, even if it led to some sort of terrible damnation. Deep down I felt an evil, uncontrollable desire for them to kiss me with those bewitching, ruby-red lips.'

Unit 7

Task 77

This exercise will help with pronunciation, and you can work with your partner to arrive at the correct answers by reading out loud to one another. Most schwas can be checked in a dictionary, but the additional ones that arise due to the words being used in a sentence, need to be identified by listening to the extract being read aloud.

Task 78

The mermaids' appearance

The mermaids have hair that they like to comb out, therefore likely to be long hair. They also have a tail (understood to be the tail of a fish in place of legs and feet).

Things that the mermaids like to do

They like to play mermaid games in the water of the lagoon. They loved to gather together at the edge of the lagoon, especially on the Marooners' Rock, where they basked, combing their hair lazily.

They also uttered strange wailing sounds at the turn of the moon. On sunny days after rain, the mermaids came up in large numbers to play with their bubbles.

The mermaids' behaviour and attitude towards all the children

They were unfriendly, and never had a civil word to say to the children. When they saw Wendy or the boys, they would dive away from them and splash their tails (Wendy thought deliberately) at them, but they behaved differently with Peter Pan, with whom they chatted.

Task 79

Writing this essay is essential to prepare yourself for the longer essay in Task 80b.

Task 80a

Writing this essay is essential to prepare yourself for the longer essay in Task 80b.

Additional Task D

This task has been designed to help students to construct an essay correctly when comparing two texts. The questions steer students towards obtaining these essential skills by guiding their analysis of the content and phraseology used in the Sample Essay.

Task 80b

Writing this essay is good practice for developing skills in analysis, especially when comparing two texts in detail.

Task 81

This will help the student to become more acquainted with poetic styles.

Task 82

These answers are easy to find.

Task 83

After careful reading, the meanings of these quotations can be easily understood, and the application to real life is unique to each person.

Task 84

There are two phrases:

'chef de train' and 'C'est une femme.'

A 'chef de train' is the chief guard of the train.

'C'est une femme' means 'It is a woman.'

Task 85

Tuppence suggests that a nice respectable Home for Elderly Ladies could be found. You would pay a visit to it, giving yourself a false name. You might even get an unsuspecting third party to make the arrangements, fixing the financial arrangements through a firm of respected solicitors. You would also somehow craftily make it known that your elderly relative has a vivid imagination and mild delusions.

Tuppence suggests this idea because everyone knows that many elderly people have a vivid imagination and mild delusions sometimes. So, nobody would take it seriously when the elderly person carried on about things like poisoned milk, dead children behind a fireplace, or a sinister kidnapping. They would just think they were having their usual fantasies and delusions.

Tommy's light-hearted suggestions were to poison them with arsenic in their soup, hit them on the head with a cosh, or push them down the stairs.

Tuppence disagreed with Tommy's suggestions for the following reasons:

She thought those methods were too extreme and it was unnecessary to be so extreme.

She thought those methods would draw too much attention from others.

Those methods and the attention they would attract would make the situation harder to deal with, making it more difficult to conceal the fact that crimes had taken place.

Task 86

'Birling' must be Mr Arthur Birling, the master of the house. 'Mrs Birling' must be Sybil, Mr Arthur Birling's wife.

Task 87

Your essay needs to be checked by your teacher.

Task 88

Ask your teacher to check your essay.

Task 89

It is well-worth becoming acquainted with the content of these pantomimes. They have stood the test of time and countless books and films have been produced based on these traditional stories.

Note, when a pantomime is not selected at Christmas-time, the school, organisation or theatre may instead use a story from English Literature such as 'Scrooge,' based on a well-respected novel by Charles Dickens called 'A Christmas Carol,' set in Victorian England at Christmas-time.

Task 90

Here are some of the similarities between these two extracts:

Beowulf	*The Hobbit*
The fire dragon belches out flames	Fire leaps from the dragon's jaws
The dragon burns homesteads	The dragon sets the town ablaze
Beowulf himself is given very bad news	The warning trumpets are suddenly sounded and joy turns to dread
The dragon destroys the coastal region and the forts and earthworks are reduced to dust and ashes	The dragon circles in the air above them lighting all the lake; the trees by the rocky shores shine like copper and like blood with leaping shadows of dense black at their feet

We can see many similarities, but the accounts are not identical. These descriptions are typical of the many western stories about dragons.

Task 91

Here is one way to rewrite the passage in today's English:

Frodo drew the Ring out of his pocket again and looked at it ... It was an admirable thing and very precious. When he took it out he had intended to fling it away into the very hottest part of the fire. But now he found that he could not do it, not without a great struggle. He weighed the Ring in his hand, hesitating, and forcing himself to remember all that Gandalf had told him ... but he found that he had to put it back in his pocket.

Gandalf laughed grimly. 'You see? It has affected you already, Frodo! Even you can't easily let it go, nor are you willing to change it ... It's been said that dragon-fire can melt and destroy the Rings of Power, but there're no more dragons left on earth in which the old fire is hot enough ... There's only one way: to find the Cracks of Doom in the depths of Orodruin, the Fire-mountain, and throw the Ring into it, if you really want to destroy it, to put it outside the grasp of the Enemy for ever.'

Task 92

'Don't hurt us! Don't let them hurt us, precious!'

'Don't hurt us! Precious, don't let them hurt us!'

'They won't hurt us will they, nice little hobbitses?'

'They won't hurt us will they, nice little hobbits?'

'We didn't mean no harm, but they jumps on us like cats on poor mices, they did, precious.'

'We didn't mean any harm, but they jumped on us like cats on poor mice, they did, Precious.'

'And we're so lonely ...'

'And we're so lonely ...'

'We'll be nice to them, very nice, if they'll be nice to us, won't we, yes, yess.'

'We'll be nice to them, very nice, if they'll be nice to us, won't we, yes, yess.'

'But that would kill us, kill us …'

'But that would kill us, kill us …'

'Cruel little hobbitses. Tie us up in the cold hard lands and leave us …'

'Cruel little hobbits. Tie us up in the cold hard lands and leave us …'

Note: Three of these quotations do not need to be changed.

Task 93

It is important to fully understand the correct usage of English today for international communication. This exercise will help you to record more examples that can be referred to in the future.

Task 94

This task will help you with your analytical skills. To fulfil this task correctly, you will have to have your wits about you. Read and study the extract and its context very carefully, otherwise you will misunderstand what Screwtape is saying, and think the opposite. However, the English is very clear if you concentrate hard.

Task 95

Sometimes it is good to simply enjoy reading. You can also study the structure of an extract to help you to form your own ideas for descriptive writing.

Task 96

Below, you can see possible updated versions of Lucy's speech, replacing words and expressions that are no longer used in the same way today.

"This must be a simply enormous wardrobe!"

"This must be an enormous wardrobe!"

"I wonder is that more mothballs?"

"I wonder if that's more mothballs!"

"This is very queer"

"This is very strange"

"Why, it is just like branches of trees!"

"What! They're just like tree branches!"

Task 97

There is enough information in the main text to help you. Have your written comments checked by your teacher.

Task 98

This is a very good opportunity to apply what you read to your life in a positive way, thereby also deepening your understanding of the subjects addressed in the Narnia series.

Additional Task E

This list will be an incredibly valuable resource to help you to write and speak in today's English rather than an outdated variety. This is vital for international communication. You have worked through this book yourself, studied the various glossaries and done the various tasks, so this will strengthen your ability to remember and understand the phrases well enough to apply them correctly in the future. Writing a full list now will consolidate that learning and serve as helpful reference material.

Unit 8

Task 99

Here are some ways in which to convert the quotations into today's English.

'… it gave one a kind of seasick feeling to watch it.'

'… it gave the observer a kind of seasick feeling.'

Or,

'… it made you feel seasick just watching it.'

'As a method of progress it looked both strenuous and clumsy'

'Its technique for moving forward looked both exhausting and clumsy'

'One felt that if it were to go on lurching for long in that fashion it would be bound to strip all its leaves'

'It looked like it would strip all its leaves off if it continued lurching forward like that for much longer'

'*… it was contriving to cover the ground at something like an average walking pace.*'

'… it was attempting to cover the ground at something like an average walking pace.'

'*… hit me one terrific slam*'

'… slammed into me really hard'

Task 100

Here is an updated version of the extract. I have underlined the areas where changes have been necessary.

Bond walked up to his room, which again showed no sign of <u>trespass</u>; <u>he threw</u> off his clothes, took a long hot bath followed by an ice-cold shower and lay down on his bed. There remained an hour in which to rest and compose his thoughts before he met the <u>woman</u> in the Splendide bar, an hour to <u>examine the details of his plans for the game in minute detail</u>, and for after the game, in all the various circumstances of victory or defeat …

As he tied his thin, double-ended, black satin tie, he paused for a moment and examined himself <u>steadily</u> in the mirror. His grey-blue eyes looked calmly back with a hint of ironical inquiry ….

….

'And now have you decided what you would like to have for dinner? Please <u>choose something</u> expensive,' he added as he sensed her hesitation, 'or you'll let down that beautiful <u>dress</u>.'

'I'd made two choices, she laughed, 'and either would have been delicious, but behaving like a millionaire occasionally is a wonderful treat and if you're sure … well, I'd like to start with caviar and then have a plain grilled rognon de veau with pommes souffles. And then I'd like to have fraises des bois with a lot of cream. Is it very <u>shameful</u> to be so <u>decisive about spending so much money</u>?' She smiled at him inquiringly.

'It's a virtue, and anyway it's only a good plain wholesome meal.' He *turned to the maitre d' hotel, 'and bring plenty of toast.'*

'The trouble <u>is always</u>,' he explained to Vesper, 'not how to get enough caviar, but how to get enough toast with it.'

Task 101

Read the book and see if you had the same idea as Philippa Pearce.

Task 102

This task will help you to get used to describing what you read to others, using words and phrases of your own.

Task 103

This will help to develop your skills in imagination.

Task 104

The key to understanding this statement is in the usage of the word 'but.' In this type of structure, the word 'but' means 'except for/apart from.'

Task 105a

In the title of the second book, we see the idea of having a restaurant at the end of the universe. This sounds ridiculous, as nobody knows if there is an 'end of the universe.' We also do not know if humans will ever go there, so the idea of a restaurant being there is nonsense. And who can say the end of the universe is so small as to only require one restaurant? ('**The** restaurant' suggests only one; '**A** restaurant' suggests one of many). Having said that, it is possible that there is a restaurant there (wherever it is) and however big the 'end of the universe' may be, there may actually only be one. The impossibility of the title combined with the incredible vague possibility of it being true, creates the humour.

The third book title starts off 'Life, the Universe …' and that is enough as the Universe actually includes **everything** already. So, adding the word 'everything' at the end of the title is humorous. But it is also quite profound, as even though 'Universe' means everything in existence, we do not often associate it with human thought or the spiritual world, such as Heaven.

The fourth book title is funny because of the reference to fish. Fish are insignificant in comparison to our galaxy or the universe, but the book is primarily about just that — the universe, and not fish in particular. 'So long' means 'Goodbye.'

For the final book, the title 'Mostly Harmless' is funny because to say something is harmless brings reassurance that no harm will come to you, whereas the addition of the word 'mostly' erases that reassurance. It is a contradictory title.

Task 105b

We are told in the extract that travelling through hyperspace is like being drunk. 'Being drunk' has two meanings. The most likely meaning is that a person is not in a controlled state of mind or behaviour due to having drunk too much alcohol. The second meaning is for an actual drink (liquid) to be 'being drunk.' Arthur understood Ford to mean the first of these, and was confused as he did not think being drunk was so unpleasant. But the humour comes when Ford says: 'You ask a glass of water.' This reveals Ford's original meaning, which was that travelling through hyperspace was like someone was actually drinking you!

Task 105c

This is an interesting topic to discuss as at first thought, we would assume better communication would create more unity and harmony, but this is not always the case as we can see from today's wars between countries and people groups that speak the same language.

Task 106

It is important not to rely too much on out-of-date articles about the education system of England as the country is always seeking to improve it and adapt it to new national and international environments, including the use of technology. Rebekah Benson's article is completely up-to-date for 2019.

Task 107

When you have written your summary, read through Extract 107 again to make sure your details are accurate. Then ask your partner or teacher to also verify that your details are correct.

Task 108

This exercise has the potential to help us to be better citizens.

Task 109

This exercise has the potential to help us to be better citizens.

Task 110

As it said in the task details, remember this simple and common structure for your own writing in the future, whether it is an academic essay or a story.

Task 111

Compare notes with your partner.

Task 112

This is a very tense and dangerous moment, so voices are raised. It is common for authors to use capital letters in this way, especially in books for children or young adults.

The phrase *'WHAT'RE YEH—?'* means 'What are you... ?' He is presumably intending to say, 'WHAT ARE YOU DOING?' or 'WHAT ARE YOU GOING TO DO?'

Task 113

This is an interesting discussion as in modern times we think of thought as something abstract, however, without thought processes we would never achieve scientific breakthroughs, artistic masterpieces or peaceful, loving relationships.

Task 114a

These are my comments on the list structure of the following original sentence from Extract 114:

'When he got home the messages were piling up, two from Claudia, one from his mother from whom he had parted three hours before, one from Martin inviting him to Sunday lunch with himself and his girlfriend.'

In this example, *'When he got home the messages were piling up'* is immediately followed by a comma. It could have been followed by a colon (:) instead, as what follows it is the list of messages. But the colon is not necessary as the meaning is clear enough from the grammatical structure. This is an example of flexibility in the use of punctuation without affecting the meaning.

However, an example of a clear, conventional structure would be as follows, my alterations being underlined. This may have an identical meaning to the original, depending on what the author intended:

'When he got home the messages were piling <u>up: two</u> from Claudia, one from his mother from whom he had parted three hours before, <u>and</u> one from Martin inviting him to Sunday lunch with himself and his girlfriend.'

This adjusted structure would indicate that when Stuart got home, he noticed he had 4 text messages in total at that point, and the author may have intended this meaning in her original text.

But Rendell's different style allows some flexibility in interpretation. She may have wanted to stress the ongoing nature of the receipt of messages even more than would be indicated in my conventional alterations. The use of a comma in place of the colon expects a shorter pause (the colon would require a stop), thereby emphasising the continuous nature of the receipt of messages, but also to avoid the assumption that he only found four messages on his phone. He may have actually received many more already. A colon would suggest Stuart had only received four texts, the list following the colon being a complete list. But the use of the comma in the colon's place, plus the fact that the final item on the list is not preceded by 'and,' implies this is not a complete list of texts; the ones listed are just a sample of the texts that have already piled up on Stuart's phone, but the author only refers to the more significant ones.

So, Rendell's structure allows us to consider that Stuart had already received more than 4 texts (only 4 of many texts being specifically referred to for some reason), and many more texts were on their way.

Task 114b

This is a good opportunity to assess whether you have become addicted to your phone, and work out how to balance its use.

Task 115

The poem 'Jabberwocky' is a nonsense poem, although the main thrust of the poem is a battle between a knight with a sword and a monster of some description. The result of this battle is victory for the knight.

Harrison capitalises on the use of the nonsense words, by inserting them into the text, allowing the reader to use his or her own imagination as to the meaning of each inserted word or phrase. The fact that the inserted words and phrases are nonsense words also stresses the fact that George's mind is confused while his mind is being taken over by another force.

The use of the Jabberwocky poem gives connotations of a battle between good and evil, similar to the battle taking place in George's mind. It also gradually unfolds that George's wife has taken on the form of the monster, and his confused mental state is telling him to kill her like a knight would kill a dragon or a monster.

Task 116

The comprehension questions should be answered clearly in full sentences.

The role play should be practiced well and performed. This process will help the readers and listeners to be much more familiar with the text.

Additional Task F

This is a good discussion to have at the end of this book, as riches is one of the most common themes in English Literature, along with Life and Death, Love and Loss, and the consequences of Position and Power.

Additional Task G

It is interesting to note that approximately a third of the extracts used in this book are written in the first person, and this has been a technique used since the beginnings of the English Language, as in the case of *The Dream of the Rood* from the eighth century.

The extracts that use the first person in this way are as follows:

Extracts 2, 15, 19, 21, 22, 24, 29, 30, 31, 32, 33, 35, 40, 41, 42, 43, 44, 45, 49, 52, 53, 54, 61, 67, 68, 72, 74, 75, 76, 87, 94, 99, 108 and 109.

These extracts represent the use of the first person in the genres of narrative, poetry, psalms, plays, letters, and diaries. They include *The Dream of the Rood* from the eighth century, a prologue by William Caxton in 1490 and of course the extracts from plays such as Shakespeare's *Hamlet and King Lear*. Shakespeare's *Sonnet 1* also uses the first person. We also have *Psalm 23* from the 1611 translation of *the Bible*, Daniel Defoe's *Robinson Crusoe* of 1719 and Jonathan Swift's *Gulliver's Travels* of 1726/1735.

The two selected poems of Robert Burns — *Auld Lang Syne* of 1788 and *My heart is in the Highlands* of 1789 — also use the first person. We have William Blake's *Jerusalem* of 1804 and Mary Shelley's *Frankenstein* of 1818. Jane Taylor's poem *The Star* of 1806 (which became the *Twinkle, Twinkle Little Star* lullaby) uses the first person and is joined by other poems like William Wordsworth's *I Wandered Lonely as a Cloud* (1807), Percy Shelley's *To a Skylark* (1820), John Keats' *Ode to a Nightingale* (1819), Alfred Tennyson's *Ulysses* (1842) and *In Memoriam A.H.H.* (1850), and Robert Browning's *The Laboratory* (1845).

Jane Eyre (1847) by Charlotte Bronte is in the first person, as is Robert Louis Stevenson's *Treasure Island* (1883). However Stevenson's *Strange Case of Dr Jekyll and Mr Hyde* (1886) from Extract 62 is not in the first person, although the author speaks in a very natural and familiar way to the reader.

The 1892 Sir Arthur Conan Doyle's story called *The Speckled Band* uses the first person as the author is the fictional Dr Watson himself. H.G. Wells' text is all the more engaging as he is writing as though he is the time-traveller himself in *The Time Machine* (1895), and Bram Stoker's journal in *Dracula* (1897) is in the first person for obvious reasons, giving the story a very personal feel. This personal effect is also evident in *Rebecca* (1938) by Daphne du Maurier and in John Wyndham's *The Day of the Triffids* (1951).

Among the last examples are the letter by Screwtape in *The Screwtape Letters* (1942) by C.S. Lewis, and Homer's *The Odyssey*. Although this latter example is a 1991 edition of a translation, it is important to remember that the original ancient Greek of the story is also in the first person, and that makes this style of writing at least 3,000 years old.

I would also like to highlight Extract 36 — Jane Austen's *Pride and Prejudice* (1813) — and Extract 46 — Robert Southey's *The Story of the Three Bears* (1837) — which are not in the first person, but the author is very chatty with the reader, as though they are telling the story to a friend. This gives a very warm feeling to the reader and helps them to engage more easily with the story. The same applies to Extract 48 which contains a passage from Charles Dickens' *A Christmas Carol* (1842), in which Dickens describes the arrival of the Ghost of Christmas Past, adding the comment that he, the author, is 'standing in the spirit at your elbow.'

Sample Essay
范文

<u>**A Comparison of Shelly's *To a Sky-Lark* (Extract 44)**</u>
<u>**with Keats' *Ode to a Nightingale* (Extract 45)**</u>
by Andrew Harrison (2019)

In this comparison of the two poems, I will focus on the content of each extract, their context and overall effect. I will also examine the relationship between the title and the content. Percy Bysshe Shelley (1792–1822) wrote *To a Sky-Lark*, and John Keats (1795–1821) wrote *Ode to a Nightingale*. Both authors were from the Romantic Period, and died at a very young age.

The two extracts in question are limited in that they are not complete poems. However there is enough material to make a reasonable comparison based on what we have available, although by word count, Shelley's *Skylark* extract is only two-thirds the length of Keats' *Nightingale* extract. In regard to the poets' use of English language, they are contemporaries, since the poems were published in 1820 and 1819 respectively. In both cases the poet is speaking in the *first person*, addressing the bird directly as *second person*.

Keats' title says *Ode to ...*, an 'ode' being a poem written to praise someone or something, in this case a species of bird. Shelley's *To a ...*, implies the same thing, the meaning being '(Ode) to a Skylark'. In regard to whether the content of the poems in the given extracts actually achieve this, we have to carefully read the content. In the *Skylark* extract, we begin with *'Hail to thee, blithe Spirit!'* This is directly praising the bird, in agreement with the title. This praise is intensified by saying, *'Bird thou never wert — that from Heaven, or near it'* as it implies the skylark is more than just a bird, and instead a heavenly being. This is also backed up by the later statement, *'Like a star of Heaven in the broad day-light.'* In the *Nightingale* extract, the only statement that would strongly support the title is: '… *thou, light-winged Dryad of the trees,'* likening the bird to a magical, human-like spirit. The *Nightingale* poem extract is more concerned with the poet's desire to enter into some sort of blissful state or a drunken trance to forget the evils of natural life. So, as far as the *Nightingale* extract is concerned, the content of the poem does not support the title as much as *Skylark*.

It is worth analysing the extent to which the poet describes the bird itself when assessing how faithful each poem is to its title. In *Skylark*, we have many descriptions of the bird; we are told that it sings in a natural and vibrant manner, and its song is like art. We are told how the skylark springs up from the earth and flies higher and higher. As it rises, it continues to sing and then hovers high in the sky. In the evening, the sunlight reflects off the skylark, but in the daylight, the bird is not so visible, although its shrill-sounding song can be easily heard.

In *Nightingale*, we are simply told that the bird is delicate and extremely happy, and that it sings melodiously in the summer. But the poet is more concerned with how the Nightingale's song effects the listener. For example, its song reminds people of summertime, and the beautiful song helps you to relax and drift into a world of imagination, enabling you to forget your troubles and the onset of old age with its characteristic limitations.

We can see from this that the poems significantly diverge in overall effect. In *Skylark*, we are to imagine the bird in all its splendour and listen to its magical song; in *Nightingale*, we are to sympathise with the poet's desire to slink into a stupor under the spell of the nightingale's song, as a type of drug to forget the troubles of life.

Skylark barely mentions the observer's emotions in the extract, but *Nightingale* is full of human emotion. *Skylark* represents Romantic Literature in its description of the magical beauty of the bird, whereas *Nightingale* represents Romantic Literature in its deep sympathy with the human spirit and its relationship with the natural environment.

It is clear that these two poems are both representative of Romantic Literature, but for different reasons, one focusing on a bird and the other on the effect of a bird's song on the listener. The poems agree in that both inspire a deep appreciation of the bird (and its song) named in the title, but *Nightingale* is less of an ode to a bird than *Skylark* is, focusing more on the listener than the bird itself.

741 words

Acknowledgements

致谢

I would like to say a huge thank you to my family: my wonderful wife Kathy, my daughters Rebekah, Ruth and Lydia, and my son Josh. I have appreciated all their suggestions, editing and support. Their endless encouragement, both in England and China, have made all my writing projects not only possible, but very rewarding. Thank you too to Lydia for helping with my research, gathering and collating information for this book, and to Kathy for her proofreading.

A big thank you too to my Chinese students, especially those who enjoy getting engrossed in my novels and text books. You have all been an inspiration to me, and made this occupation of mine both challenging and worthwhile.

Andrew Harrison

June 2020

我想要对我的家人说一声非常感谢,包括我了不起的妻子凯西,我的女儿丽贝卡、露丝和莉迪亚,还有我的儿子乔希。我感谢他们的建议、编辑和支持。在英格兰和中国,他们无尽的鼓励,使我所有的写作计划不仅变成可能,而且非常有回报。我还要特别感谢莉迪亚对我的研究、收集和整理这本书的信息所带来的帮助,也谢谢凯西的校对。

非常感谢我的中国学生,特别是那些喜欢全神贯注于阅读我的小说和课本的学生。你们都是我的灵感来源,让我的这份工作充满挑战和价值。

安德鲁·哈里森

2020年6月